Yum!

Irresistible, Fun-to-Create, Reliable Recipes

To Nancy,
Enjoy creative cooking!
all best wishes, John

JOHN L. LEONARD

Heron Hill Press
Wilmington, North Carolina

Illustrations by Laurie E. Dalton

Library of Congress Catalog Card Number 95-94321

ISBN 0-9646465-5-2

FOR ADDITIONAL COPIES, PLEASE USE THE ORDER FORMS AT THE BACK OF THE BOOK OR WRITE:

Heron Hill Press
7915 Masonboro Sound Road
Wilmington, NC 28409-2674

Price $17.95 plus $3.00 shipping and handling.
North Carolina residents add 6% sales tax ($1.08).

Printed on recycled paper in the United States of America by
KEEPSAKE COOKBOOKS • FUNDCO PRINTERS
1815 Wayne Road, Savannah, Tennessee 38372
1-800-426-9827

Contents

INTRODUCTION 5

COOKING EQUIPMENT 9

INGREDIENTS 15

APPETIZERS 21

SOUPS 41

SALADS AND SALAD DRESSINGS 63

FISH AND SHELLFISH 79

POULTRY 97

BEEF, PORK, AND LAMB 131

VEGETABLES 147

PASTA 175

SAUCES 189

YEAST BREADS 201

QUICK BREADS 237

CAKES 249

COOKIES 301

PASTRIES 315

DESSERTS AND DESSERT SAUCES 353

TABLE FOR CHANGING THE YIELD OF A RECIPE 375

INDEX 377

Introduction

Yum! Put away those instant "convenience" foods and get ready to create dishes you, your family, and friends will truly enjoy. Consider cooking an art form rather than a daily chore. Let preparing food become a delightful pastime, an active hobby, or even a lifelong avocation. Let **Yum!** keep your family and friends asking for more and wondering how you became so creative!

Being a veterinarian has kept me quite busy. Still, I always look forward to a great meal and for me cooking is a great stress reliever. The transformation of raw ingredients into a taste treat has always provided me with a unique satisfaction. This book started out as a personal collection of reliable recipes that pleased my family and friends. After more than 40 years of cooking as a hobby, I am sharing these recipes, as well as techniques, with others who may not have much time to invest in learning culinary skills yet want to create exciting and inviting cuisine worthy of a professional chef.

This book gives you confidence to tackle new recipes and develop additional skills. Remember, the worst that can happen is that the results of your efforts may wind up in the waste can. Hopefully, the easy-to-follow, step-by-step directions in this book will prevent that from happening. Choose a recipe you've never prepared and give it a try. My wife, who had never used yeast before, produced excellent French bread on her first attempt by following the directions in this book.

My family helped determine which recipes were included in this collection. When I was in the kitchen, my wife and sons would usually be waiting to see if I was cooking something good. With my more successful ventures, they would dive into the pot with fork and spoon before the recipe was even finished. This irked me, since I was usually trying to determine the yield of the recipe.

By the time the nibblers were finished, I had no idea how much was in the pot before their invasion. However, their interest and appetites suggested that I might have a successful recipe. If they couldn't wait for dinner and scraped the dish clean, I knew I had a "hit."

My greatest satisfaction has come from cooking for and with my wife and children. I enjoy watching my sons learn to appreciate new foods and flavors. It pleases me to see them become interested in cooking. In fact, they are becoming quite proficient cooks. Spending time in the kitchen with your family builds togetherness, and I will always cherish the happy times we have shared in our kitchen. Your children will acquire skills such as mathematics, coordination, and the ability to plan ahead. Teaching my sons about fractions with a set of measuring cups and spoons was fun for all of us. They will always remember what one-third of three-quarters of a cup equals. Welcome your children into the kitchen and discover how creative and helpful they can be!

Many of this book's recipes are adaptations of familiar dishes that have been favorites of mine since childhood such as: Chicken Pot Pie, Sauerbraten, German Potato Salad, Applesauce Cake, Linzer Cookies, Cream Puffs with Chocolate Fudge Sauce, and Lemon Sponge Pudding.

Some inventive taste sensations include: Fresh Beet Soup, which uses the greens as well as the roots; Peanut Pumpkin Soup; Tuna Salad, flavored with ginger and sesame seeds; Lemon and Wine Barbecued Chicken; Orange Pecan Rice Pilaf; Seafood Lasagna, in which the seafood topping is prepared separately from the lasagna to prevent overcooking the seafood; Cornmeal and Honey Bread; Pecan Bundt Cake; Blueberry Sour Cream Pie, made with crumbs for both the crust and topping; Toasted Almond Wafers; and Coconut Ambrosia Pie.

The Improvisational Stir-Fry recipe shows you how to create an infinite variety of stir-fry combinations using your choice of seafood, meat, poultry, and vegetables.

Several recipes feature chicken in dishes typically prepared using beef, with delicious results. Among them are: Chicken Meatballs in Sour Cream Sauce, Turkey or Chicken Loaf with Parsley Cream Sauce, Chicken and Tomato Pasta Sauce, and Chicken and Vegetable Lasagna.

I know you will enjoy the yeast breads which are light in texture and full of flavor. Try the Pecan Caramel Buns or Cinnamon Raisin Buns for a real treat.

Also included are recipes with innovative techniques such as using a broiler to brown cubes of meat for stews (such as Braised Beef in Red Wine and Lamb Stew) which results in faster, easier, and more efficient browning than in a skillet. This same method is also used for browning Swedish Meatballs and browning ground beef to prepare Beef Broth. Rice Pudding is made in a unique way to ensure a rich, creamy, and smooth custard base.

For most recipes, the yield is given in cups so you may decide for yourself the size of each serving and how many servings each recipe will produce. The number of servings listed for each recipe is only a suggestion.

Most recipes use commonly available ingredients. Feel free to add or substitute any of your favorite herbs, spices, and other ingredients.

During the past few years, I have become more health conscious so I try to reduce the amount of cholesterol, fat, sugar, and salt in the dishes I prepare. Most of the recipes generally follow this trend but there are exceptions for occasional splurges such as Strawberry Cheesecake and Chocolate Mocha Bavarian Cream.

Enjoy using this collection to go beyond the ordinary — keep your family and friends saying

Yum!

Cooking Equipment

CONTAINERS

Store dry ingredients such as flour, sugar, salt, and cornstarch in labeled wide-mouthed plastic containers with snap-on lids. Measuring and removing ingredients from these containers is easier than using the original containers, and ingredients will stay fresh longer. A variety of sizes can be obtained from restaurant supply stores.

COOKWARE

Some foods react chemically with the cookware in which they are prepared. Spinach and acidic foods such as wine, citrus juice, vinegar, and tomatoes react with aluminum or cast iron to create a metallic taste. Milk or eggs react with aluminum to cause an unpleasant taste as well as an unwanted gray or green color. Use nonreactive cookware such as nonstick aluminum, stainless steel, enameled cast iron, anodized aluminum, ceramic, and glass in the preparation of chemically reactive foods.

Avoid pots made of thin metal. Lightweight pots may be used for boiling but food may burn in them if they are used for any other purpose. Heavy cookware with thick bottoms are essential for sautéing or frying and the preparation of sauces and stews.

For sautéing and pan-frying, heavy aluminum skillets with nonstick lining are my preference. Skillets of unlined cast iron diffuse heat well for even cooking, are inexpensive, and last forever. However, they should not be used with chemically reactive foods. Enameled cast iron skillets are not very effective for sautéing or frying.

For preparing sauces or stews, stainless steel pots with heavy aluminum bottoms or enameled cast iron pots are excellent.

Some of the recipes in this book use a 4 1/2-quart pot. There are a variety of names for this pot, such as Dutch oven, casserole, roaster, and stew pan. Any 4 1/2-quart pot with a heavy bottom that does not chemically react with the food being prepared in it can be used. I use either an enameled cast iron pot or a stainless steel pot with a heavy aluminum bottom. Both have two loop handles.

Avoid using metal utensils in enameled cast iron or nonstick cookware since they are easily scratched. Use wooden or plastic spoons, spatulas, whisks, and forks.

COOKBOOK PROTECTION

Use a clear plastic cookbook protector to hold your cookbook and protect the pages from being spattered with food. A cookbook or recipe may be covered with plastic wrap or placed in a plastic bag for protection.

DISHWASHER

Do not put any kitchen utensil with a cutting edge in the dishwasher. The heat will dull its cutting ability. This includes knives, cleavers, graters, peelers, and food processor blades. Also, wooden ware such as spoons, spatulas, and rolling pins should not be washed in a dishwasher. The water will raise the grain of the wood, causing rough surfaces, and the wood will eventually split.

DUPLICATE EQUIPMENT

Purchase duplicates of commonly used equipment such as mixer and food processor bowls and measuring cups and spoons. This will prevent stopping to wash a piece of equipment or looking for a misplaced item at an inopportune moment.

KNIVES

A serrated steak knife, about 8 1/2-inches long, is very useful for slicing and chopping fruits and vegetables. This knife is easier and safer to use than larger knives when slicing and coring apples (p. 15), chopping onions (p. 18), and mincing garlic (p. 17).

Large serrated knives make quick work of slicing bread and vegetables such as cabbage, squash, and rutabagas.

OVENS

When an oven is installed, be sure the racks are level to ensure even rising of cakes. Oven temperatures should be checked periodically and the temperature dial adjusted accordingly. An oven thermometer is a wise investment. The mercury type is much more accurate than the dial and spring type. Whenever an appliance repairman visits your home, have your ovens calibrated.

PASTRY BAG AND TIPS

These are great fun to use and will give your creations professional flair. A 12-inch bag is useful for piping frostings. A 16-inch bag is used for Eclairs (p. 348) and Duchess Potatoes (p. 162). Buy tips (also called tubes) as you need them. The two tips I use most often are 1/2-inch in diameter, have fluted openings, and are known as rosette or star tips. One has wide teeth (#5) and the other has narrow teeth (#5B). I use them to pipe rosettes of frosting or whipped cream and to shape cookies. A 3/4-inch plain round tip (#9) is useful for making Eclairs. See Rosettes (p. 251) for information about using a pastry bag and making rosettes.

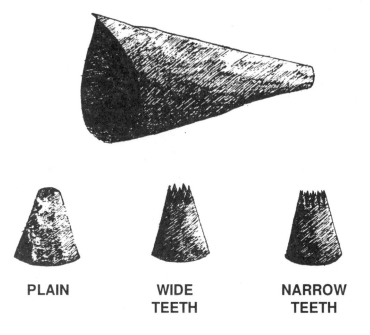

| PLAIN | WIDE TEETH | NARROW TEETH |

PASTRY SCRAPER

This utensil is also known as a dough blade, dough scraper, or dough knife. It is a rectangular piece of thin but rigid stainless steel with a wooden or plastic handle on one of the long sides. I prefer a 6 x 5-inch scraper which may be obtained from a restaurant supply house.

The scraper is useful in the early stages of kneading dough by hand and for dividing dough into pieces. The utensil can also be used to scrape work surfaces clean and to transfer items such as chopped vegetables from a cutting board to a pot. A pancake turner, wide spatula, or putty knife may be substituted.

RECIPE COLLECTIONS

Anyone interested in cooking has a collection of recipes from different sources: cookbooks, magazines, relatives, friends, flour bags, boxes, newspapers, etc. In order to be useful, recipes must be accessible. Shelve all your cookbooks in one place. Obtain a file box that will hold 5 x 8-inch cards on which you can write or attach your favorite recipes. Use paste or staples to attach recipes to the cards since tape will eventually come off and damage the recipes. Label a set of card dividers with the categories of your recipes (Appetizers, Salads, etc.). Place blank cards behind each of the dividers and list the names and pages of favorite recipes in your cookbooks on the cards. Any comments, such as what to serve with the recipe, may be included. Put all other recipes in a box until you are ready to file them. Then, cut out the recipes and place them in folders with category labels. Transfer the most interesting recipes to a loose-leaf notebook with clear plastic pages and index dividers. This notebook provides an easy way to select a new recipe. A successful recipe can be removed from the notebook and copied or stapled onto an index card in your permanent collection.

RESTAURANT EQUIPMENT SUPPLIERS

These stores are excellent resources for the home cook. Their equipment is usually more durable than that available elsewhere. I especially like their baking sheets known as half-bun or half-sheet pans. These heavy pans measure 18 x 13-inches and have a 1-inch rim. They are excellent for producing evenly browned cookies and breads. Large offset spatulas (pancake turners), 14-inches long with 7 1/2 x 3-inch blades, are useful for removing several rolls at a time from baking sheets and for transferring cakes and roasts to serving dishes. Large rubber spatulas (13 1/2-inches long with a 4 1/2 x 2 3/4-inch blade) make quick work of folding in ingredients and scraping bowls especially when making cakes. Spring-type tongs function like an extension of your hand to pick up and turn hot items. I prefer the 12-inch size. Large 20 x 15-inch plastic cutting boards are more useful than smaller sizes. Candy/deep-fry thermometers from such suppliers are less likely to break and are more accurate than those available elsewhere.

THERMOMETER

An instant-reading thermometer provides a fast and accurate method to determine the desired doneness of meat and poultry. This thermometer also ensures ideal liquid temperatures when baking with yeast.

TOWELS

Terry cloth hand towels and face cloths are more absorbent than the usual kitchen towels. They are especially useful for drying meat and absorbing spills. Face cloths are excellent for wiping counters and washing dishes.

WHISKS

Stainless steel whisks ensure smooth sauces and pastry fillings. A whisk is more efficient than a rubber spatula for folding in ingredients. Purchase 10 and 12-inch sizes from a restaurant supply house or a kitchen shop. Use plastic-coated whisks in enameled and nonstick pans to prevent scratching their surfaces.

Ingredients

ALMONDS
Blanching: Drop almonds into just enough boiling water to cover. Remove from heat. Leave in the water until the skins loosen, about 2 minutes. Drain. Hold the broad end of an almond between your thumb and index finger. Squeeze this end and the nut will pop through the skin.

Toasting: Spread almonds in one layer on a rimmed baking sheet. Place in a 350° F oven. Stir occasionally until the almonds are light brown, being careful not to let them burn. A toaster oven is useful for small quantities.

APPLES
Coring and Slicing: First peel and quarter the apples. Then use a small knife with a serrated edge to cut the core out of each quarter in a semicircular piece. Slice each cored quarter.

BROWNING SAUCE
I prefer Bovril Concentrated Beef Flavored Liquid Bouillon because it contains beef stock. Kitchen Bouquet and Gravy Master do not contain beef stock but are also quite good.

BUTTER AND MARGARINE

The recipes in this book are based on the use of lightly salted butter since it is readily available and less expensive than unsalted butter. However, I often use unsalted butter since it has a fresher taste. If unsalted butter is used, additional salt (1/8 to 1/4 teaspoon for each 1/2 cup of unsalted butter) may be added to the recipe.

Bring chilled butter or margarine to room temperature quickly by cutting the measured amount into thin slices and separating them on a plate.

COCONUT

To Open: Stand coconut in a 2-cup measuring cup or a small bowl with the 3 "eyes" directed upward. Use an ice pick or nail and a mallet or hammer to puncture the "eyes." Invert coconut and drain the watery liquid. Wrap coconut loosely in a cloth towel and use the mallet to split the coconut into several pieces. Use the tip of a knife to remove coconut from the shell. If coconut is difficult to separate from the shell, break the shell into smaller pieces. A vegetable peeler or knife will remove the brown skin. Wash pieces of coconut in cold water.

To Grate: Grate coconut in a food processor with a shredding disc or use a hand grater. Coconut may be frozen for up to several months. One coconut yields about 4 cups of loosely packed grated coconut.

To Remove Sweet Packaged Taste: Place packaged coconut in a strainer and rinse with cold water. Press out the water. Spread the coconut on a rimmed baking sheet. Bake in a 350° F oven, stirring frequently, until dry. This will give the coconut a fresher taste.

CORNSTARCH

One tablespoon of cornstarch has the same thickening ability as 2 tablespoons of all-purpose flour.

EGGS

Bring chilled eggs to room temperature or until warm by cracking them into a bowl and placing the bowl over hot water. Stir occasionally.

EGG WHITES

When beating egg whites, be sure bowl and beaters are very clean. Any trace of yolk or fat will prevent proper beating of the whites. Even though a rubber spatula is commonly used to fold in beaten egg whites, a large whisk is more efficient.

FLOUR

All-purpose flour is available in unbleached and bleached forms. I usually use the unbleached form.

If a recipe calls for sifted flour, use a wire strainer to sift a third more flour than needed into a bowl. A wire strainer is easier, faster, and more efficient than a flour sifter. Scoop flour into a measuring cup and level it off with a knife. Even though the flour package may state that the flour has been presifted and sifting is not necessary, flour should be sifted for the recipes in this book.

GARLIC

Garlic cloves may be minced using the same method described for mincing onions (p. 18). A garlic press may also be used.

GINGER

Fresh ginger may be kept in the refrigerator for up to a year if it is peeled, placed in a jar, and covered with dry sherry.

HERBS AND SPICES

For variety and to please your own taste, feel free to change the amounts and types of herbs and spices used in the recipes in this book. I prefer to use herbs and spices sparingly so as not to overpower the taste of the main ingredients. Dried herbs, rather than fresh, have been used in most of the recipes since they are readily available. Dried herbs can be crushed with a mortar and pestle to release their flavor. If you have fresh herbs, use 2 to 4 times the amount of dried herbs.

LEMON RIND, GRATED

A flat stainless steel grater is much easier to use than a lemon zester or citrus-peel shredder. Use the medium (1/8-inch diameter) holes of the grater. Be sure to grate only the yellow part of the rind since the white part is bitter. Measuring spoons should be firmly packed with the lemon rind to ensure correct measurement.

ONIONS

When a recipe calls for onions, I usually use yellow onions. However, feel free to use any variety that appeals to you. Shallots, which have a mild garlic taste, or green onions are interesting alternatives when only a small amount of onion flavor is needed.

If onions have been chilled, you are less likely to cry when they are cut.

A serrated knife, about 8 1/2-inches long, is very efficient for slicing, chopping, and mincing onions. First cut off root and stem ends. Then halve the onion by cutting from the stem end to the root end. Pull off peel and place halves cut side down on the cutting board.

If you are going to chop or mince onion, first slice it in the stem-root direction by pressing the knife downward without any back-and-forth motion (A). This will keep the slices barely joined together at the base of the onion half. When slices are left attached, they are easier to cut crosswise. Use a back-and-forth motion to chop or mince the onion (B). Before cutting the attached slices crosswise, two or three horizontal cuts can be made through the onion half. These cuts will make the chopped pieces more even in size. This method may also be used to mince garlic.

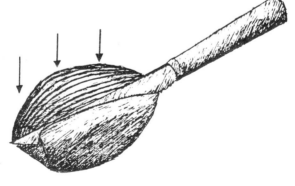

A

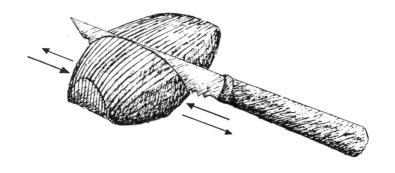

B

PEPPERS, BELL
Slicing: First cut the top and bottom off the pepper. Halve the pepper lengthwise. Cut out core and remove the seeds from each half. Place the pepper, skin side down, on a cutting surface. Press firmly and slice.

SALT
Kosher salt dissolves faster than regular salt and clings better to food (e.g. corn on the cob, salads).

Wine intensifies the taste of salt. If the food contains wine, always taste before adding salt.

TOMATOES
To Peel: Plunge each tomato into boiling water for 10 seconds. Immediately transfer the tomato to cold water and peel off the skin.

To Seed: Halve each tomato by cutting through the middle section rather than through the stem end. Squeeze each tomato half to press out the seeds. Use a finger or small spoon to remove the remaining seeds.

Appetizers

Cheese Wafers

Crisp and flaky, these wafers are perfect with cocktails.

1 cup all-purpose flour
1/4 teaspoon salt
1/8 teaspoon cayenne pepper
(Southerners may wish to
use 1/4 teaspoon or more)
6 tablespoons (3/4 stick)
butter (no substitute),
chilled

6 ounces extra sharp
Cheddar cheese, grated
(1 1/2 cups, loosely packed)
1 large egg yolk
Pecan pieces (optional)

1. Combine flour, salt, and cayenne pepper in a food processor with a steel blade. Process a few seconds until mixed.

2. Cut butter into 1/2-inch cubes and add to flour mixture. Process with a pulsing action until mixture resembles cornmeal. If a food processor is not available, use a pastry blender to cut butter into flour mixture.

3. Add cheese and egg yolk. Process or mix only until blended.

4. Form mixture into a ball, wrap in plastic wrap, and place in freezer or refrigerator until firm.

5. Use a lightly floured pastry cloth and a rolling pin with a cloth cover to roll out half the dough at a time. The rolled dough should be about 1/8-inch thick. Use a 2-inch biscuit cutter to cut out wafers. Place wafers about 1 1/2-inches apart on unbuttered baking sheets.

6. A piece of pecan may be pressed into the center of each wafer.

7. Bake wafers in a preheated 350° F oven until light brown at the edges, about 12 minutes.

8. Remove wafers from baking sheet and cool on a wire rack. Store in an airtight container.

Yield: About 8 dozen wafers.

Green Beans, Carrots, Broccoli, and/or Cauliflower with Vinaigrette and Mustard Mayonnaise

These vegetables are one of the most popular items on my party buffets. Any of them may be prepared alone or in combination. Boiling the vegetables for a few minutes enhances their bright colors, removes their raw taste, and helps them absorb the vinaigrette.

VINAIGRETTE (1 recipe for each vegetable)
1/2 clove garlic
1/2 teaspoon salt
2 teaspoons Dijon mustard
1 tablespoon vinegar
  (wine or cider)
1 tablespoon lemon juice
1/4 teaspoon ground black
  pepper

1/4 teaspoon dried basil
  (optional)
1/4 teaspoon dried oregano
  (optional)
1/2 cup vegetable oil

GREEN BEANS
2 1/2 pounds fresh green string beans

CARROTS
2 pounds carrots

BROCCOLI
1 large head broccoli, cut into 1 1/2 to 2-inch florets

CAULIFLOWER
1 large head cauliflower, cut into 1 1/2 to 2-inch florets

MUSTARD MAYONNAISE (p. 76) (OPTIONAL)
1/4 to 1/2 recipe for each vegetable

VINAIGRETTE

Use either food processor or hand method:

Food Processor Method

1. Mince garlic by dropping it into a food processor with a steel blade and the motor running.

2. Add all remaining ingredients except oil. Process a few seconds to mix ingredients.

3. With processor running, add oil in a fine stream to produce an emulsion.

Hand Method

1. Mince garlic. In a small bowl, use a spoon to mash garlic and salt into a paste. Use a whisk to stir in all remaining ingredients except the oil.

2. Add oil, in a fine stream, while whisking to form an emulsion. An emulsion does not have to be formed but it will create a dressing with a better appearance.

Yield: 2/3 cup.

Note: The dressing may be refrigerated but let it reach room temperature before using.

GREEN BEANS

1. Cut or snap ends off beans and pull off any attached strings.

2. Drop beans into a large pot of boiling water. Boil until they just begin to become tender, about 6 to 7 minutes. Do not overcook or they will lose their bright green color. Drain immediately. Refrigerate until ready to serve.

3. Immediately before serving, toss beans in vinaigrette. The beans will lose their bright green color after being in the vinaigrette for more than an hour or two. Season with salt and pepper.

4. On a circular or rectangular serving dish, arrange beans parallel to each other.

5. Place a band of mustard mayonnaise over the middle of the beans.

CARROTS

1. Peel the carrots and cut them in half crosswise. Then cut them into 4 x 1/4 x 1/4-inch sticks. The carrots may also be cut into 1/4-inch round slices.

2. Drop carrots into boiling water and boil for 4 to 5 minutes. Drain immediately and cool to room temperature.

3. Toss carrots in vinaigrette. Season with salt and pepper. Refrigerate and marinate for several hours or overnight.

4. Serve with mustard mayonnaise.

BROCCOLI

1. Drop broccoli florets into boiling water. Boil for 3 minutes. Drain immediately. Refrigerate broccoli until served.

2. Immediately before serving, toss broccoli in vinaigrette. The broccoli will lose its bright green color after being in the vinaigrette for more than an hour or two. Season with salt and pepper.

3. Serve with mustard mayonnaise.

CAULIFLOWER

1. Drop cauliflower florets into boiling water. Boil until barely tender, about 8 minutes. Drain immediately and cool to room temperature.

2. Toss cauliflower in the vinaigrette. Season with salt and pepper. Refrigerate and marinate for several hours or overnight.

3. Serve with mustard mayonnaise.

Notes:

1. The serving dish may be lined with lettuce and garnished with whole cherry tomatoes or tomatoes cut into decorative shapes.

2. For a spectacular display, arrange the vegetables on a large rectangular silver platter. Arrange the green beans in a band in the middle of the platter. The beans should be parallel to each other and to the long side of the platter. On both sides of the beans place a row of cauliflower. Next to each row of cauliflower, arrange a row of broccoli. Place a row of carrot sticks on top of each of the two borders where the broccoli and cauliflower meet. The carrot sticks should be parallel to each other and to the short side of the platter. Whole cherry tomatoes may be placed at the edges of the platter.

Mushrooms Stuffed with Ham

These may be prepared ahead and broiled just before serving.

6 ounces mushrooms
(about 12 to 14 medium
mushrooms)
4 tablespoons (1/2 stick)
butter or margarine,
divided
2 tablespoons finely chopped
onion
1/3 cup (2 ounces) finely
chopped cooked ham

3 tablespoons finely grated
Parmesan cheese
2 teaspoons finely chopped
parsley
1/4 teaspoon Worcestershire
sauce
1/8 teaspoon ground white
pepper, or to taste
Toothpicks, for serving

1. Clean mushrooms by wiping them with a towel. Cut off stems. Remove remaining stem from inside each cap. Finely chop stems. Reserve.

2. In a 10-inch skillet, melt 2 tablespoons of butter. Add onion and sauté over low heat until tender but not brown. Add chopped stems. Sauté until tender.

3. Transfer stems and onion to a small bowl. Stir in ham, Parmesan cheese, parsley, Worcestershire sauce, and pepper.

4. Melt 2 tablespoons of butter in the skillet. Add caps and sauté over moderate heat until barely tender.

5. Stuff caps with ham mixture. Place on a lightly oiled baking sheet. Refrigerate until ready to broil.

— This recipe may be prepared ahead to this point. —

6. Place baking sheet on a rack about 6-inches below the heating element of a broiler. Broil until the filling begins to brown, about 6 to 8 minutes. Watch closely to prevent burning.

7. Insert a toothpick in each mushroom and serve immediately.

Yield: About 12 to 14 stuffed mushrooms.

Salmon Pâté

I enjoy decorating this tasty pâté in an elaborate fashion (see illustration, next page) but it will be equally flavorful if served in a crock. You may use any or all of Steps 5 to 9 when decorating your pâté. This pâté will have better flavor if made a day or so before serving.

1 pound salmon broiled with tarragon (see Broiled Fish with Wine, p. 80)
1 teaspoon finely grated shallot or other onion
1/4 cup (1/2 stick) butter (no substitute), at room temperature
1/4 cup Mayonnaise (p. 75) or commercial mayonnaise
1 teaspoon lemon juice
2 teaspoons Cognac or brandy

1/2 teaspoon salt, or to taste
1/4 teaspoon ground white pepper, or to taste
Lettuce to cover the serving dish (optional)
1 lemon for garnish (optional)
3 Hard-Cooked Eggs (p. 29) for garnish (optional)
1 red and 1 green bell pepper for garnish (optional)

1. Remove skin and bones from salmon. In a food processor with a steel blade or electric mixer, combine salmon with shallot, butter, mayonnaise, lemon juice, Cognac, salt, and pepper. Process or beat until blended.

2. The pâte may be packed into a crock or molded.

3. If the pâté is to be molded, use a 2-cup mold shaped like a fish. Spray mold with nonstick cooking spray or brush with vegetable oil. Line mold with plastic wrap extending out of mold. Fill mold with pâté and press out any air pockets. Chill until pâté is firm.

4. Invert mold onto a serving dish. Unmold by pulling the plastic wrap and lifting the mold away from the pâté.

5. The serving dish may be covered with lettuce. Score the lemon lengthwise with a single channel zester to make decorative parallel grooves about 1/2-inch apart. Slice the lemon and cut each slice in half. Arrange 6 or 8 of these slices around the pâté with the curved sides pointing outward.

6. Cut 2 eggs lengthwise into quarters. Place an egg quarter between each lemon slice.

7. Cut out small hearts or other shapes from the red and green peppers. Alternate a red and green pepper shape on the center of each

lemon slice. Place a red shape on the head of the fish to resemble an eye. Arrange narrow strips of red and green pepper on the fins to simulate rays in the fins. Alternate red and green strips on each fin.

8. To make shapes resembling scales of the fish, cut thin slices of egg white from remaining egg. Cut small oval shapes from the egg white slices. A 7/8-inch oval canapé cutter may be used. Cut each shape in half lengthwise. Arrange these scale shapes on the fish with the curved sides pointing away from the head of the fish.

9. Small circles of red and green pepper may be placed between the scales. The end of a plain round pastry bag tip (#4) may be used to cut circles 3/8-inch in diameter.

10. Refrigerate until served.

Yield: 2 cups.

Note: This recipe is easily doubled or halved.

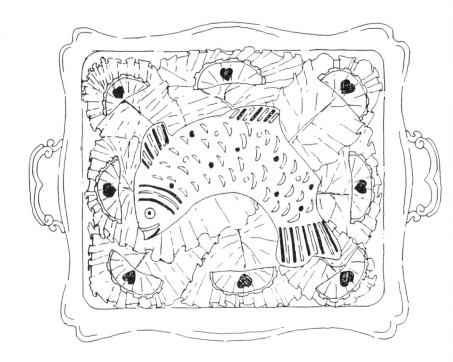

Hard-Cooked Eggs

1. Place refrigerated large eggs in a nonreactive saucepan. Add enough cold water to cover eggs with at least an inch of water.
2. Bring to a boil, reduce heat, and simmer very gently for 14 minutes.
3. Immediately place eggs in cold water. Crack eggs all over on a flat surface and return to cold water. This will make them easier to peel.
4. When cool, peel each egg under cold running water. Start at the large end.

Lemon-Lime Marinated Shrimp

Serve these shrimp in a bowl with toothpicks or arrange them on plates covered with lettuce.

2 3/4 to 3 pounds unshelled
  shrimp
1/4 cup lime juice
1 1/2 tablespoons lemon juice
1/4 cup vegetable oil
1/4 teaspoon finely grated
  lime rind
1/2 teaspoon finely grated
  onion

1/2 teaspoon Dijon mustard
1/2 teaspoon finely chopped
  fresh dill or 1/8 teaspoon
  dried dill weed (optional)
1/4 teaspoon ground black
  pepper, or to taste
1 1/4 teaspoons salt, or to
  taste

1. Drop shrimp into a 2-quart saucepan half full of boiling water. Cook until pink, about 2 or 3 minutes. Do not overcook. Drain, peel, and devein.
2. Whisk remaining ingredients together in a 2-quart covered dish or bowl. Add shrimp and toss to coat.
3. Cover and refrigerate for several hours before serving. Toss occasionally.

Yield: About 4 cups.

Note: The shrimp may be served with Garlic Lime Mayonnaise (p. 76).

Crab Salad for Appetizers

1 pound (2 cups) crab meat,
  preferably lump or backfin
1/2 cup finely chopped celery
1/2 teaspoon grated shallot or
  other onion
1 cup Mayonnaise (p. 75)

1 teaspoon Dijon mustard
1 teaspoon lemon juice
Pinch cayenne pepper
1/4 teaspoon salt, or to
  taste

Mix all ingredients together and refrigerate until served.

Yield: 2 2/3 cups.

Notes:

1. I like to serve this salad on buttered crackers that have been covered with a thin slice of cucumber. Before slicing the cucumber, use a single channel zester to score the cucumber lengthwise making decorative parallel grooves about 1/2-inch apart. Garnish with diamond shaped pieces of red pepper and/or fresh dill leaves.

2. For elegant canapés, spread the salad on sliced French Bread (p. 222), Italian Bread (p. 225), or Pain de Mie (Sandwich Bread) (p. 213) cut into attractive shapes. The canapés may be garnished with finely chopped red and green pepper or parsley.

Grouper Salad for Appetizers

1 1/2 cups cooked grouper
1/2 cup finely chopped celery
1/3 cup unpeeled, seeded,
  chopped tomato or red bell
  pepper
2 tablespoons chopped
  parsley

1 1/2 teaspoons grated onion
3/4 cup Mayonnaise (p. 75)
1 teaspoon Dijon mustard
1/4 teaspoon salt, or to taste
1/4 teaspoon ground white
  pepper, or to taste
Pinch cayenne pepper

Mix all ingredients together and refrigerate until served.

Yield: 2 1/2 cups.

Note: See notes above for Crab Salad for Appetizers.

Miniature Cream Puffs with Assorted Fillings

1. Fill Miniature Cream Puffs (p. 350) with any of the following fillings: Crab Salad for Appetizers (p. 30), Grouper Salad for Appetizers (p. 30), Curried Chicken Salad (p. 72), Tuna Salad (p. 71), or Vegetable Cheese Spread (p. 40).

2. Garnish with chopped parsley, chives, or paprika.

3. Refrigerate until served.

Oysters with Mornay Sauce

MORNAY SAUCE
2 tablespoons (1/4 stick) butter or margarine
2 tablespoons all-purpose flour
3/4 cup half-and-half
2 tablespoons finely grated Parmesan cheese
3/4 teaspoon Dijon mustard
1/4 teaspoon salt, or to taste
1/16 teaspoon ground white pepper, or to taste
Pinch grated nutmeg

OYSTERS
36 oyster half shells, well scrubbed
5 pounds rock salt (optional)
1 quart shucked oysters with their juice
1/4 cup dry white wine
4 to 6 tablespoons finely grated Parmesan cheese
Ground paprika (optional)
Finely chopped parsley, about 1/4 cup (optional)

1. Prepare sauce: Melt the butter in a 1 1/2-quart saucepan. Whisk in flour until smooth. Stir over low heat for 2 minutes without browning. Add half-and-half. Stir over moderate heat until smooth and thick. Add Parmesan cheese, mustard, salt, pepper, and nutmeg. Heat and stir until cheese is melted and sauce is smooth. Reserve.

2. Prepare oysters: Arrange the shells on rimmed baking sheets lined with aluminum foil. The sheets may be filled with rock salt to support the shells. Butter the shells.

3. In a 2-quart saucepan, bring the oysters, their juice, and wine to a boil. Reduce heat and simmer for 5 minutes. Drain oysters reserving 1/4 cup of the liquid.

4. Fill shells with oysters.

5. Boil reserved liquid down to about 2 tablespoons. Stir into sauce. Spoon sauce over oysters. They will be barely covered. Sprinkle with Parmesan cheese and then paprika.

— This recipe may be prepared ahead to this point. —

6. Place oysters on a rack about 3-inches below the heating element of a broiler. Broil until sauce is golden brown, about 3 to 4 minutes.

7. Sprinkle with chopped parsley.

8. The oysters may be served on the baking sheets or transfer them to a serving dish. Serve immediately.

Yield: 36 oysters on the half shell, 18 to 36 servings.

Note: This recipe is easily halved, doubled, or quadrupled.

Broiled Clams on the Half Shell

2 dozen clams in shells,
about 2-inches long or 1
dozen clams in shells,
2 1/2 to 3 1/2-inches long
2 1/2 pounds rock salt
(optional)
Salt, to taste
Ground black pepper, to taste
7 tablespoons butter or
margarine, divided

1/4 cup finely chopped green
onions or shallots
4 ounces mushrooms, finely
chopped
1/2 cup peeled, seeded, and
chopped tomato
3/4 cup fresh bread crumbs
from White Bread (p. 210) or
firm commercial bread
Finely chopped parsley or
paprika (optional)

1. Scrub clams well. Place in a large flat pan such as a roasting pan. Heat in a 450° F oven until clams begin to open, about 10 minutes.

2. Use a clam knife, oyster knife, or other heavy knife to open clams and scrape them from their shells. Save clam juice for another purpose. Chop clams into small pieces.

3. Arrange two dozen of the half shells on rimmed baking sheets lined with aluminum foil. The sheets may be filled with rock salt to support the shells.

4. Divide chopped clams equally between the shells.

5. Taste a piece of clam to determine saltiness. If needed, sprinkle clams with salt. Season with pepper.

6. In a 9-inch skillet, melt 4 tablespoons of butter. Add onion and sauté over low heat until tender but not brown. Remove from heat and stir in mushrooms and chopped tomato. Spread over clams.

7. Melt 3 tablespoons of butter in the skillet. Add bread crumbs and stir until evenly coated with butter. Spread over the clams. The clams may be refrigerated until ready to serve.

— This recipe may be prepared ahead to this point. —

8. Place clams on a rack about 6-inches below the heating element of a broiler. Broil until the crumbs are golden brown, about 5 minutes.

9. Sprinkle with chopped parsley or paprika.

10. The clams may be served on the baking sheets or transfer them to a serving dish.

Yield: 2 dozen half shells with clams.

Ham and Egg Canapés

3 Hard-Cooked Eggs (p. 29)
3 tablespoons Mayonnaise
  (p. 75)
1/2 teaspoon lemon juice
1/4 teaspoon grated onion
  (optional)
1/2 teaspoon Dijon mustard
Pinch salt, or to taste
Pinch pepper (white or
  cayenne), or to taste
1 tablespoon finely chopped
  parsley

Crackers, French Bread
  (p. 222), Italian Bread
  (p. 225), Pain de Mie
  (Sandwich Bread) (p. 213),
  or firm commercial bread,
  sliced and buttered or
  spread with Mayonnaise
  (p. 75) or commercial
  mayonnaise
Ham, cooked and thinly
  sliced
Red bell pepper for garnish
  (optional)

1. Prepare egg yolk filling: Halve eggs and remove yolks. In a small bowl, mash yolks. Add mayonnaise, lemon juice, onion, mustard, salt, and pepper. Beat until smooth. Yield: 6 tablespoons.

2. Use a food processor with a steel blade or a knife to finely chop the egg whites. Add parsley. Mix thoroughly. Reserve.

3. Cover the crackers or bread with ham. A round cutter is useful for fitting the ham to the crackers. Sprinkle egg white and parsley mixture on top of the ham. Avoid placing any of the mixture in the center of the canapé.

4. Use a pastry bag with a 1/2-inch star tip (#5 or #5B) to pipe the egg filling into a rosette in the center of each canapé.

5. Garnish each rosette with a tiny piece of red pepper. Serve as soon as possible.

Yield: 2 to 3 dozen canapes.

Chicken Mushroom Meatballs in Velouté Sauce

A savory alternative to beef meatballs.

MEATBALLS

3 1/2 to 4 pounds chicken pieces or 3 pounds chicken breasts (bone-in)
4 cups water
5 tablespoons butter or margarine, divided
1 clove garlic, minced
1/2 cup chopped onion
1 cup fresh bread crumbs from White Bread (p. 210) or firm commercial bread

1/2 cup finely grated Parmesan cheese
1/2 teaspoon dried tarragon
1 teaspoon salt, or to taste
1/4 teaspoon ground white pepper, or to taste
4 ounces mushrooms, finely chopped
1 teaspoon lemon juice

SAUCE

3 tablespoons butter or margarine
1/4 cup all-purpose flour
1/4 teaspoon dried tarragon
1/2 teaspoon salt, or to taste

1/8 teaspoon ground white pepper, or to taste
2 tablespoons dry sherry
1/2 cup sour cream

1. Prepare meatballs: Remove skin and bones from chicken. In a 2-quart saucepan, combine the bones, skin, and water. Bring to a boil, reduce heat, and simmer for 30 to 60 minutes. Strain and reserve broth.

2. In a food processor or meat grinder, grind chicken to yield 2 1/2 to 3 cups of meat. Reserve.

3. In a 9-inch skillet, melt 2 tablespoons of butter. Add garlic and onion and sauté over low heat until tender but not brown. Transfer to a food processor with a steel blade.

4. Add chicken, bread crumbs, Parmesan cheese, tarragon, salt, and pepper. Process until blended. Transfer to a bowl. If a food processor is not available, mix ingredients thoroughly with a wooden spoon.

5. Melt 3 tablespoons of butter in the skillet. Add mushrooms. Sprinkle with lemon juice and sauté until just tender. Stir into chicken mixture.

6. Form into 48, 1-inch meatballs. Discard any tendons you find as you shape the meatballs. Place meatballs in a buttered 10-inch skillet.

7. Cover the meatballs with the broth. Bring to a boil, reduce heat, and simmer for 20 minutes. Turn meatballs occasionally. Remove meatballs from broth. Reserve broth for sauce.

8. Prepare sauce: Melt butter in a 2-quart saucepan. Whisk in flour until smooth. Stir over low heat for 2 minutes without browning.

9. Stir in 1 1/2 cups of reserved broth, tarragon, salt, pepper, and sherry. Stir over moderate heat until smooth and thick. Remove from heat and stir in sour cream.

10. Add meatballs. The meatballs may be refrigerated until ready to serve.

— This recipe may be prepared ahead to this point. —

11. Gently simmer meatballs until heated through. Do not boil or the sauce may separate.

12. The meatballs may be served in a chafing dish.

Yield: 4 dozen meatballs with sauce.

Swedish Meatballs for Appetizers

Follow the recipe for Swedish Meatballs (p. 141) with the following changes:

1. In Step 4, shape the meat mixture into 72 instead of 36 meatballs.

2. In Step 5, the meatballs will be browned in about 10 rather than 15 minutes.

3. Serve in a chafing dish.

Yield: 72 meatballs.

Turkey or Chicken Breasts Marsala for Appetizers

Follow the recipe for Turkey or Chicken Breasts Marsala (p. 116) with the following changes:

1. After the sautéed breasts are seasoned with salt and pepper and sprinkled with Parmesan cheese, cut them into 1-inch squares.
2. For each appetizer, insert a toothpick through a sautéed mushroom slice and then through a square of turkey or chicken. If desired, pass the toothpick through another slice of mushroom.
3. Place the appetizers in a heatproof dish or pan.
4. Prepare the sauce and pour it over the appetizers.

— This recipe may be prepared ahead to this point. —

5. Heat the appetizers in a 350° F oven for a few minutes until they are just hot. Do not overcook.
6. Sprinkle with chopped parsley and serve immediately.

Yield: About 35 to 40 appetizers.

Pineapple with Rum

Fresh pineapple, cut into chunks and chilled

Dark Jamaican rum
Granulated sugar (optional)

Flavor pineapple with rum, sweeten to taste, and serve in a crystal bowl with toothpicks.

Fresh Fruit with Honey Lemon Salad Dressing

Fresh fruit such as:
  strawberries,
  grapes (red and green
    seedless),
  orange wedges,
  pineapple chunks,
  kiwi fruit, and
  melon balls (cantaloupe,
    honeydew, and
    watermelon)

Honey Lemon Salad
Dressing (p. 78)

1. Arrange fruit on a serving dish.
2. Immediately before serving, spoon dressing over fruit.

Cheddar Cheese with Port Wine

This cheese spread may be served in a crock or molded and decorated with pecans for an easily decorated yet strikingly attractive buffet item.

12 ounces Cheddar cheese
3 tablespoons butter
  (no substitute)
2 tablespoons port wine
Salt, to taste
Cayenne or white pepper,
  to taste

Pecan halves for garnish
  (optional)
Finely chopped pecans for
  garnish (optional)

1. Cut cheese into 1-inch cubes. In an electric mixer with a paddle attachment, beat cheese until smooth.
2. Add butter and beat until blended.
3. Gradually beat in wine and continue to beat until light and fluffy. Season with salt and pepper. The cheese may be packed into a crock or molded.

4. If cheese is to be molded, spray an oval or round 2 1/2-cup mold with nonstick cooking spray or brush with vegetable oil. Line mold with plastic wrap extending out of the mold. Fill mold with cheese mixture being sure to press out any air pockets. Chill until cheese is firm. Unmold by pulling on the plastic wrap and lifting mold away from the cheese.

5. Place cheese in the middle of a serving dish. Place a pecan half on top of the cheese in the center. Surround this pecan with 8 other halves. The decoration should resemble a daisy. Surround the cheese with enough chopped pecans to cover the dish. Arrange pecan halves on top of the chopped pecans.

Yield: 2 1/3 cups.

Note: This recipe is easily doubled or tripled. If so, gradually add the pieces of cheese to the mixer to prevent overloading the motor.

Sliced Apples with Cheese Spread and Pecans

Apples, cheese, and pecans — all in one tasty bite.

1 1/2 apples, unpeeled, quartered, and cored
Calvados or other apple liqueur

Cheese Spread (p. 40)
1/2 cup chopped pecans
Lettuce (optional)

1. Cut each apple quarter into 4 slices. Brush apple slices with Calvados.

2. Spread one side of each apple slice with about 1 1/2 teaspoons of cheese spread. Dip the cheese side into chopped pecans.

3. Arrange the slices on a serving dish lined with lettuce leaves. Refrigerate until served.

Yield: 24 apple slices.

Cheese Spread

4 ounces grated sharp
Cheddar cheese, at room
temperature (1 cup, loosely
packed)
1 tablespoon butter
(no substitute), at room
temperature

1 to 2 tablespoons Calvados
or other apple liqueur

1. In an electric mixer, beat cheese and butter together until light and fluffy. Gradually beat in the Calvados.
2. If the spread is made ahead and refrigerated, beat until fluffy before using.

Yield: 2/3 cup, enough to cover 24 apple slices.

Note: This cheese spread may be used to prepare Sliced Apples with Cheese Spread and Pecans (p. 39). The cheese may also be spread on crackers. Garnish the center of each cracker with a pecan half.

Vegetable Cheese Spread

The vegetables in this spread are best minced by hand since a food processor tends to overprocess them.

8 ounces cream cheese
4 teaspoons minced carrot
4 teaspoons minced celery

2 teaspoons minced green
pepper
2 teaspoons minced green
onion

1. In an electric mixer, whip the cream cheese. Stir in remaining ingredients.
2. Refrigerate until served. This spread may be prepared a day or so before serving.
3. Spread on crackers, bread, or celery.

Yield: 1 cup.

Soups

Chicken Broth

Broth of excellent quality is essential for any recipe in which it is used. This broth is much more flavorful, less salty, and more economical than canned broth. Be sure to have plenty of broth in the freezer at all times. Delicious broth may be made with just chicken, water, and a little salt for flavor.

8 cups cold water
1 chicken (3 to 3 1/2 pounds) including giblets except liver, cut up, OR 3 to 3 1/2 pounds bones such as backs and necks
1 1/2 teaspoons salt, or to taste
1/4 teaspoon ground white pepper, or to taste (optional)

1 medium carrot, peeled and sliced (optional)
1 medium onion, coarsely chopped (optional)
1 medium celery rib, coarsely chopped (optional)
1/2 small bay leaf (optional)
1 clove garlic, chopped (optional)

1. Combine all ingredients in a 6-quart pot. Bring to a simmer and skim off any scum. Simmer slowly, uncovered, for 1 hour. Do not stir or let boil or the broth may become cloudy.

2. The broth may be used at this point (Yield: 9 1/2 cups) but it will not be as flavorful as when Steps 3 and 4 are completed.

3. If you have used chicken pieces, remove them from the broth. Use two forks to separate the meat from the skin and bones. Reserve the chicken for another purpose. Return the skin and bones to the broth.

4. Simmer broth for an additional hour.

5. Strain broth. Skim off fat or refrigerate broth and lift off the solid fat.

6. Refrigerate or freeze.

Yield: 8 cups.

Beef Broth

This broth derives its rich flavor and dark brown color from broiled beef.

2 pounds ground or finely
  chopped lean beef
3 tablespoons vegetable oil
1 medium onion, finely
  chopped
1 medium carrot, finely
  chopped
10 cups cold water
1 celery rib, finely chopped
1 clove garlic, chopped
1/2 medium tomato,
  unpeeled, seeded, and
  chopped

1 teaspoon salt
1/4 teaspoon cracked black
  peppercorns
1/2 small bay leaf
2 sprigs parsley (optional)
Pinch dried thyme (optional)
Pinch dried marjoram
  (optional)
2 whole cloves (optional)

1. Spread beef on an oiled broiling pan with the rack removed or use a similar pan measuring about 14 1/2 x 12 x 1-inches. Place the pan on a rack 3-inches below the heating element of a broiler. Broil, stirring every few minutes, until meat forms dark brown granules, about 15 minutes. Reserve.

2. Meanwhile, heat the oil in a heavy 4 1/2-quart pot. Add onion and carrot. Sauté over moderate heat until vegetables are golden brown.

3. Add beef. Pour a little of the water into the broiling pan and scrape loose any browned particles. Add this liquid and the remaining ingredients to the pot.

4. Bring to a simmer and skim off any scum. Simmer slowly, uncovered, for 3 hours. Do not stir or let boil or the broth may become cloudy.

5. Strain broth and discard meat and vegetables. Skim off fat or refrigerate broth and lift off the solid fat.

6. Refrigerate or freeze.

Yield: 8 cups.

Beef and Barley Soup

1/4 cup + 2 tablespoons
  vegetable oil, divided
2 to 2 1/2 pounds boneless
  beef for stew, such as chuck
2 medium carrots, sliced
2 medium celery ribs,
  finely chopped
1 large onion, chopped
8 cups Beef Broth (p. 43),
  cold water, or a combination
  of both
1/2 cup fine barley
1 medium tomato, peeled,
  seeded, and chopped

1/2 small bay leaf
1/8 teaspoon dried thyme
1/8 teaspoon dried marjoram
1 1/2 teaspoons salt, or to
  taste
1/4 teaspoon ground black
  pepper, or to taste
2 cups fresh green beans cut
  into 1-inch lengths or 1
  package (9 ounces) frozen
  green beans

1. Pour 1/4 cup of vegetable oil into a broiler pan with the rack removed or use a pan measuring about 14 1/2 x 12 x 1-inches.

2. Cut meat into 3/4-inch cubes and add to pan. Toss beef with oil until the cubes are evenly coated. Arrange the beef cubes in one layer. Place the pan on a rack 3-inches below the heating element of a broiler. Broil, turning frequently, until beef cubes are brown on all sides, about 15 minutes. Reserve.

3. Heat 2 tablespoons of oil in a heavy 4 1/2-quart pot. Add carrots, celery, and onion. Sauté over moderate heat until vegetables begin to become tender.

4. Add beef and juices to pot. Use part of the broth to scrape loose any browned particles in the broiler pan. Add this liquid and remaining broth to the pot.

5. Add barley, tomato, bay leaf, thyme, marjoram, salt, and pepper. Bring to a simmer and skim off any scum. Simmer slowly, uncovered, for 1 hour and 15 minutes. Do not stir or let boil or the broth may become cloudy.

6. Add green beans and continue to simmer until just tender, 20 to 25 minutes.

7. Skim off fat. Season with salt and pepper. Serve.

Yield: 11 cups, 10 servings.

French Onion Soup

6 tablespoons (3/4 stick) butter
1 3/4 pounds onions, thinly sliced (about 5 1/2 cups)
6 cups Beef Broth (p. 43) (no substitute)
1/4 cup Madeira or dry sherry
1 teaspoon salt, or to taste
1/4 teaspoon ground black pepper, or to taste
6 slices (1/4 to 1/2-inch thick) French Bread (p. 222) or firm commercial bread, toasted
6 ounces sliced Swiss cheese, divided

1. In a heavy 4 1/2-quart pot, melt the butter. Add onions. Sauté over moderate heat until onions begin to brown. Then reduce heat to low and continue to cook, stirring occasionally, until onions are dark brown, about 30 minutes.

2. Stir in broth, Madeira, salt, and pepper. Cover and simmer gently for 30 minutes.

3. Meanwhile, grate about 1 1/2 ounces of the cheese to make 6 tablespoons of grated cheese. Reserve.

4. Place bread slices close together on a baking sheet. Cover bread with remaining cheese slices. Reserve.

— This recipe may be prepared ahead to this point. —

5. When ready to serve, heat the soup. Also, broil the bread slices until the cheese is bubbly.

6. Spoon soup into individual casseroles or bowls. Top each serving with a bread slice. Sprinkle 1 tablespoon of grated cheese over each serving. Serve immediately.

Yield: 6 cups, 6 servings.

Chicken and Bok Choy Soup

1 chicken (3 to 3 3/4 pounds),
  cut into pieces
8 cups water
1/2 cup chopped green
  onions
1 large clove garlic, minced

1 1/2 teaspoons salt, or to
  taste
1/4 teaspoon ground white
  pepper, or to taste
1 pound bok choy (celery
  cabbage or Chinese chard)

1. In a heavy 4 1/2-quart pot, combine all ingredients except bok choy. Bring to a simmer and skim off any scum. Simmer slowly, uncovered, for 45 minutes. Do not stir or let boil or the broth may become cloudy.

2. Remove chicken from broth. Discard the skin and bones and tear chicken into bite-size pieces. Reserve.

3. Wash bok choy and cut the leaves off the stems. Cut stems into 1-inch square or diamond pieces and reserve. Cut leaves into 1 1/2-inch square or diamond pieces and reserve.

4. Bring broth to a boil. Drop bok choy stems into the broth and boil gently for 4 minutes. Add leaves and boil for 2 minutes. Remove from heat.

5. Add chicken. Season to taste with salt and pepper. Reheat and serve.

Yield: 12 cups, 12 servings.

Cream of Carrot Soup

1/4 cup (1/2 stick) butter or
  margarine
1 pound carrots, finely
  chopped or grated (about
  2 cups, firmly packed)
3/4 cup finely chopped onion
2 tablespoons all-purpose
  flour

3 cups Chicken Broth (p. 42)
  or canned broth
1 cup half-and-half or milk
1/2 teaspoon salt, or to taste
1/8 teaspoon ground white
  pepper, or to taste
Chopped parsley or chives
  for garnish (optional)

1. In a heavy 4 1/2-quart pot, melt the butter. Add carrots and onion and sauté over moderate heat for 5 minutes without letting the vegetables brown.

2. Add flour and stir until blended. Add broth and stir until smooth.

3. Bring to a boil, cover, reduce heat, and simmer until carrots are tender, about 20 to 30 minutes.

4. Strain the vegetables from the liquid. Use a food processor or food mill to purée vegetables. Return puréed vegetables and liquid to pot.

5. Stir in half-and-half, salt, and pepper.

6. Simmer for 10 minutes, garnish, and serve.

Yield: 4 1/2 cups, 4 to 5 servings.

Cream of Corn Soup

6 tablespoons (3/4 stick) butter or margarine
1 medium onion, finely chopped
6 tablespoons all-purpose flour
3 cups Chicken Broth (p. 42) or canned broth
3 cups milk
3 cups cooked fresh corn or 2 packages (10 ounces each) cooked frozen corn (I prefer Silver Queen white corn)

1 teaspoon salt, or to taste
1/8 teaspoon ground white pepper, or to taste
1/4 teaspoon dried marjoram (optional)
Crumbled crisp fried bacon, finely chopped parsley, or chives for garnish (optional)

1. In a heavy 4 1/2-quart pot, melt the butter. Add onion and sauté over moderate heat until tender but not brown.

2. Add flour. Stir over low heat for 2 minutes without browning. Add broth and milk. Stir over moderate heat until thick.

3. Purée corn in a food processor or food mill. Add to pot along with salt, pepper, and marjoram. Stir until blended.

4. For a smoother texture, the soup may be forced through a strainer using a rubber spatula or wooden spoon.

5. Reheat, garnish, and serve.

Yield: 8 cups, 8 to 10 servings.

Cream of Broccoli Soup

1 pound broccoli
1/4 cup (1/2 stick) butter or
  margarine
3/4 cup finely chopped onion
1/3 cup all-purpose flour
3 cups Chicken Broth (p. 42)
  or canned broth

2 cups half-and-half or milk
Pinch grated nutmeg
1 teaspoon salt, or to taste
1/4 teaspoon ground white
  pepper, or to taste

1. Cut the broccoli florets off the stalks. Remove and discard the fibrous ends of the stalks. Peel stalks and cut them into 1/4-inch cubes. Drop florets and stalks into boiling water. Boil until just tender, about 8 minutes. Do not overcook or the broccoli will lose its bright green color. Drain. Finely chop the broccoli in a food processor. Reserve.

2. In a heavy 4 1/2-quart pot, melt the butter. Add onion and sauté over moderate heat until tender but not brown. Add flour. Stir over low heat for 2 minutes without browning. Purée in a food processor and return to pot.

3. Add broth and half-and-half. Stir over moderate heat until smooth and thick. Stir in broccoli, nutmeg, salt, and pepper. Heat and serve.

Yield: 6 1/2 cups, 6 to 8 servings.

Cream of Asparagus Soup

Follow the above recipe for Cream of Broccoli Soup with the following changes:

1. Substitute 1 to 1 1/4 pounds of fresh asparagus for the broccoli. Peel the asparagus. Remove and discard the fibrous ends. Cut into 1-inch lengths. Boil until just tender. Do not overcook or the asparagus will lose its bright green color. Purée asparagus in a food processor.

2. Omit nutmeg.

Yield: 6 1/2 cups, 6 to 8 servings.

Cream of Chicken Soup

1/4 cup (1/2 stick) butter or
  margarine
1/3 cup all-purpose flour
3 cups Chicken Broth (p. 42)
  (no substitute)
1 cup half-and-half or milk
1/4 cup dry sherry (optional)
Pinch grated nutmeg
  (optional)
3/4 teaspoon salt, or to taste
1/8 teaspoon ground white
  pepper, or to taste

3/4 cup cooked chicken,
  cut into cubes or small
  pieces (optional)
1/3 cup cooked green peas
  (optional)
1/3 cup cooked sliced, cubed,
  or julienned carrots
  (optional)
Finely chopped parsley,
  chives, or other fresh herb
  for garnish (optional)

1. Melt the butter in a 2-quart saucepan. Whisk in flour until smooth. Stir over low heat for 2 minutes without browning.

2. Add broth, half-and-half, sherry, nutmeg, salt, and pepper. Stir over moderate heat until smooth and thick. Do not boil or the cream may separate.

3. Stir in chicken and vegetables.

4. Heat while stirring gently, garnish, and serve.

Yield: 4 1/2 cups, 4 to 5 servings.

Cream of Mushroom Soup

1. Prepare Cream of Chicken Soup (see above) omitting the chicken, peas, and carrots.

2. Wipe 4 ounces of mushrooms clean with a towel. Cut the caps into thin slices and finely chop the stems. Add to soup. Simmer until mushrooms are just tender, about 10 minutes.

3. Garnish and serve.

Yield: 4 1/2 cups, 4 to 5 servings.

Cream of Spinach Soup

Your children may hate spinach but I bet they'll love this soup. My kids, when young, called it "Popeye Soup."

1 package (10 ounces) frozen
 chopped spinach
1/4 cup water
1/4 cup (1/2 stick) butter or
 margarine
3/4 cup finely chopped onion
1 clove garlic, minced
 (optional)

1/3 cup all-purpose flour
3 cups Chicken Broth (p. 42)
 or canned broth, divided
2 cups half-and-half or milk
3/4 teaspoon salt, or to taste
1/8 teaspoon ground white
 pepper, or to taste

1. Place spinach and water in a heavy, nonreactive 1 1/2-quart saucepan. Bring to a boil, breaking up the spinach as it thaws. When completely thawed and warm, remove from heat. Do not overcook or the spinach will lose its bright green color. Reserve spinach and liquid.

2. In a heavy 4 1/2-quart pot, melt the butter. Add onion and garlic and sauté over moderate heat until tender but not brown. Add flour. Stir over low heat for 2 minutes without browning. Add 1 cup of broth. Stir over moderate heat until smooth and thick.

3. Stir in spinach and liquid. If desired, purée mixture in a food processor or blender.

4. Add remaining broth, half-and-half, salt, and pepper. Stir over low heat until thick. Do not overcook. Serve.

Yield: 5 to 6 cups, 6 to 8 servings.

Cream of Tomato Soup

Use only fresh, ripe, delicious tomatoes for this summertime treat.

1/4 cup (1/2 stick) butter or
  margarine
3/4 cup chopped onion
1 clove garlic, minced
1/4 cup all-purpose flour
2 cups Chicken Broth (p. 42)
  or canned broth
2 pounds (5 medium) fresh,
  ripe tomatoes, peeled,
  seeded, and coarsely
  chopped
1 cup half-and-half or milk

1/4 teaspoon dried basil
1 teaspoon salt, or to taste
1/8 teaspoon ground white
  pepper, or to taste
Pinch sugar (optional)
Fresh, ripe tomatoes, peeled,
  seeded, and coarsely
  chopped for garnish
  (optional)
Fresh chopped basil or dill
  leaves for garnish (optional)

1. In a heavy, nonreactive 4 1/2-quart pot, melt the butter. Add onion and garlic. Sauté over moderate heat until tender but not brown.

2. Add flour. Stir over low heat for 2 minutes without browning. Add broth. Stir over moderate heat until smooth and thick. Simmer for 10 minutes. Purée in a food processor or blender. Return to pot.

3. Add tomatoes, half-and-half, dried basil, salt, and pepper. Bring to a boil, reduce heat, and simmer for 20 minutes. Stir occasionally to prevent scorching.

4. The soup may be forced through a strainer.

5. If the soup has an acidic taste, stir in a pinch or two of sugar.

6. Reheat, garnish with tomatoes and basil or dill leaves, and serve.

Yield: 4 1/2 cups, 4 to 6 servings.

Acorn Squash and Apple Soup

The flavors of acorn squash, apples, and spices combine to make this a taste-tempting soup.

2 1/2 pounds acorn squash
1/4 cup (1/2 stick) butter or
  margarine
1 large clove garlic, minced
1 medium onion, chopped
2 medium apples, peeled,
  cored, and chopped
1/4 cup all-purpose flour
2 cups Chicken Broth (p. 42)
  or canned broth
2 cups half-and-half or milk

3/4 teaspoon salt, or to taste
1/4 teaspoon ground white
  pepper, or to taste
1/2 teaspoon dry mustard
1/8 teaspoon ground
  cinnamon
1/8 teaspoon ground cloves
1/8 teaspoon ground dried
  ginger

1. Cut squash in half. Use a spoon to scoop out the seeds. Cut into 2 or 3-inch pieces. Drop squash into boiling water, and boil until tender, about 10 to 15 minutes. Drain. Use a knife to remove peel.

2. Meanwhile, melt butter in a heavy 4 1/2-quart pot. Add garlic and onion. Sauté over moderate heat until tender but not brown.

3. Add apples. Sauté until tender but not brown. Stir in flour.

4. Purée apple mixture and cooked squash in a food processor or blender. Return to pot.

6. Add broth and half-and-half. Stir over moderate heat until smooth and thick.

7. Stir in remaining ingredients and simmer for 10 minutes. Serve.

Yield: 6 cups, 6 to 8 servings.

Sweet Potato Soup

2 1/2 pounds sweet potatoes
2 tablespoons (1/4 stick)
  butter or margarine
1 medium onion, finely
  chopped
2 tablespoons all-purpose
  flour
3 cups Chicken Broth (p. 42)
  or canned broth
1 1/2 cups half-and-half or
  milk
1/2 cup orange juice
1 1/2 teaspoons salt, or to
  taste
1/4 teaspoon ground white
  pepper, or to taste
1/4 teaspoon ground dried
  ginger
1/4 teaspoon ground
  cinnamon
1/8 teaspoon ground cloves
1/8 teaspoon grated nutmeg

1. Wash sweet potatoes. Cut them crosswise into 1 1/2-inch slices. Boil until just tender, about 20 minutes. Drain and peel. Purée potatoes in a food processor or food mill. Reserve.

2. Meanwhile, in a heavy 4 1/2-quart pot, melt the butter. Add onion and sauté over moderate heat until tender but not brown.

3. Add flour. Stir over low heat for 2 minutes without browning. Add broth. Stir over moderate heat until smooth and thick.

4. Add puréed sweet potatoes and remaining ingredients. Stir until smooth.

5. Strain the soup. Reheat and serve.

Yield: 7 1/2 cups, 8 servings.

Cheddar Cheese Soup

1/4 cup (1/2 stick) butter or margarine
1 clove garlic, minced
6 tablespoons all-purpose flour
1 2/3 cups Chicken Broth (p. 42) or 1 can (14 1/2 ounces) broth
8 ounces Cheddar cheese, grated (2 cups, loosely packed)
1 1/2 cups half-and-half and 1 1/2 cups milk OR 3 cups milk

1/4 cup dry white wine (optional)
1/2 teaspoon salt, or to taste
1/8 teaspoon cayenne pepper, or to taste
Pinch grated nutmeg
Crumbled crisp fried bacon, croutons, finely chopped chives, or parsley for garnish (optional)

1. In a heavy 4 1/2-quart pot, melt the butter. Add garlic. Sauté over low heat for a few minutes until tender but not brown.

2. Add flour. Stir over low heat for 2 minutes without browning. Add broth. Stir over moderate heat until smooth and thick.

3. Add cheese. Heat and stir until cheese is melted.

4. Stir in half-and-half, milk, wine, salt, pepper, and nutmeg.

5. Strain the soup. Reheat, garnish, and serve.

Yield: 5 1/2 cups, 5 to 6 servings.

Fresh Beet Soup

The beet greens make this a full-flavored soup.

**1 1/2 pounds beets including
  greens
4 tablespoons (1/2 stick)
  butter or margarine, divided
1 medium onion, chopped
1 clove garlic, minced
3 1/2 cups Chicken Broth
  (p. 42) or canned broth
1/2 teaspoon dried tarragon**

**1/4 teaspoon dried marjoram
3/4 teaspoon salt, or to taste
1/4 teaspoon ground black
  pepper, or to taste
Sour cream for garnish
  (optional)
Chopped chives or fresh dill
  leaves for garnish (optional)**

1. Cut the greens off the beets and reserve. Wash beets, cover with water, and boil until tender, about 25 to 30 minutes.

2. Wash greens. Pull off and discard the thick stems.

3. In a heavy 4 1/2-quart pot, melt 2 tablespoons of butter. Add greens. Do not add any water as the water droplets on the greens will provide enough moisture.

4. Cover and cook over moderate heat, stirring occasionally, until greens are wilted but still bright green, about 3 to 4 minutes.

5. Finely chop greens in a food processor or blender. Remove and reserve.

6. Melt 2 tablespoons of butter in the pot. Add onion and garlic. Sauté over moderate heat until tender but not brown. Transfer to the food processor.

7. Peel beets, chop coarsely, and add to food processor. Purée beet and onion mixture. A little broth added to the food processor will make this easier.

8. Return beets and part or all of the greens to the pot. Stir in broth, tarragon, marjoram, salt, and pepper.

9. Heat and serve. Each bowl of soup may be garnished with a dollop of sour cream and chopped chives or dill leaves.

Yield: 6 cups, 6 servings.

Minestrone

This hearty soup is a complete meal.

2 tablespoons olive oil
2 medium carrots, cut into
  1/4-inch cubes
2 celery ribs, finely chopped
2 medium onions, thinly
  sliced
3 cloves garlic, minced
1 can (16 ounces) tomatoes,
  undrained and coarsely
  chopped
6 cups Chicken Broth (p. 42)
  (no substitute)
1/2 teaspoon dried basil
1 teaspoon salt, or to taste
1/4 teaspoon ground black
  pepper, or to taste

1 medium zucchini
  (about 7 ounces), cut into
  1/2-inch cubes
1 can (15 ounces) Great
  Northern beans or cannellini
  (white kidney beans),
  undrained
1 package (10 ounces) frozen
  spinach
4 ounces small pasta such
  as ditalini, salad macaroni,
  fusilli, elbow macaroni, or
  shells
1/4 cup finely grated
  Parmesan cheese for
  garnish

1. In a heavy 4 1/2-quart pot, heat the olive oil. Add carrots, celery, onions, and garlic. Sauté over moderate heat until tender but not brown.

2. Add tomatoes, broth, basil, salt, and pepper. Bring to a boil, reduce heat, and simmer for 15 minutes.

3. Add zucchini and simmer until barely tender, about 15 minutes.

4. Add beans and spinach. Simmer until spinach is thawed.

5. Boil pasta until just tender and add to soup. Season with salt and pepper.

6. Sprinkle each serving with a teaspoon of Parmesan cheese.

Yield: 13 cups, 13 servings.

Kidney Bean and Tomato Soup

1/4 cup (1/2 stick) butter or margarine
1 medium onion, finely chopped
1 medium carrot, grated
1/2 celery rib, finely chopped
3 cups Chicken Broth (p. 42) (no substitute)
1 can (16 ounces) red kidney beans, drained

1/8 teaspoon dried basil
1/4 teaspoon salt, or to taste
1/8 teaspoon ground black pepper, or to taste
1 small bay leaf
2 medium tomatoes, peeled, seeded, and cut into 1-inch cubes
4 to 6 tablespoons finely grated Parmesan cheese

1. In a heavy 4 1/2-quart pot, melt the butter. Add onion, carrot, and celery. Sauté over moderate heat until tender but not brown.

2. Add broth, beans, basil, salt, pepper, and bay leaf.

3. Bring to a boil, cover, reduce heat, and simmer for 20 minutes.

4. Add tomatoes and continue to simmer for an additional 10 minutes.

5. Immediately before serving, sprinkle 1 tablespoon of Parmesan cheese over each portion.

Yield: 5 cups, 4 to 6 servings.

Sausage and Bean Soup

In this robust soup, half the beans are puréed, creating an appealing contrast of textures.

6 small sausage links, each
  weighing about 1 ounce
1 celery rib, finely chopped
1 medium carrot, finely
  chopped
1 medium onion, chopped
1 large clove garlic, minced
2 cups Chicken Broth (p. 42)
  or canned broth

1 can (15 ounces) cannellini
  (white kidney beans) or
  Great Northern beans,
  undrained
1/2 teaspoon salt, or to taste
1/8 teaspoon ground black
  pepper, or to taste

1. In a heavy 4 1/2-quart pot, brown the sausage links on all sides over moderate heat. Remove links and cut into 1/2-inch slices. Reserve.

2. Add celery, carrot, onion, and garlic to the fat in the pot. Sauté over moderate heat until vegetables are tender.

3. Add broth. Bring to a boil, cover, reduce heat, and simmer 30 minutes.

4. Strain vegetables from broth. Skim fat off broth and return broth to pot.

5. In a food processor or blender, purée the vegetables with half the beans. Transfer to pot.

6. Add remaining beans and sausage slices. Season with salt and pepper.

7. Heat and serve.

Yield: 4 cups, 4 servings.

Split Pea Soup

1/2 pound (1 1/8 cups)
 dried split peas
2 tablespoons (1/4 stick)
 butter or margarine
1 large onion, chopped
1 medium carrot, chopped
1 clove garlic, minced
3 cups Chicken Broth (p. 42),
 canned broth, or water
1/4 teaspoon celery seed
1/8 teaspoon ground black
 pepper, or to taste

1/8 teaspoon ground allspice
1/4 teaspoon dried marjoram
1/2 bay leaf
1 ham bone or 1/3 cup
 chopped cooked ham
1 teaspoon salt, or to taste
1 1/2 cups milk
Chopped cooked ham for
 garnish (optional)

1. Cover split peas with cold water, soak overnight, and drain. If you do not have time to soak the peas overnight, use a covered pot to simmer them in the broth or water for 30 minutes. Reserve.

2. Melt the butter in a heavy 4 1/2-quart pot. Add onion, carrot, and garlic. Sauté over moderate heat until tender but not brown.

3. Add peas, broth, celery seed, pepper, allspice, marjoram, bay leaf, ham bone or 1/3 cup of chopped ham, and salt.

4. Bring to a boil, reduce heat, cover, and simmer until peas are soft when pressed between the fingertips, about 1 hour.

5. Remove the ham from the bone. Chop ham and return to soup. Discard bone and bay leaf.

6. Strain the vegetables and return the liquid to the pot. Purée vegetables in a food processor or blender. Return to pot. Stir in milk.

7. Heat, garnish with chopped ham, and serve.

Yield: 5 cups, 5 to 6 servings.

Shrimp Bisque

This rich, lavish soup uses shrimp shells to create an intensely flavorful broth.

2 tablespoons vegetable oil
1 pound unshelled shrimp
6 tablespoons (3/4 stick) butter (no substitute), divided
1 celery rib, finely chopped
1 medium carrot, finely chopped
1 medium onion, finely chopped
1 large clove garlic, minced
2 medium tomatoes, unpeeled, seeded, and chopped
2 cups water
1 cup dry white wine
1/4 teaspoon dried tarragon
1 teaspoon salt, or to taste
1/8 teaspoon ground white pepper, or to taste
1/2 bay leaf
1/4 cup all-purpose flour
1 cup (1/2 pint) whipping cream
2 tablespoons Cognac or brandy (optional)

1. In a heavy 10 to 12-inch skillet, heat the oil. Add shrimp and sauté over high heat until pink. Remove from heat and reserve.

2. In a heavy 4 1/2-quart pot, melt 3 tablespoons of butter. Add celery, carrot, onion, and garlic. Sauté over moderate heat until tender but not brown. Reserve.

3. Shell and devein shrimp. Place the shells in the pot and reserve peeled shrimp.

4. Add tomatoes, water, wine, tarragon, salt, pepper, and bay leaf to pot. Bring to a boil, cover, reduce heat, and simmer for 1 hour. Strain broth and discard shell mixture. There should be about 3 cups of broth. Reserve.

5. In the pot, melt 3 tablespoons of butter. Add flour. Stir over low heat for 2 minutes without browning. Add broth and whipping cream. Stir over moderate heat until smooth and thick. Reserve.

6. In a food processor with a steel blade, purée two-thirds of the shrimp with about 1/2 cup of the soup. Return to pot. Add Cognac. Season to taste with salt and pepper.

7. Split remaining shrimp lengthwise and reserve.

8. Reheat bisque, garnish with shrimp, and serve.

Yield: 5 cups, 5 to 6 servings.

Clam Chowder

2 dozen clams in shells,
 about 2 1/2 to 3-inches long,
 or enough to yield 1 cup
 shucked clams and 1 cup
 clam juice
1/4 cup (1/2 stick) butter or
 margarine
1/2 cup finely chopped onion
1/4 cup finely chopped celery
1 tablespoon grated carrot
1/3 cup all-purpose flour

1 1/2 cups Chicken Broth
 (p. 42) or canned broth
2 cups milk and 1 cup
 half-and-half OR 3 cups milk
1 tablespoon dry sherry
Salt, to taste
Ground white pepper, to taste
2 cups peeled boiling
 (preferably new) potatoes,
 cut into 1/2-inch cubes

1. Scrub clams and place them in a large flat pan, such as a roasting pan. Heat in a 450° F oven until the clams begin to open, about 10 minutes. Use a clam or oyster knife or other heavy knife to open the clams and scrape them from their shells. Chop clams into small pieces. Reserve clams and juice. If the clam juice is excessively salty, substitute water or chicken broth for part of the juice.

2. In a heavy 4 1/2-quart pot, melt the butter. Add onion, celery, and carrot. Sauté over low heat until tender but not brown, about 8 to 10 minutes.

3. Add flour. Stir over low heat for 2 minutes without browning. Add broth, milk, half-and-half, sherry, and clam juice. Stir over moderate heat until smooth and thick. Reserve.

4. Boil potatoes until just tender. Drain. Add potatoes and clams to pot. Season with salt and pepper. Simmer just long enough to heat the clams, about 5 minutes. Do not overcook. Serve.

Yield: 7 cups, 4 to 8 servings.

Peanut Pumpkin Soup

This rich soup makes an unusual and tasty first course.

2 tablespoons (1/4 stick)
  butter or margarine
1/3 cup finely chopped onion
3 1/3 cups Chicken Broth
  (p. 42) or 2 cans (14 1/2
  ounces each) broth
3/4 cup smooth peanut butter
1 can (16 ounces) pumpkin
1/8 teaspoon ground allspice

Salt, to taste
Ground white pepper, to
  taste
1/3 cup heavy cream,
  whipped (optional)
Chopped chives or grated
  nutmeg for garnish
  (optional)

1. In a heavy 2-quart saucepan, melt the butter. Add onion and sauté over low heat until tender but not brown.

2. Add broth, peanut butter, pumpkin, allspice, salt, and pepper.

3. Stir over moderate heat until smooth and heated.

4. Garnish each serving with a dollop of whipped cream and chives or nutmeg.

Yield: 6 cups, 8 servings.

Salads
and
Salad
Dressings

Caesar Salad

All ingredients must be fresh and the croutons made from quality bread for this to be a perfect salad. Serve as soon as prepared.

1/2 cup olive oil, other vegetable oil, or a combination of both
2 cloves garlic, minced
1 1/2 cups French Bread (p. 222), Italian Bread (p. 225), White Bread (p. 210), or firm commercial bread, cut into 1/2-inch cubes
1 large egg OR 1/4 cup heavy cream

1 1/2 to 2 tablespoons lemon juice
1/4 teaspoon Worcestershire sauce
1/2 teaspoon salt, or to taste
1/8 teaspoon ground black pepper, or to taste
7 cups bite-size pieces of romaine lettuce, loosely packed
5 tablespoons finely grated Parmesan cheese, divided

1. Combine the oil and garlic. Allow the oil to absorb the garlic flavor for at least 30 minutes. Strain and reserve.

2. On a rimmed baking sheet, toast the bread cubes in a 350° F oven, turning frequently, about 8 to 10 minutes. A toaster oven is useful for this. Put the croutons in a small bowl. Pour 2 tablespoons of the garlic olive oil over the croutons and toss. Add 1 tablespoon of Parmesan cheese and toss again. Reserve.

— This recipe may be prepared ahead to this point. —

3. In a large bowl, whisk the egg or cream, remaining oil, 1 1/2 tablespoons of lemon juice, Worcestershire sauce, salt, and pepper together until smooth.

4. Add lettuce to salad bowl and toss salad. Taste and adjust seasoning with additional lemon juice, salt, and pepper. Sprinkle 4 tablespoons of Parmesan cheese over salad. Toss again.

5. Place on salad plates. Sprinkle with croutons. Serve immediately.

Yield: 4 servings.

Note: This recipe (Steps 1 and 2) may be used to prepare tasty croutons for use in other salads.

Molded Cranberry Salad

1 1/2 cups cold water, divided
1/2 cup orange juice
2 envelopes (2 tablespoons) unflavored gelatin
12 ounces fresh or frozen cranberries
1 cup granulated sugar
Finely grated rind of an orange
1 can (15 1/4 ounces) crushed pineapple, drained
1 cup finely chopped celery
1 1/4 cups coarsely chopped pecans
Lettuce to cover plates
Mayonnaise (p. 75) or commercial mayonnaise for garnish (optional)
Grated orange rind for garnish (optional)
Honey Lemon Salad Dressing (p. 78) (optional)

1. Soften gelatin in 1/2 cup of water and orange juice. Reserve.

2. In a heavy 2-quart saucepan, combine 1 cup of water, cranberries, sugar, and orange rind. Bring to a boil stirring occasionally. Boil until cranberries pop and become soft, about 5 minutes.

3. Remove from heat. Add gelatin and stir until dissolved. Stir in pineapple, celery, and pecans.

4. Spoon into ten 4-ounce (1/2-cup) lightly oiled molds or use one 1 1/2-quart mold.

5. Refrigerate until firm. Unmold by placing each mold in hot water for a minute or so. Refrigerate unmolded salads until ready to serve. Serve on lettuce.

6. Each salad may be garnished with a rosette of mayonnaise and sprinkled with grated orange rind. Spoon dressing over each serving.

Yield: Ten 4-ounce (1/2-cup) molds or one 1 1/2-quart mold, 10 servings.

Ambrosia

2 1/2 cups orange sections (about 4 oranges)
1 cup grated fresh or frozen coconut (p. 16)
1/4 cup orange juice
2 tablespoons granulated sugar, or to taste
2 tablespoons Grand Marnier or other orange liqueur (optional)

1. Combine all ingredients in a bowl. Toss gently.
2. Refrigerate for several hours before serving.
3. Serve in crystal dishes or on salad plates covered with lettuce.

Yield: 3 cups, 6 servings.

Apple and Cheese Salad

The dressing for this salad is light and tangy.

1 tablespoon cider vinegar
1 tablespoon lemon juice
1/4 teaspoon brown sugar
1 teaspoon Dijon mustard
1/4 teaspoon salt, or to taste
1/8 teaspoon ground black
  pepper, or to taste
1/4 cup vegetable oil
1 cup celery, cut into 1/4-inch
  cubes

1/2 cup raisins
1/2 cup chopped walnuts
  or pecans
1 cup Monterey Jack cheese,
  cut into 1/2-inch cubes
2 medium apples, unpeeled
Lettuce to cover 4 salad
  plates (optional)

1. In a small jar, combine vinegar, lemon juice, brown sugar, mustard, salt, and pepper. Cover and shake until sugar is dissolved. Add oil. Reserve.

2. In a salad bowl, combine celery, raisins, walnuts, and cheese.

— This recipe may be prepared ahead to this point. —

3. When ready to serve, cut apples into 1/2 to 3/4-inch cubes. Add to salad bowl. Toss the salad with the dressing. Serve on plates covered with lettuce.

Yield: 4 1/2 cups, 4 servings.

Crab and Grapefruit Salad

My wife and I first enjoyed this salad at the Hong Kong Hilton. This colorful salad may be used as a special first course.

Lettuce to cover 4 salad
  plates
Endive leaves (optional)
3/4 to 1 cup (6 to 8 ounces)
  crab meat, preferably lump
  or backfin
1 can (16 ounces) grapefruit
  sections in light syrup,
  drained
1/2 cup Mayonnaise (p. 75) or
  commercial mayonnaise

2 teaspoons ketchup
2 teaspoons minced dill
  pickle
2 tablespoons milk
4 teaspoons finely grated red
  cabbage
24 thin radish slices
20 cooked tiny whole shrimp
  (optional)
Paprika for garnish

1. Tear lettuce into small pieces and cover 4 salad plates. Endive may be substituted for part of the lettuce.

2. Use one-quarter of the crab, divided into five spoonfuls, for each salad. Place one spoonful in the center of the plate and equally space the other four in a circle about 2-inches in from the edge of the plate.

3. Arrange grapefruit sections between the mounds of crab.

4. In a small bowl, stir mayonnaise, ketchup, pickle, and milk together. Spoon over each mound of crab.

5. Sprinkle each salad with a teaspoon of grated cabbage.

6. Arrange 6 radish slices in a circle around the edge of each plate.

7. Place a shrimp on each mound of crab. Sprinkle the shrimp with paprika.

8. Chill before serving.

Yield: 4 servings.

Cole Slaw

1/4 cup granulated sugar
1/3 cup cider vinegar
1/3 cup vegetable oil
1 teaspoon salt, or to taste
1/4 teaspoon ground pepper,
  or to taste
1/4 teaspoon celery seed
  (optional)
1 teaspoon finely grated
  onion (optional)

1/2 teaspoon prepared
  horseradish (optional)
1/2 medium head (1 pound)
  cabbage, sliced 1/4-inch
  thick
1 medium carrot, grated
1/4 green pepper, thinly
  sliced

1. In a nonreactive 1/2-quart saucepan, combine sugar, vinegar, oil, salt, pepper, and celery seed. Heat and stir until sugar is dissolved. Cool to room temperature. Stir in onion and horseradish. Reserve.

2. In a large bowl, combine remaining ingredients.

3. Pour dressing over vegetables. Toss well.

4. Refrigerate for at least several hours before serving.

Yield: 4 cups, 4 to 6 servings.

Hot German Potato Salad

2 pounds boiling (preferably
  new) potatoes, unpeeled
4 ounces thinly sliced bacon
  (about 5 strips)
1 medium onion, finely
  chopped
3/4 cup Chicken Broth (p. 42),
  Beef Broth (p. 43), or canned
  broth

1/4 cup white wine vinegar
1/2 teaspoon granulated
  sugar
3/4 teaspoon salt, or to taste
1/4 teaspoon ground black
  pepper, or to taste
1/4 cup finely chopped
  parsley

1. Boil potatoes until just tender. Use an ice pick or fork to test for doneness. Drain. When potatoes have cooled enough to handle, peel them and cut into 1/2-inch slices.

2. Arrange the slices in layers in an 11 x 7-inch (2-quart) baking dish. Reserve.

3. Fry bacon in a heavy 10-inch skillet until crisp. Drain on paper towels. Crumble bacon. Reserve.

4. Sauté onion in bacon fat over moderate heat until tender and golden brown. Spread on top of the potatoes.

5. In a nonreactive 1/2-quart saucepan, combine broth, vinegar, sugar, salt, and pepper. Bring to a boil and pour over potatoes. Let potatoes absorb liquid for at least 30 minutes. Cover with a lid or aluminum foil. Refrigerate if salad will be served later.

— This recipe may be prepared ahead to this point. —

6. Reheat the covered salad in a 350° F oven until potatoes are warm.

7. Sprinkle bacon and parsley over potatoes. Gently toss salad with two forks and serve immediately.

Yield: 6 cups, 6 to 8 servings.

Cold German Potato Salad

I have enjoyed this potato salad ever since I first tasted it in a German delicatessen when I was a child.

2 pounds boiling (preferably
  new) potatoes, unpeeled
1/3 cup commercial
  mayonnaise
2/3 cup sour cream
2 teaspoons grated onion
1 teaspoon Dijon mustard
1/4 teaspoon celery seeds
1/4 cup finely chopped celery
2 tablespoons finely chopped
  carrot

3 tablespoons vinegar
  (cider or white wine)
1/4 cup cold water
1 teaspoon salt, or to taste
1/4 teaspoon ground black
  pepper, or to taste
1 tablespoon finely chopped
  parsley

1. Boil potatoes until just tender. Use an ice pick or fork to test for doneness. Peel potatoes and cut into slices 1/8 to 1/4-inch thick. Reserve.

2. In a small bowl, combine remaining ingredients. Mix thoroughly.

3. Arrange a layer of potatoes in an 11 x 7-inch (2-quart) baking dish. Pour a little of the dressing on the slices and use a rubber spatula to

spread it evenly. Cover with additional layers of potatoes and dressing until all are used.

4. Toss gently with a rubber spatula. The salad may be garnished with additional parsley.

5. Refrigerate until served.

Yield: 6 cups, 6 to 10 servings.

Shrimp and Pasta Salad

A beautiful salad of contrasting vibrant colors. This recipe is easily doubled or tripled and may be prepared ahead for a large luncheon or supper.

2 to 2 1/4 pounds raw shrimp, shelled and deveined
1 tablespoon vegetable oil
8 ounces sea shell or rotini (tri-color vegetable type or plain) pasta
2 1/2 cups bite-size broccoli florets
2 recipes Lemon Basil Salad Dressing (p. 74)
1 teaspoon Dijon mustard
1/4 teaspoon dried basil
1 tablespoon lemon juice and possibly more, to taste
1 cup finely chopped celery
1 can (5 3/4 ounces) jumbo pitted ripe olives, drained and quartered lengthwise

8 ounces shredded mozzarella cheese (2 cups, loosely packed)
1/2 red bell pepper, cut into 2-inch x 1/4-inch strips
1 teaspoon salt, or to taste
Ground white pepper, to taste
Lettuce to cover 8 to 10 plates
15 cherry tomatoes, halved (optional)
Finely grated Parmesan cheese for garnish (optional)

1. Drop shrimp into a 2-quart saucepan one-third full of boiling water. Boil just until pink and firm, about 2 minutes. Do not overcook. Drain and reserve.

2. Drop pasta into lightly salted boiling water to which the vegetable oil has been added. Boil until just tender, about 9 to 12 minutes. Drain, rinse with cold water, and reserve in a large bowl.

3. Drop broccoli into boiling water. Boil for 2 minutes. Drain immediately. Reserve.

4. Whisk salad dressing, mustard, basil, and 1 tablespoon of lemon juice together until blended. Pour over pasta. Toss gently with a rubber spatula until the pasta shells are evenly coated.

5. Add shrimp, broccoli, celery, olives, mozzarella cheese, and bell pepper. Toss gently. Season to taste with lemon juice, salt, and pepper. Refrigerate for 2 hours or up to a day before serving.

— This recipe may be prepared ahead to this point. —

6. Toss gently before serving. Spoon onto plates covered with lettuce. Arrange 3 cherry tomato halves, cut side down, around the edge of each serving. Sprinkle each serving with about 1/4 teaspoon Parmesan cheese.

Yield: 12 cups, 8 to 10 servings.

Tuna Salad

The flavors of ginger and sesame seeds are perfect complements to the taste of tuna.

2 tablespoons sesame seeds
1 can (6 1/2 ounces) tuna fish, drained
1/3 cup finely chopped celery
2 teaspoons finely grated onion
6 tablespoons Mayonnaise (p. 75) or commercial mayonnaise

1/2 teaspoon lemon juice
1/2 teaspoon grated fresh ginger or 1/4 teaspoon ground dried ginger
Pinch salt, or to taste
1/8 teaspoon ground white pepper, or to taste

1. On a rimmed baking sheet, toast sesame seeds in a 350° F oven. A toaster oven is useful for this. Stir frequently as the seeds are easily burned.

2. Mix all ingredients together.

3. Refrigerate until served.

Yield: 1 1/4 cups, 2 to 3 servings.

Vegetable Sandwich Spread

Low-calorie, nutritious, and especially delicious. I like to include lettuce, tomato, and mayonnaise in sandwiches made with this spread.

12 ounces (1 1/4 cups)
  cottage cheese
2 tablespoons finely chopped
  carrot
2 tablespoons finely chopped
  celery
2 tablespoons finely chopped
  green pepper

2 tablespoons peeled,
  seeded, and finely chopped
  cucumber
1 tablespoon minced green
  onion
1/8 teaspoon ground white
  pepper, or to taste

1. Mix all ingredients together.
2. Refrigerate until served.

Yield: 1 1/2 cups, enough for 4 sandwiches.

Curried Chicken Salad

Something different for soup and sandwich meals. I like to serve this salad with lettuce in pockets of whole wheat pita bread.

3 to 3 1/2 cups cooked
  chicken, cut into small
  pieces
1/4 cup finely chopped green
  pepper
1/4 cup finely chopped celery
1/2 cup sliced almonds,
  toasted or untoasted
1 can (8 ounces) tidbit (or
  chunks, halved) pineapple,
  drained

1/2 cup halved red seedless
  grapes (optional)
1/2 cup sour cream
1/4 cup Mayonnaise (p. 75) or
  commercial mayonnaise
1/2 teaspoon curry powder,
  or to taste
1 teaspoon salt, or to taste
1/4 teaspoon ground white
  pepper, or to taste

1. In a bowl, combine chicken, green pepper, celery, almonds, pineapple, and grapes. Reserve.

2. In a small bowl, stir sour cream, mayonnaise, curry powder, salt, and pepper together until blended. Pour over chicken mixture.

3. Use a rubber spatula to gently mix the ingredients.

4. Refrigerate. This chicken salad is best served the day it is made.

Yield: 4 cups, 6 to 8 servings.

Mustard Vinaigrette Salad Dressing

Try a variety of vinegars and oils to find the flavors and brands you like. Use ingredients of the highest quality.

1 small clove garlic (optional)
1/2 teaspoon salt, or to taste
1 tablespoon Dijon mustard
2 tablespoons wine vinegar
1/4 teaspoon ground black
**   pepper, or to taste**

1/4 teaspoon dried basil or
**   tarragon (optional)**
1/2 cup vegetable oil
1 to 2 pinches granulated
**   sugar (optional)**

FOOD PROCESSOR METHOD

1. Mince garlic by dropping it into a food processor with a steel blade and the motor running.

2. Add salt, mustard, vinegar, pepper, and basil or tarragon. Process a few seconds to mix ingredients.

3. With processor running, add oil in a fine stream to produce an emulsion.

4. Taste the dressing. If it is too acidic, add sugar and process for a few seconds.

HAND METHOD

1. Mince garlic. In a small bowl, use a spoon to mash garlic and salt into a paste. Whisk in mustard, vinegar, pepper, and basil.

2. Add oil, in a fine stream, while whisking to form an emulsion. An emulsion does not have to be formed but it will create a dressing with a better appearance.

3. Taste the dressing. If it is too acidic, add sugar and process for a few seconds.

Yield: 2/3 cup, 6 to 8 servings.

Italian Salad Dressing

Prepare Mustard Vinaigrette Salad Dressing (p. 73) with the following changes:

1. Use basil rather than tarragon.
2. Add 1/4 teaspoon dried oregano.
3. Use olive oil.
4. Sprinkle finely grated Parmesan cheese, about 1 teaspoon, over each serving.

Yield: 2/3 cup, 6 to 8 servings.

Lemon Basil Salad Dressing

1/2 clove garlic (optional)
1/2 teaspoon salt, or to taste
1/4 teaspoon finely grated
 lemon rind
2 tablespoons lemon juice
1/4 teaspoon ground white
 pepper, or to taste

1/4 teaspoon dried basil
1/2 cup vegetable oil
Pinch granulated sugar
 (optional)

FOOD PROCESSOR METHOD

1. Mince garlic by dropping it into a food processor with a steel blade and the motor running.
2. Add salt, lemon rind and juice, pepper, and basil. Process a few seconds to mix ingredients.
3. With processor running, add oil in a fine stream to produce an emulsion.
4. Taste the dressing. If it is too acidic, add sugar and process for a few seconds.

HAND METHOD

1. Mince garlic. In a small bowl, use a spoon to mash garlic and salt into a paste. Whisk in lemon rind and juice, pepper, and basil.
2. Add oil, in a fine stream, while whisking to form an emulsion. An emulsion does not have to be formed but it will create a dressing with a better appearance.

3. Taste the dressing. If it is too acidic, add sugar and process for a few seconds.

Yield: 10 tablespoons, 6 to 8 servings.

Mayonnaise

Once you make your own mayonnaise, the store-bought kind will never be as satisfying. With a food processor, this recipe can be made in a flash.

3 large egg yolks	**1 teaspoon Dijon mustard**
1 tablespoon lemon juice	**3/4 teaspoon salt, or to taste**
2 teaspoons vinegar	**Pinch cayenne pepper or**
(white wine, tarragon, or	**1/8 teaspoon ground white**
cider)	**pepper, or to taste**
2 teaspoons water	**2 cups vegetable oil**

1. In a food processor bowl with a plastic or steel blade, combine all ingredients except vegetable oil. Process until blended.
2. With processor running, add oil in a fine stream until a smooth, thick emulsion is formed.
3. If a food processor is not available, a blender or electric mixer with a wire whisk attachment may be used. Mayonnaise may also be made by hand using a whisk.
4. Cover and refrigerate.

Yield: 2 1/4 cups.

Mustard Mayonnaise

Add 1 tablespoon of Dijon mustard to 1 cup of Mayonnaise (p. 75).

Herb Mayonnaise

Add 1/2 teaspoon of fresh, finely chopped tarragon, thyme, or dill to 1 cup of Mayonnaise (p. 75) or Mustard Mayonnaise (see above).

Garlic Lime Mayonnaise

A zesty mayonnaise for vegetables, seafood (e.g. Lemon-Lime Marinated Shrimp, p. 29), and sandwiches.

2 cloves garlic
3 large egg yolks
1 teaspoon finely grated lime rind
2 tablespoons lime juice
1 teaspoon tarragon vinegar
1 teaspoon Dijon mustard

3/4 teaspoon salt, or to taste
1/8 teaspoon ground white pepper, or to taste
1 teaspoon finely grated onion
2 cups vegetable oil

1. Mince garlic by dropping it into a food processor with a steel blade and the motor running. Add all remaining ingredients except vegetable oil. Process until blended.
2. With processor running, add oil in a fine stream until a smooth, thick emulsion is formed.
3. If a food processor is not available, a blender or electric mixer with a wire whisk attachment may be used. Mayonnaise may also be made by hand using a whisk.
4. Cover and refrigerate.

Yield: 2 1/4 cups.

Blue Cheese Salad Dressing

1 cup sour cream
1/2 cup Mayonnaise, (p. 75) or
 commercial mayonnaise
1 teaspoon lemon juice
1/2 teaspoon white wine
 vinegar
2 tablespoons milk
1/2 teaspoon salt, or to taste

Pinch ground white pepper,
 or to taste
1/4 teaspoon granulated
 sugar
1/2 small clove garlic, minced
3 ounces (1/2 cup) blue
 cheese, crumbled

1. In a small bowl, combine all ingredients except blue cheese. Whisk until smooth. Add blue cheese and mix gently. The dressing may be thinned with additional milk.

2. The flavor is improved if the dressing is refrigerated for at least 8 hours before serving.

Yield: 2 cups.

Creamy Italian Salad Dressing

For garlic and onion lovers.

1 cup Mayonnaise (p. 75) or
 commercial mayonnaise
1/8 teaspoon garlic, minced
1 teaspoon grated onion
2 teaspoons milk

Pinch ground white pepper,
 or to taste
Finely grated Parmesan
 cheese (optional)

1. In a small jar, mix together all ingredients except Parmesan cheese. Additional milk may be added for a thinner dressing.

2. Refrigerate for at least 30 minutes before serving.

3. Drizzle dressing over each individual salad.

4. Sprinkle salads with Parmesan cheese and serve.

Yield: 1 cup, 8 servings.

Honey Lemon Salad Dressing

This dressing is the perfect complement for fruit salads.

1/3 cup honey
1/4 cup lemon juice

1/2 teaspoon grated fresh ginger or 1/4 teaspoon ground dried ginger (optional)

1. In a small jar, mix all ingredients together.
2. Refrigerate until served.
3. Pour dressing over salad immediately before serving.

Yield: 1/2 cup, 8 servings.

Note: The illustration below shows an enticing fruit salad that can be served with this sweet and tangy salad dressing. Cover the salad plate with leaf lettuce. Place a pineapple ring in the center. Surround the pineapple ring with six strawberry halves and place a whole strawberry in the center of the pineapple ring. The salad may be covered with plastic wrap and refrigerated for up to 6 hours before serving.

Fish
and
Shellfish

Broiled Fish with Wine

The wine enhances the taste of the fish and keeps it moist.

6 tablespoons (3/4 stick)
  butter or margarine, melted,
  OR olive oil or other
  vegetable oil
3 tablespoons dry white wine
1 1/2 pounds fish fillets or
  steaks
Salt, to taste

Ground white pepper, to
  taste
1/4 teaspoon dried tarragon,
  basil, thyme, marjoram, or
  other dried herb (optional)
Paprika (optional)

1. Combine butter and wine. Use part of this mixture to brush a broiling pan with the rack removed or use a similar pan measuring about 14 1/2 x 12 x 1-inches. The pan should be nonreactive such as enamel or stainless steel.

2. Arrange fish, skin side down, in one layer in the pan. If necessary, fold the tail ends under the fillets. Brush fish with remaining butter and wine. Sprinkle with salt, pepper, and herb or paprika.

3. Place pan on a rack 3-inches below the heating element of a broiler. Be prepared to place the pan on the next lower rack (6-inches) if the fish browns too quickly. Use a pastry brush to occasionally baste the fish and brush the pan to prevent the pan juices from burning. If needed, use additional butter or oil. Broil until the fish just begins to flake when touched with a fork, about 8 minutes for flounder fillets.

4. Serve immediately.

Yield: 4 servings.

Notes:

1. The broiled fish may be served with Lemon Butter Sauce (Beurre Blanc) (p. 194), Orange Butter Sauce (Beurre Blanc) (p. 195), Hollandaise Sauce (3/4 cup, p. 193), Mustard Hollandaise Sauce (3/4 cup, p. 194), Sour Cream and Mustard Sauce (p. 197), or Sour Cream and Shallot Sauce (p. 197).

2. If less than 1 1/2 pounds of fish are broiled, use a pan just large enough to hold the pieces in one layer. Use 4 tablespoons of butter and 2 tablespoons of wine for 1 pound of fish and 3 tablespoons of butter and 1 1/2 tablespoons of wine for 1/2 pound.

Broiled Fish with Wine and Garlic Butter

3 tablespoons butter
1/2 clove garlic, minced
Broiled Fish with Wine (p. 80)

Chopped parsley for
garnish (optional)

1. Prepare garlic butter either before or while fish is broiling. Melt butter in a 1/2-quart saucepan. Add garlic and let stand for at least 5 minutes.

2. Immediately before serving, heat garlic butter, strain, and spoon over the broiled fish. Garnish with parsley.

Yield: 4 servings.

Broiled Mackerel with Mustard Sauce

1 1/2 pounds mackerel fillets
broiled according to the
recipe for Broiled Fish with
Wine (p. 80)
1/4 cup (1/2 stick) butter or
margarine
1 tablespoon finely chopped
green onion, shallot, or
other onion

5 tablespoons Dijon mustard
Chopped fresh tarragon,
basil, parsley, or chives
for garnish (optional)

1. Prepare sauce either before or while fish is broiling. Melt butter in a heavy 2-quart saucepan. Add green onion and sauté over moderate heat until tender.

2. Add mustard. Whisk until mixture is the consistency of mayonnaise.

3. Spread sauce on broiled fillets. Sprinkle with the herb and serve.

Yield: 4 servings.

Broiled Mackerel with Mustard Hollandaise

Broil mackerel fillets with dried tarragon according to the recipe for Broiled Fish with Wine (p. 80). Place a spoonful of Mustard Hollandaise (3/4 cup, p. 194) on each serving. Garnish with chopped parsley.

Yield: 4 servings.

Broiled Salmon with Tarragon

Broil salmon using dried tarragon according to the recipe for Broiled Fish with Wine (p. 80). Serve with Sour Cream and Shallot Sauce (p. 197). Use dried tarragon in the sauce.

Yield: 4 servings.

Baked Fish with Wine

In this method, the fish bakes in intense heat with a small amount of wine. The result is juicy and flavorful.

1 1/2 pounds fish fillets or steaks
1/3 cup dry white wine
3 tablespoons butter, margarine, olive oil, or other vegetable oil
Salt, to taste
Ground white pepper, to taste
1/4 teaspoon dried basil, tarragon, or another herb (optional)

1. Butter a nonreactive baking dish or roasting pan measuring about 14 1/2 x 10-inches.
2. Arrange fish, skin side down, in one layer in the pan. If necessary, fold the tail ends under the fillets. Pour wine over fillets.
3. Dot fish with butter. Sprinkle with salt, pepper, and herb.

4. Bake, uncovered, in a preheated 450° F oven until the fish just begins to flake when touched with a fork, about 10 to 15 minutes. Baste occasionally.

5. Transfer fish to a serving dish. Spoon juices over fish.

6. Serve immediately.

Yield: 4 servings.

Note: The baked fish may be served with Lemon Butter Sauce (Beurre Blanc) (p. 194), Orange Butter Sauce (Beurre Blanc) (p. 195), Hollandaise Sauce (3/4 cup, p. 193), Mustard Hollandaise Sauce (3/4 cup, p. 194), Sour Cream and Mustard Sauce (p. 197), or Sour Cream and Shallot Sauce (p. 197).

Flounder Amandine

Bake flounder according to the recipe for Baked Fish with Wine (p. 82) but omit the herb and sprinkle the fillets with 1/3 cup of slivered almonds before baking.

Yield: 4 servings.

Baked Cod in Onion Mustard Sauce

1 1/2 to 2 pounds fresh or
  thawed frozen cod fillets
  or steaks
1/8 teaspoon dried thyme
1/8 teaspoon dried marjoram
9 tablespoons butter or
  margarine, divided
2 medium onions, sliced
  1/8-inch thick

1 large clove garlic, minced
1/4 cup all-purpose flour
1 3/4 cups milk
2 teaspoons Dijon mustard
1/2 teaspoon salt, or to taste
1/8 teaspoon ground white
  pepper, or to taste
1/4 cup dry bread crumbs

1. Arrange cod in one layer in a buttered 11 x 7-inch or 8-inch square (2-quart) baking dish. Sprinkle with thyme and marjoram.

2. In a heavy 10-inch skillet, melt 4 tablespoons of butter. Add onions and sauté over moderate heat until light golden brown. Add garlic and cook for a few minutes over low heat. Spread over fish.

3. Melt 3 tablespoons of butter in the skillet. Whisk in flour until smooth. Stir over low heat for 2 minutes without browning. Stir in milk, mustard, salt, and pepper. Stir over moderate heat until smooth and thick.

4. Pour sauce over cod. Cover baking dish with a lid or aluminum foil.

5. Bake in a preheated 375° F oven until the fish just begins to flake when touched with a fork, about 35 minutes.

6. While cod is baking, prepare bread crumbs: Melt 2 tablespoons of butter in a small skillet. Add bread crumbs and sauté over moderate heat until golden brown.

7. Sprinkle baked fish with bread crumbs and serve.

Yield: 4 servings.

Broiled or Baked Fish with Tomato and Green Pepper

The striking colors of tomato and green pepper make this a particularly attractive dish.

Broiled or Baked Fish with
 Wine (p. 80 or p. 82)
1/4 cup (1/2 stick) butter or
 margarine
1 medium onion, chopped
1 clove garlic, minced
1/2 green bell pepper,
 seeded, and cut into
 1/4-inch squares

1 large tomato, peeled or
 unpeeled, seeded, and cut
 into 1-inch by 1/4-inch strips
3/4 teaspoon chopped fresh
 basil or 1/4 teaspoon dried
 basil
Salt, to taste
Ground white or black
 pepper, to taste

1. While fish is cooking, melt the butter in a 9-inch skillet. Add onion and garlic. Sauté over moderate heat until tender but not brown. Reserve.

2. Transfer fish to a serving plate and keep warm.

3. Add green pepper, tomato, and basil to skillet. Heat only until hot.
4. Spoon vegetables over fillets. Season with salt and pepper.
5. Serve immediately.

Yield: 4 servings.

Broiled or Baked Fish with Orange Butter Sauce and Pecans

I prefer to use grouper or flounder in this recipe.

**Broiled or Baked Fish with
  Wine (p. 80 or p. 82)
Orange Butter Sauce
  (Beurre Blanc) (p. 195)**

4 teaspoons chopped pecans

1. Prepare sauce while fish is cooking.
2. Spoon sauce over fish and sprinkle with pecans.
3. Serve immediately.

Yield: 4 servings.

Flounder Dugléré

**Baked Flounder Fillets with
  Wine (p. 82) (use a
  nonreactive, broiler-proof
  baking dish or pan)
5 tablespoons butter or
  margarine, divided
2 tablespoons all-purpose
  flour
1 1/2 cups half-and-half or
  milk
1/2 teaspoon salt, or to taste**

**1/8 teaspoon ground white
  pepper, or to taste
3 tablespoons finely grated
  Parmesan cheese
4 ounces mushrooms, sliced
  1/4-inch thick
1 teaspoon lemon juice
1 medium tomato, peeled,
  seeded, and cut into
  1-inch x 1/4-inch strips**

1. Prepare sauce either before or while fillets are cooking. Melt 3 tablespoons of butter in a heavy 2-quart saucepan. Whisk in flour until smooth. Stir over low heat for 2 minutes without browning. Add half-and-half or milk, salt, pepper, and Parmesan cheese. Stir over moderate heat until smooth and thick. Reserve.

2. In a heavy 9-inch skillet, melt 2 tablespoons of butter. Add mushrooms, sprinkle with lemon juice, and sauté over high heat until barely tender. Reserve.

3. When fillets are done, pour liquid from fish into sauce. Heat and stir until sauce is thick. Spoon over fillets.

4. Sprinkle the sauced fish with the mushrooms and tomato.

5. Place dish on a rack 6-inches below the heating element of a broiler. Broil until sauce begins to brown, about 5 minutes.

6. Serve immediately.

Yield: 4 servings.

Sautéed Fish Fillets in Cracker Meal

Cracker meal, as needed
Salt, to taste
Pepper, to taste
Dried tarragon, basil, thyme, marjoram, or other dried herb, to taste (optional)
Egg(s), as needed

Fish fillets
Butter, margarine, olive oil, or other vegetable oil, as needed
Fresh chopped chives or parsley for garnish (optional)

1. In a pie pan, mix cracker meal, salt, pepper, and herb together. Reserve.

2. In another pie pan, lightly beat the egg.

3. Dip each fillet in egg and then coat it with cracker meal mixture.

4. Heat butter in a heavy, preferably nonstick, 10 to 12-inch skillet. Use just enough butter to cover the bottom of the skillet. Add fillets and, over moderately high heat, brown them on both sides. The fish is done when it just begins to flake when touched with a fork.

5. Sprinkle with chives or parsley and serve immediately.

Shallow-Poached Fish in Wine

This cooking method creates moist fish with exceptional flavor. Even those who don't care much for fish will enjoy this recipe.

1/4 cup (1/2 stick) butter or margarine
1/2 cup carrot, cut into 1/4-inch cubes
1/2 cup celery, cut into 1/4-inch cubes
1/2 cup finely chopped onion
1 clove garlic, minced (optional)
1/4 teaspoon dried basil

1/2 teaspoon salt, or to taste
1/4 teaspoon ground white pepper, or to taste
1 cup dry white wine
1 1/2 pounds fish fillets or steaks
1/2 cup peeled, seeded, and chopped tomato (optional)
Chopped parsley for garnish (optional)

1. In a heavy, nonreactive 10 to 12-inch skillet, melt the butter. Add carrot, celery, onion, and garlic. Sauté over moderate heat until tender but not brown.

2. Stir in basil, salt, pepper, and wine. Add fish. If necessary, fold the tail ends under the fillets. Spoon some of the vegetables on top of the fish. Heat just until the boiling point is reached. Immediately reduce heat, cover, and simmer until fish just begins to flake when touched with a fork, about 6 to 8 minutes. Transfer fish and vegetables to a serving dish and keep warm.

3. Boil the contents of the skillet, stirring constantly, until the liquid becomes syrupy. Stir in tomato and pour over fish.

4. Garnish with parsley and serve immediately.

Yield: 4 servings.

Note: Try this variation:

1. Omit the tomato.

2. After the liquid becomes syrupy in Step 3, add 1/2 cup of whipping cream to the skillet. Boil and stir until thickened. Pour over fish, garnish with parsley, and serve.

3. Do not use tomato and whipping cream together because juices from the tomato give the cream an unattractive color.

Codfish Cakes

9 tablespoons butter or
  margarine, divided
10 ounces fresh or thawed
  frozen cod fillets or steaks
3 tablespoons finely chopped
  onion
1 clove garlic, minced
  (optional)
1 cup mashed potatoes from
  boiled or baked potatoes

1 large egg
1/4 cup dry bread crumbs
  (Italian style or plain)
1/4 teaspoon salt, or to taste
1/8 teaspoon ground white
  pepper, or to taste
1/4 cup all-purpose flour

1. Melt 2 tablespoons of butter in a heavy 10 to 12-inch skillet. Add cod to skillet. Cook over moderate heat until the fish just begins to flake, about 3 to 4 minutes on each side.

2. Grind fish in a food processor or meat grinder. There should be about 1 to 1 1/4 cups of fish. Reserve.

3. Melt 1 tablespoon of butter in the skillet. Add onion and garlic. Sauté over low heat until tender but not brown. Transfer to a bowl.

4. Add fish, potatoes, egg, bread crumbs, salt, and pepper to bowl. Mix thoroughly.

5. On a work surface, flatten mixture until it is 1/2-inch thick. Use a 2 1/2-inch cutter to cut mixture into rounds.

6. Dust fish cakes with flour. Refrigerate until ready to serve.

— This recipe may be prepared ahead to this point. —

7. Fry fish cakes in 6 tablespoons of butter. Serve.

Yield: 12 fish cakes, 4 servings.

Note: These fish cakes are delicious served with spaghetti and Tomato Sauce (p. 190). Prepare 2/3 to 1 pound of spaghetti for 4 servings.

Shrimp Scampi

5 tablespoons butter
(no substitute), divided
1 clove garlic, minced
1 pound raw shrimp, shelled
and deveined (about 2 cups)
2 to 3 tablespoons lemon
juice

1/2 teaspoon dried basil
3/4 teaspoon salt, or to taste
1/4 teaspoon ground black
pepper, or to taste
Chopped parsley for garnish
(optional)

1. In a heavy 1/2-quart saucepan, melt 2 tablespoons of butter. Add garlic and stir over low heat until tender but not brown. Reserve.

2. In a heavy, nonreactive, preferably nonstick, 10 to 12-inch skillet, melt 3 tablespoons of butter. Add shrimp and sauté over high heat until pink.

3. Add garlic butter and 2 tablespoons of lemon juice to skillet. Season shrimp with basil, salt, and pepper.

4. Add more lemon juice to taste. Garnish with parsley and serve.

Yield: 4 servings.

Note: These shrimp may be served over fettuccine or linguine. Prepare 2/3 to 1 pound of pasta for 4 servings.

Scallops Mornay

These scallops and the following Shrimp and Scallops Mornay are the seafood recipes I serve most frequently to guests. They are always a hit and may be prepared ahead. They are best served in large scallop shells or individual heatproof dishes.

MUSHROOMS
1/4 cup (1/2 stick) butter or margarine
2 tablespoons minced shallots or green onions

8 ounces mushrooms, sliced 1/4-inch thick
2 teaspoons lemon juice

SCALLOPS
1 1/4 cups half-and-half or milk

1 1/2 pounds scallops

SAUCE
3 tablespoons butter or margarine
3 tablespoons all-purpose flour
1/3 cup finely grated Parmesan cheese
2 tablespoons dry sherry

1/2 teaspoon Dijon mustard (optional)
Pinch grated nutmeg
1/4 teaspoon salt, or to taste
1/8 teaspoon ground white pepper, or to taste

TOPPING
1/3 cup grated Swiss cheese

Chopped parsley for garnish (optional)

1. Prepare mushrooms: In a heavy 4 1/2-quart pot, melt the butter. Add shallots and sauté over low heat for 1 minute. Add mushrooms, sprinkle with lemon juice, and sauté over high heat until barely tender. Transfer to a bowl. Reserve.

2. Prepare scallops: In the 4 1/2-quart pot, scald the half-and-half. Add scallops and simmer until they become opaque, about 3 to 5 minutes. Stir frequently with a wooden spatula or spoon to prevent scorching. Strain scallops and add to mushrooms. Reserve the half-and-half.

3. Prepare sauce: Melt butter in a heavy 2-quart saucepan. Whisk in flour until smooth. Stir over low heat for 2 minutes without browning. Add

the reserved half-and-half and any juices that have escaped from the shellfish and mushrooms. Stir over moderate heat until smooth and thick. Add Parmesan cheese, sherry, mustard, nutmeg, salt, and pepper. Heat and stir until the cheese is melted and sauce is smooth.

4. Add scallops and mushrooms to sauce. If desired, the sauce may be thinned with a little milk. Spoon mixture into 4 to 6 buttered large scallop shells or other individual serving dishes. Sprinkle with Swiss cheese. Arrange shells on a baking sheet. The shells may be refrigerated until ready to serve. Let reach room temperature before broiling.

— This recipe may be prepared ahead to this point. —

5. Place baking sheet on a rack 6-inches below the heating element of a broiler. Broil until contents are bubbly hot and cheese is golden brown.

6. Garnish with parsley and serve.

Yield: 5 cups, 4 to 6 servings.

Shrimp and Scallops Mornay

Prepare the above Scallops Mornay with the following changes:

1. Use only 3/4 pound of scallops.
2. After Step 2, melt 3 tablespoons of butter in a 10-inch skillet. Add 3/4 pound shrimp, shelled and deveined (about 1 1/2 cups). Sauté over high heat until shrimp are pink. Add shrimp to scallops and mushrooms.

Yield: 5 cups, 4 to 6 servings.

Crab and Shrimp Hollandaise

Must be prepared at the last minute but can be done quickly.

1 1/4 cups Hollandaise Sauce
(p. 193)
8 tablespoons (1 stick) butter
(no substitute), divided
8 ounces mushrooms, sliced
1/4-inch thick
2 tablespoons lemon juice,
divided
2 pounds raw shrimp, shelled
and deveined (about 4 cups)

1 pound fresh crab meat,
preferably lump or backfin
1/4 teaspoon salt, or to taste
Pinch ground white pepper,
or to taste
1/4 teaspoon grated nutmeg
(optional)
Chopped parsley for garnish

1. Keep the hollandaise sauce warm over hot water.

2. In a heavy, nonreactive, preferably nonstick, 10 to 12-inch skillet, melt 3 tablespoons of butter. Add mushrooms and sprinkle with 1 tablespoon of lemon juice. Sauté over high heat until just tender. Transfer to a large bowl.

3. Melt 5 tablespoons of butter in the skillet. Add shrimp and sauté over high heat until pink. Place shrimp in bowl with mushrooms.

4. Add crab to skillet. Heat only until warm. Combine with shrimp and mushrooms. Stir in 1 tablespoon of lemon juice, salt, pepper, and nutmeg.

5. Spoon mixture into 8 large scallop shells or individual serving dishes or serve on plates.

6. Spoon a ribbon of hollandaise sauce over the middle of each portion.

7. Garnish with parsley and serve.

Yield: 8 servings.

Improvisational Stir-Fry

Here are some suggestions for preparing an infinite variety of your own creative stir-fries.

1. Choose any combination of vegetables and poultry, meat, or seafood.

2. Have all ingredients and equipment ready before cooking.

3. Cut each vegetable or meat into pieces of the same size and shape to ensure even cooking.

4. Dry cut pieces of poultry or meat with paper towels. If the meat is dry, it will brown better when fried. If the meat is moist, it may boil in watery juices rather than fry.

5. Generally, each item should be cooked separately. If not, one food may become overcooked before another is done. Place a large bowl near the wok into which the individual foods may be transferred as soon as they are cooked.

6. Use as little vegetable oil (preferably canola or peanut) as possible to avoid an oily taste. Keep a bowl and strainer nearby. If there is too much oil on the food, transfer the contents of the wok to the strainer, allow the oil to drain, and return the food to the wok or place it in the large bowl. The oil can be reused. Some or all of the vegetables may be boiled instead of stir-frying them in oil. I prefer to boil broccoli and cauliflower in water for 3 to 7 minutes until barely tender. Other vegetables, such as carrots and bok choy, may be boiled in broth which is added later.

7. Stir-fries are commonly sauced with broth thickened with cornstarch. One cup of broth and a cornstarch mixture of 2 tablespoons each of cornstarch and dry sherry and 1 to 2 tablespoons of soy sauce are used for about 6 cups of meat and vegetables. This will yield 4 servings.

8. After all the vegetables and meat have been cooked and transferred to the large bowl, add broth to the empty wok. Stir over high heat while scraping loose any attached food particles (deglazing). When broth boils gently, add cornstarch mixture and stir quickly until thick.

9. Add vegetables and meat to sauce in wok. Heat while stirring gently. Serve immediately.

10. Read the recipes for Shrimp and Vegetable Stir-Fry (p. 94), Chicken and Vegetable Stir-Fry (p. 117), and Beef and Broccoli Stir-Fry (p. 139) for additional suggestions.

Shrimp and Vegetable Stir-Fry

2 cups broccoli florets
1 small yellow summer
  squash, sliced into 1/4-inch
  rounds (about 1/2 to 3/4
  cup) (optional)
1 package (6 ounces) frozen
  snow peas or 1 package
  (8 ounces) frozen snap peas
2 tablespoons cornstarch
2 tablespoons dry sherry
1 tablespoon soy sauce
7 tablespoons vegetable oil,
  preferably canola or peanut,
  divided
8 ounces mushrooms, sliced
  1/4-inch thick (include cap
  and stem in each slice)

2 teaspoons lemon juice
1 large white or purple onion,
  sliced (about 1 1/4 cups)
1 large clove garlic, minced
1/2 teaspoon grated fresh
  ginger (optional)
1 red bell pepper, seeded
  and sliced 1/8-inch thick
1 1/2 pounds raw shrimp,
  shelled and deveined
  (about 3 cups)
1 cup Chicken Broth (p. 42) or
  canned broth
1 teaspoon salt, or to taste
1/4 teaspoon ground black
  or white pepper, or to
  taste

1. Drop broccoli into boiling water. Boil until barely tender, about 6 minutes. Do not overcook or the broccoli will lose its bright green color. Immediately add squash and frozen snow peas and boil for 1 minute. Drain vegetables and place them in a large bowl. Reserve.

2. In a small bowl, combine cornstarch, sherry, and soy sauce. Stir until blended. Reserve.

3. Heat a wok or heavy 10 to 12-inch skillet over high heat. Pour in 3 tablespoons of oil. Add mushrooms and sprinkle with lemon juice. Stir-fry until just tender and transfer to the large bowl. Reserve.

4. Heat 2 tablespoons of oil in wok. Add onion, garlic, and ginger. Stir-fry over moderate heat until tender but not brown. Add red bell pepper and continue to stir-fry for another minute. Transfer to the large bowl. Reserve.

5. Add 2 tablespoons of oil to wok. Add shrimp and sauté over high heat until pink. Transfer to the large bowl. Reserve.

6. Pour off any oil remaining in wok. Add broth to wok and bring to a boil while scraping loose coagulated juices. Add cornstarch mixture and stir until liquid is thickened. Add shrimp and vegetables. Heat and stir until hot. Season with salt and pepper. Serve immediately.

Yield: About 7 cups, 6 servings.

Crab and Mushroom Crêpes

SAUCE
2 large egg yolks
1 cup (1/2 pint) whipping
  cream, divided
8 tablespoons (1 stick) butter
  (no substitute), divided
3 tablespoons all-purpose
  flour
3/4 cup milk

1/4 cup grated Parmesan
  cheese
1 teaspoon Dijon mustard
Pinch grated nutmeg
2 teaspoons lemon juice
1/4 teaspoon salt, or to taste
Pinch cayenne pepper, or
  to taste

FILLING
3 tablespoons butter
  (no substitute)
2 tablespoons finely chopped
  shallots or onion
6 ounces mushrooms,
  sliced 1/4-inch thick
2 teaspoons lemon juice

1 pound crab meat, preferably
  lump or backfin
Pinch cayenne pepper, or to
  taste

CRÊPES
Crêpes for Entrées (p. 247)

3 tablespoons melted butter
  (no substitute)

GARNISH
Chopped Parsley (optional)

1. Prepare sauce: Place egg yolks in a small bowl. Add 2 tablespoons of the cream. Reserve.

2. In a 1 1/2 quart saucepan, melt 2 tablespoons of butter. Whisk in flour until smooth. Stir over low heat for 2 minutes without browning.

3. Add milk and remaining cream. Stir over moderate heat until smooth and thick. Add Parmesan cheese. Heat and stir until cheese is melted and sauce is smooth.

4. Whisk yolks and cream until blended. Add about a third of the sauce to the yolks and cream. Whisk until smooth. Return mixture to saucepan. Stir constantly over moderate heat until sauce is thick, about 2 minutes.

5. Reduce heat to low. Add remaining butter, 1 tablespoon at a time, whisking continuously until each piece is melted before adding the next one. Do not overheat or the sauce will separate.

6. Season sauce with mustard, nutmeg, lemon juice, salt, and cayenne pepper.

7. Prepare filling: In a heavy, nonreactive, preferably nonstick, 10 to 12-inch skillet, melt the butter. Add shallots and sauté over moderate heat until barely tender.

8. Add mushrooms and sprinkle with lemon juice. Sauté over high heat until just tender. Remove from heat and stir in crab. Stir in 1/2 cup of the sauce. Season to taste with cayenne pepper.

9. Place about 1/4 cup of filling on the edge of each crêpe. Roll crêpes like a jelly roll and place them in a buttered baking dish. Brush with melted butter. The crêpes may be refrigerated until ready to serve.

— This recipe may be prepared ahead to this point. —

10. Bake crêpes, uncovered, in a 350˚ F oven until heated through, about 20 to 30 minutes.

11. Heat remaining sauce over low heat. Spoon sauce over center of crêpes. Garnish with parsley and serve.

Yield: 12 crêpes, 6 servings.

Poultry

Roast Chicken

1 whole chicken (3 1/2 to 5 1/2 pounds)
Salt and pepper, to taste
1 clove garlic, peeled (optional)
1 tablespoon fresh rosemary, tarragon, sage, or basil, finely chopped, or 1 teaspoon dried herb (optional)
Old-Fashioned Poultry Stuffing (p. 126), Cornbread and Sausage Stuffing (p. 127), Apple and Prune Stuffing (p. 128), or Apricot and Raisin Stuffing (p. 129) (optional)

1/4 cup (1/2 stick) butter or margarine, melted, or olive oil, or other vegetable oil
1 small onion, chopped
1/2 carrot, chopped
1/2 celery rib, chopped
Gravy for Poultry or Meat Using Cornstarch (Jus Lié) (p. 99), Poultry or Meat Gravy with Mushrooms (p. 100), or Cream Gravy for Poultry (p. 101) (optional)

1. Pull off and discard fat deposits at opening of body cavity. Season inside of chicken with salt and pepper. Place garlic and herb inside chicken or fill cavity with one of the stuffings.

2. Place chicken, breast side up, on a rack in a heavy roasting pan measuring about 14 x 10 x 2 1/2-inches. Brush chicken with butter.

3. Add giblets, neck, onion, carrot, and celery to roasting pan or use them to prepare broth (see Note 1, p. 100). Stir giblets and vegetables every 15 minutes during roasting time.

4. Roast chicken, uncovered, in a 400° F oven for 15 minutes. Baste chicken and turn it back side up. Roast for 15 minutes and baste.

5. Turn chicken, breast side up, sprinkle with salt, and reduce oven temperature to 375° F. Roast for 15 minutes and baste. Turn chicken, back side up, roast for 15 minutes, and baste.

6. Finish roasting the chicken with the breast side up. A 3 1/2 to 4 pound chicken will be done in about 1 hour and 15 minutes. A 5 to 5 1/2 pound chicken will take about 1 1/2 hours. Test for doneness by piercing the inside of the upper part of the thigh with a fork. The juices should be clear with no trace of pink. Another test is to make a small cut in the skin between the thigh and breast. The thigh meat should have no more than a trace of pink color. An instant-reading thermometer inserted into the thickest part of the thigh will indicate 160° F when the chicken is done.

7. When chicken is done, baste, and let stand at room temperature for 15 to 20 minutes before carving. This will reduce the amount of juices that escape from the meat.

8. Carve chicken with a knife or poultry shears. Arrange chicken on a serving dish, spoon gravy over chicken, and serve.

Yield: 4 to 6 servings.

Gravy for Poultry or Meat Using Cornstarch (Jus Lié)

Fat and juices in roasting pan
1 2/3 cups Chicken Broth
  (p. 42) (also see Notes, next
  page), Beef Broth (p. 43), or
  1 can (14 1/2 ounces) broth
2 tablespoons cornstarch
2 tablespoons cold water
1 teaspoon browning sauce,
  or to desired color (optional)

1/4 teaspoon Worcestershire
  sauce (optional)
1/4 teaspoon salt, or to taste
1/8 teaspoon ground
  pepper, or to taste
1/2 teaspoon dried tarragon,
  basil, thyme, marjoram, or
  other herb (optional)

1. Gravy may be prepared before the meat is fully roasted. When the roast is almost done, transfer it to another roasting pan. Prepare the gravy while the meat finishes roasting.

2. Remove any vegetables and giblets that may have been roasted with the meat. They may be simmered in the broth for 15 minutes or longer to infuse the broth with additional flavor.

3. Skim fat off juices in roasting pan.

4. Measure the pan juices: 1/3 cup is needed. If there is less than 1/3 cup, add water to equal 1/3 cup. If there is more than 1/3 cup, the excess may be substituted for part of the broth or the juices may be boiled down to equal 1/3 cup.

5. Add the 1/3 cup of pan juices and broth to the roasting pan. Scrape loose coagulated roasting juices.

6. Strain the liquid into a 2-quart saucepan. Bring to a boil. Mix cornstarch and water together until blended. Pour into the boiling broth. Whisk until smooth and thick.

7. Add remaining ingredients. Stir while boiling gently until the gravy reaches the desired thickness, about 5 minutes.

8. Add any juices that have escaped from the roast while the gravy was prepared. The gravy may need to be thickened by simmering and stirring. Serve.

Yield: 2 cups.

Notes:
1. Poultry broth may be prepared from the neck and giblets. In a 2-quart saucepan, place the neck and giblets. Add half a carrot, half a celery rib, and a small onion, all coarsely chopped, and enough water to cover them. Simmer for 1 hour or longer. If needed, add water to the broth to equal 1 2/3 cups.

2. One-third cup of dry white wine may be substituted for 1/3 cup of chicken broth.

Poultry or Meat Gravy with Mushrooms

3 tablespoons butter or margarine
8 ounces mushrooms, sliced 1/4-inch thick

1 teaspoon lemon juice
Gravy for Poultry or Meat Using Cornstarch (Jus Lié) (p. 99)

1. In a heavy 10-inch skillet, melt the butter. Add mushrooms and sprinkle with lemon juice. Sauté over high heat until just tender. Add mushrooms to gravy.
2. Reheat and serve.

Yield: 3 cups.

Cream Gravy for Poultry

I especially like to serve this gravy with Roast Chicken (p. 98) and Noodle and Mushroom Dressing (p. 130).

Fat and juices in roasting pan
Up to 3 tablespoons butter
 or margarine
1 2/3 cups Chicken Broth
 (p. 42) (also see Notes,
 p. 100) or 1 can (14 1/2
 ounces) broth

1/4 cup all-purpose flour
1/4 cup whipping cream
1/4 teaspoon dried
 tarragon (optional)
1/4 teaspoon salt, or to taste
1/8 teaspoon ground white
 pepper, or to taste

1. Gravy may be prepared before the poultry is fully roasted. When the roast is almost done, transfer it to another roasting pan. Prepare the gravy while the meat finishes roasting.

2. Remove any vegetables and giblets that may have been roasted with the meat. They may be simmered in the broth for 15 minutes or longer to infuse the broth with additional flavor.

3. Skim fat off juices in roasting pan. Reserve 3 tablespoons of the fat in a 2-quart saucepan. If there is less fat than this, use butter to make up the difference.

4. Measure the pan juices: 1/3 cup is needed. If there is less than 1/3 cup, add broth or water to equal 1/3 cup. If there is more than 1/3 cup, the excess may be substituted for part of the broth or the juices may be boiled down to 1/3 cup.

5. Add the 1/3 cup of pan juices and broth to the roasting pan. Scrape loose coagulated roasting juices. Strain and reserve.

6. Add flour to fat in saucepan. Whisk over low heat for 2 minutes without browning. Add broth. Stir over moderate heat until smooth and thick. Add whipping cream and remaining ingredients. Stir over moderate heat until smooth and thick.

7. Add any juices that may have escaped from the roast while the gravy was prepared. The gravy may need to be thickened by simmering and stirring. Serve.

Yield: 2 1/4 cups.

Roast Boneless Turkey Breast with Stuffing

This method produces a juicy flavorful roast that is easily cut into slices of turkey with colorful swirls of stuffing. The boneless roast cooks in less than half the time a bone-in turkey breast would take. Boning and butterflying the breast is not as hard as it seems. The whole process is accomplished quickly. This is a special entrée for company that is easily prepared ahead.

1 turkey breast (bone-in) (5 to
  6 pounds)
Salt and pepper, to taste
Apricot and Raisin Stuffing
  (p. 129), Apple and Prune
  Stuffing (p. 128), or 1/2
  recipe Old-Fashioned
  Poultry Stuffing (p. 126)

1/4 cup (1/2 stick) butter or
  margarine, melted
Gravy for Poultry or Meat
  Using Cornstarch
  (Jus Lié) (p. 99)

1. Place turkey breast on a work surface with the skin side down. Bone the turkey breast by cutting close to the breastbone on each side. Be careful when you reach the ridge of the breastbone where it is attached to the skin. Carefully cut the skin off the ridge of the breastbone without puncturing the skin. The two breast halves will be connected by just the skin.

2. Butterfly the two breast halves: See illustration, next page. Place the boned turkey breast, skin side down, on the work surface (A). Using your fingers, find the natural separation between the upper and lower portions of the breast meat of one breast half. Work your fingers between the two layers to separate them. Lift the top layer of breast meat and fold it out like opening a book (B). Repeat with the other breast half.

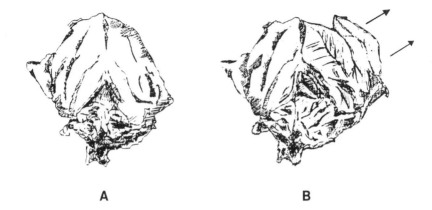

A   B

3. Cover the turkey with a piece of plastic wrap. Use a mallet or rolling pin to flatten the breast until it is about 1/2-inch thick.

— This recipe may be prepared ahead to this point. —

4. Season the meat with salt and pepper. Spread the stuffing on the turkey. Start at a long edge and roll the breast and stuffing together to form a smooth roll. Tie the roll at 2 1/2-inch intervals with kitchen twine.

5. Place the turkey on a rack in a roasting pan that is no deeper than 4-inches. Brush the turkey with the butter. Roast in a preheated 350° F oven until clear juices escape when the turkey is punctured with a fork, about 1 hour. An instant-reading meat thermometer placed in the center of the turkey will indicate 160° F when the meat is done. Baste several times during the roasting period.

6. While the turkey is roasting, the breastbone may be cut up and used instead of the neck and giblets to prepare turkey broth for the gravy (see Note 1, p. 100).

7. After the turkey is roasted, remove the twine. Cut the turkey into 1/2-inch slices.

8. Arrange 2 or 3 overlapping slices on each plate. Place a spoonful of gravy over the center of the slices. Serve.

Yield: 8 servings.

Broiled Chicken with Wine

The wine gives the chicken a golden brown glaze.

3 tablespoons butter or
  margarine, melted, and 1
  tablespoon olive oil or
  other vegetable oil OR 1/4
  cup olive oil or other
  vegetable oil
4 tablespoons dry white wine,
  sherry, or Madeira, divided

1 chicken (2 1/2 to 3 1/2
  pounds), cut into pieces
Salt, to taste
Ground white or black
  pepper, to taste
3/4 teaspoon dried herb such
  as tarragon, rosemary, sage,
  or basil (optional)

1. Combine butter, oil, and 2 tablespoons of wine. Use part of this mixture to brush a broiling pan with the rack removed or use a pan measuring about 14 1/2 x 12 x 1-inches. The pan should be nonreactive such as enamel or stainless steel. The pan must be no deeper than 1-inch or the chicken will not brown properly.

2. Arrange chicken pieces, skin side up, in the pan. Brush chicken with remaining butter and wine mixture.

3. Place pan on a rack about 6-inches below the heating element of a preheated broiler.

4. After the first 8 or 9 minutes, use a pastry brush to baste the chicken and brush the pan to prevent the juices from burning. Repeat the basting every few minutes. If needed, add additional butter or oil. Broil the chicken until golden brown, about 15 minutes.

5. Pour 2 tablespoons of wine over the chicken. Sprinkle chicken with salt, pepper, and herb. Turn chicken. Broil and baste until chicken is brown and clear juices, with no trace of pink, escape from the meat when pierced with a fork, about 7 to 10 minutes.

6. Arrange chicken on a serving dish and keep warm. Skim fat off juices, spoon juices over chicken, and serve.

Yield: 4 servings.

Broiled Rock Cornish Hens

A fast and easy way to prepare Rock Cornish hens.

Follow the recipe for Broiled Chicken with Wine (p. 104) with the following changes:

1. Use two Rock Cornish hens, each weighing about 24 ounces, in place of the chicken.
2. Use poultry shears or other heavy scissors to halve the hens. First cut the backbone in half with the shears. Then use a knife to cut the breast meat in half by cutting along one side of the ridge of the breastbone. Cut the breastbone in half with the shears.

Yield: 4 Rock Cornish hen halves, 2 to 4 servings.

Baked Chicken Dijon

12 tablespoons (1 1/2 sticks)
  butter or margarine, divided
1 medium onion, finely
  chopped
1 large clove garlic, minced
1/2 teaspoon dried herb such
  as rosemary, tarragon, or
  basil

1/2 cup Dijon mustard
1 1/2 cups dry bread crumbs
1/2 teaspoon salt, or to taste
1/2 teaspoon ground white or
  black pepper, or to taste
3 to 3 1/2 pounds chicken
  pieces

1. Melt 8 tablespoons of butter in a heavy 2-quart saucepan. Add onion and garlic. Sauté over moderate heat until tender but not brown. Remove from heat.
2. Add herb and mustard. Whisk until mixture resembles mayonnaise. Reserve.
3. In a pie pan, mix bread crumbs, salt, and pepper together.
4. Brush each chicken piece with the mustard mixture and coat it with bread crumbs.
5. Arrange chicken pieces on an oiled wire rack placed over a broiling pan or similar pan measuring about 14 1/2 x 12 x 1-inches. The rack allows air to circulate around the pieces of chicken so the bottom

surfaces brown evenly. The pan may be lined with aluminum foil for easy cleanup.

6. Drizzle 4 tablespoons of melted butter over the chicken.

7. Bake in a preheated 375° F oven until the chicken is brown and clear juices, with no trace of pink, escape when the chicken is pierced with a fork, about 30 to 35 minutes. Serve.

Yield: 4 servings.

Baked Chicken with Wine

1/4 cup (1/2 stick) butter or margarine, melted, OR olive oil or other vegetable oil
1/4 cup dry white wine, sherry, or Madeira
2 1/2 to 3 1/2 pounds chicken pieces
Salt, to taste
Ground white or black pepper, to taste

2 to 3 teaspoons fresh rosemary, tarragon, sage, or basil, finely chopped or 3/4 teaspoon dried herb (optional)
1 large clove garlic, minced (optional)

1. Combine butter and wine. Use part of this mixture to brush a baking dish measuring about 15 x 10-inches or use a metal pan. The pan should be nonreactive such as enamel or stainless steel.

2. Place chicken pieces, skin side up, in the pan. Brush chicken with remaining butter and wine mixture. Sprinkle with salt, pepper, herb, and garlic.

3. Bake in a preheated 375° F oven until the chicken is golden brown and clear juices, with no trace of pink, escape from the meat when pierced with a fork, about 30 to 40 minutes. Baste occasionally.

4. Arrange chicken on a serving dish and keep warm.

5. Skim fat off juices, spoon juices over chicken, and serve.

Yield: 4 servings.

Sautéed Chicken

2 1/2 to 3 1/2 pounds chicken
  pieces
1 to 3 tablespoons olive oil or
  other vegetable oil
1/2 teaspoon dried herb such
  as tarragon, rosemary, basil,
  or sage
1/2 teaspoon salt, or to taste

1/4 teaspoon ground white or
  black pepper, or to taste
2 tablespoons finely chopped
  shallots or onion (optional)
1 clove garlic, minced
  (optional)
1 cup dry white wine
1 tablespoon butter (optional)

1. Wash chicken pieces and dry thoroughly.

2. Heat the oil in a heavy, nonreactive, preferably nonstick, 10 to 12-inch skillet. Add chicken pieces and, over moderately high heat, brown them all over, about 3 minutes on each side. If all the pieces do not fit in the pan with at least 1/2-inch between each piece, brown half the chicken at a time.

3. Remove chicken from skillet. Pour off all but about 2 tablespoons of the fat from the skillet. Add dark meat pieces, cover, and cook gently over low heat for 7 minutes. Turn the pieces once halfway through cooking time.

4. Add white meat pieces to skillet. Sprinkle with herb, salt, and pepper. Cover and continue to cook for 12 to 14 minutes. Turn chicken pieces once halfway through cooking time. The chicken is done when clear juices, with no trace of pink, escape when the pieces are pierced with a fork. Transfer chicken to a serving plate and keep warm.

5. Skim fat off juices in skillet. Add shallots and garlic. Sauté over low heat until tender. Add wine and butter. Boil and stir until syrupy.

6. Season sauce with salt and pepper. Pour over chicken and serve as soon as possible.

Yield: 3 to 4 servings.

Sautéed Chicken with Sour Cream or Heavy Cream

Sautéed Chicken (p. 107),
  prepared through Step 5
1/2 cup sour cream or
  whipping cream
1 teaspoon Dijon mustard
  (optional)

1/2 teaspoon salt, or to taste
1/4 teaspoon ground white
  pepper, or to taste
Chopped parsley for garnish
  (optional)

1. After completing Step 5, add cream and mustard to skillet. Stir constantly while boiling over moderate heat until thick.

2. Season sauce with salt and pepper, pour over chicken, garnish with parsley, and serve.

Yield: 3 to 4 servings.

Sautéed Chicken with Vinegar

Prepare Sautéed Chicken (p. 107) but use 1/4 cup of vinegar (wine or balsamic) and 3/4 cup of wine instead of 1 cup of wine.

Yield: 3 to 4 servings.

Barbecued Chicken

2 1/2 to 3 1/2 pounds chicken
  pieces
1 to 2 cups Barbecue Sauce
  (p. 196)

Chopped chives or green
  onion for garnish (optional)

1. In a baking dish or pan measuring about 15 x 10-inches and brushed with vegetable oil, arrange the chicken pieces, skin side down.

2. Brush 1/2 cup of the barbecue sauce over the chicken. Turn the chicken pieces over and brush with another 1/2 cup of sauce.

3. Bake in a preheated 375° F oven until chicken is tender and clear juices, with no trace of pink, escape from the meat when pierced with a fork, about 35 minutes. Baste occasionally.

4. Transfer chicken to a serving dish and keep warm. Skim fat off sauce in pan. Spread sauce over chicken.

5. Serve immediately, or refrigerate and reheat in a 350° F oven.

6. The remaining barbecue sauce may be heated and brushed over the chicken. Garnish with chives and serve.

Yield: 4 servings.

Lemon and Wine Barbecued Chicken

Lots of flavor without lots of effort.

2 1/2 to 3 1/2 pounds chicken
 pieces
2 tablespoons olive oil or
 other vegetable oil
1/4 cup dry white wine
3 tablespoons lemon juice
1 tablespoon tarragon wine
 vinegar

1 clove garlic, minced
1/2 teaspoon crushed
 dried rosemary or basil
1 teaspoon salt, or to taste
1/2 teaspoon ground black
 pepper, or to taste

1. Arrange chicken pieces, skin side up, in a baking dish or metal pan measuring about 15 x 10-inches. The pan should be nonreactive such as enamel or stainless steel.

2. Combine remaining ingredients. Pour over chicken.

3. Bake in a preheated 375° F oven until chicken is brown, about 20 to 25 minutes. Baste occasionally. Turn chicken. Continue to bake and baste until chicken is brown and clear juices, with no trace of pink, escape when the chicken is pierced with a fork, about 10 to 15 minutes.

4. Transfer chicken to a serving dish and keep warm.

5. Skim fat off juices. Spoon juices over chicken and serve.

Yield: 4 servings.

Greek Chicken

Follow the directions for Lemon and Wine Barbecued Chicken (p. 109) with the following changes:

1. Omit vinegar.
2. Use 1/2 teaspoon of dried oregano instead of rosemary or basil.

Yield: 4 servings.

Sautéed Chicken Breasts with Mushrooms and Cream

2 tablespoons (1/4 stick)
  butter or margarine
6 ounces mushrooms, sliced
  1/4-inch thick
1 teaspoon lemon juice
4 chicken breast halves,
  skinned and boned
1 to 2 tablespoons olive oil or
  other vegetable oil
2 tablespoons finely chopped
  shallots

1/4 cup dry white wine
1 tablespoon butter or
  margarine (optional)
1/2 cup whipping cream
1/4 teaspoon dried
  tarragon (optional)
1/4 teaspoon salt, or to taste
1/8 teaspoon ground white
  pepper, or to taste

1. In a heavy, preferably nonstick, 10 to 12-inch skillet, melt 2 tablespoons of butter. Add mushrooms and sprinkle with lemon juice. Sauté over high heat until just tender. Transfer from skillet and reserve.

2. Dry chicken breasts. Use a mallet or rolling pin to flatten each breast between a folded piece of plastic wrap until about 1/4-inch thick.

3. Heat the oil in the skillet. Add chicken breasts and sauté over moderately high heat until light brown, about 2 to 3 minutes on each side. The cooked breasts should be springy to the touch. If a small incision is made in the center of the breast, the meat should be opaque. Do not overcook or the chicken will lose its juices and become tough and stringy. Transfer to a serving dish and keep warm.

4. Add shallots to skillet. Sauté over low heat until tender. Add wine and 1 tablespoon of butter. Boil and stir until syrupy. Add whipping cream. Boil and stir until thickened. If desired, the sauce may be strained. Stir in tarragon, salt, and pepper.

5. Add mushrooms to sauce. Reheat, spoon over chicken, and serve.

Yield: 4 servings.

Sautéed Chicken Breasts with Dijon Sauce

Prepare Sautéed Chicken Breasts with Mushrooms and Cream (p. 110) with the following changes:

1. Omit mushrooms, lemon juice, and the 2 tablespoons of butter in which they are cooked. Start with Step 2.

2. Add 1 1/2 tablespoons of Dijon mustard after adding the cream in Step 4.

3. If desired, garnish with chopped parsley.

Yield: 4 servings.

Chicken Divan

7 tablespoons butter or
  margarine, divided
1/3 cup all-purpose flour
1 2/3 cups Chicken Broth
  (p. 42) or 1 can (14 1/2
  ounces) broth
3 tablespoons dry sherry
1/2 cup whipping cream
Pinch grated nutmeg
1 teaspoon Dijon mustard

1/2 teaspoon salt, or to taste
1/4 teaspoon ground white
  pepper, or to taste
1 teaspoon lemon juice
1 to 1 1/2 pounds broccoli
4 chicken breast halves,
  skinned and boned
1/3 cup (2 ounces) grated
  Swiss cheese

1. Prepare sauce: In a heavy 2-quart saucepan, melt 4 tablespoons of butter. Whisk in flour. Stir over low heat for 2 minutes without browning. Add broth, sherry, and whipping cream. Stir over moderate heat until smooth and thick. Stir in nutmeg, mustard, salt, pepper, and lemon juice. Reserve.

2. Cut broccoli into 4-inch pieces that include a floret and a stem. Split each stem lengthwise. This will allow the stems to cook as fast as the attached florets. Drop the broccoli into boiling water. Boil until barely tender, about 7 minutes. Do not overcook or the broccoli will lose its bright green color. Drain immediately. In a buttered 11 x 7-inch or 8-inch square (2-quart) broiler-proof dish or pan, arrange the broccoli with the florets at the edge and the stem ends in the center. Reserve.

3. Dry chicken breasts. Use a mallet or rolling pin to flatten each breast between a folded piece of plastic wrap until about 1/4-inch thick.

— This recipe may be prepared ahead to this point. —

4. Melt 3 tablespoons of butter in a heavy, preferably nonstick, 10 to 12-inch skillet. Add chicken breasts and sauté over moderately high heat until brown, about 2 to 3 minutes on each side. The cooked breasts should be springy to the touch. If a small incision is made in the center of the breast, the meat should be opaque. Do not overcook or the chicken will lose its juices and become tough and stringy. Keep warm.

5. Meanwhile, heat the sauce and pour half of it over the broccoli. Arrange chicken breasts on top of broccoli. Cover with remaining sauce. Sprinkle with Swiss cheese.

6. Place the dish on a rack about 6-inches below the heating element of a broiler. Broil until sauce is golden brown, about 5 minutes. Serve.

Yield: 4 servings.

Italian Chicken Breasts

This is my wife Betsy's recipe — quick, easy, and superb.

**4 chicken breast halves,
  boned or bone-in
1 to 2 tablespoons olive oil
  or other vegetable oil**

**2 cups Tomato Sauce (p. 190)
  or commercial meatless
  spaghetti sauce
1 cup shredded mozzarella
  cheese**

1. Dry chicken breasts. In a heavy, preferably nonstick, 10 to 12-inch heavy skillet, heat the oil. Add chicken breasts. Sauté over moderately high heat until brown, about 2 to 4 minutes on each side.

2. Remove chicken from skillet and pour off fat.

3. Pour tomato sauce into skillet. Return chicken, skin side down, to skillet. Spoon some of the sauce over the chicken.

4. Bring to a boil, cover, reduce heat, and simmer until the chicken is tender. Boned chicken breasts will require about 8 to 10 minutes of cooking whereas bone-in chicken breasts will need about 15 to 20 minutes.

5. When tender, turn breasts skin side up. Sprinkle cheese over chicken, cover, and simmer until cheese melts, about 3 minutes. Serve.

Yield: 4 servings.

Note: I like to serve these chicken breasts with spaghetti or noodles. Boil 1/2 to 2/3 pound of spaghetti for 4 people. Spoon the tomato sauce over the pasta.

Chicken Cordon Bleu

A popular dish for company in which most of the preparation can be completed before the guests arrive.

4 chicken breast halves,
  skinned and boned
4 thin slices cooked ham
4 thin slices Swiss cheese
2 teaspoons Dijon mustard,
  smooth or coarse grained
  (optional)
1 large egg
1/3 cup milk
1/2 cup all-purpose flour

3/4 cup fine dry bread crumbs
1/4 cup (1/2 stick) butter or
  margarine
1/2 recipe Chicken Allemande
  Sauce (p. 195) or 3/4 cup
  Hollandaise Sauce (p. 193)
  (optional)
Chopped parsley for garnish
  (optional)

1. Dry chicken breasts. Use a mallet or rolling pin to flatten each breast between a folded piece of plastic wrap until about 1/4-inch thick.

2. Cover half of each breast with a slice of ham and cheese. The slices should not extend over the edge of the breast. Spread 1/2 teaspoon of mustard on top of each cheese slice.

3. Fold each chicken breast in half so the ham and cheese are covered by the chicken. The folded breast should be no thicker than 1-inch.

4. In a pie pan, lightly beat the egg. Stir in milk. Place flour and bread crumbs in separate pans. Dip each chicken breast in the egg mixture and then coat it with flour. Dip the floured breast in the egg mixture and then coat it with bread crumbs.

5. Cover chicken breasts with plastic wrap and refrigerate for at least 1/2 hour.

— This recipe may be prepared ahead to this point. —

6. Melt butter in a heavy, preferably nonstick, 10 to 12-inch skillet. Add chicken breasts and sauté over moderately high heat until brown, about 3 to 4 minutes on each side. Transfer to a baking dish. Bake in a preheated 350° F oven until done, about 10 to 15 minutes.

7. Immediately before serving, a spoonful of chicken allemande sauce or hollandaise sauce may be placed over each chicken breast.

8. Garnish with parsley and serve.

Yield: 4 servings.

Chicken Cutlets Tarragon

If you're into haute cuisine, the tapered end of each cutlet may be garnished with a paper frill. These cutlets are perfect for a ladies' luncheon.

3 chicken breast halves,
  skinned and boned
6 tablespoons (3/4 stick)
  butter or margarine, at
  room temperature, divided
1 1/2 teaspoons Dijon
  mustard
1/8 teaspoon dried tarragon
1/4 teaspoon salt, or to taste
1/8 teaspoon ground white
  pepper, or to taste

1/4 cup all-purpose flour
1 large egg
1/2 cup dry bread crumbs
Chicken Allemande Sauce
  (p. 195) or 1 1/4 cups
  Hollandaise Sauce (p. 193)
  (optional)
Chopped parsley for garnish
  (optional)

1. Grind chicken in a food processor or meat grinder. Add 2 tablespoons of butter, mustard, tarragon, salt, and pepper. Process until blended. Chill thoroughly.

2. Shape chicken mixture into 8 cutlets (see illustration, below) or oval shapes, each measuring about 4 x 2 1/2 x 1/2-inches. Use the flour to dust the work surface and to flour both sides of each cutlet.

3. In a pie pan, lightly beat the egg. Place bread crumbs in another pie pan. Dip each cutlet in egg and then coat with bread crumbs.

4. Cover cutlets with plastic wrap and refrigerate until ready to serve.

— This recipe may be prepared ahead to this point. —

5. In a heavy, preferably nonstick, 10 to 12-inch skillet, melt 4 tablespoons of butter. Add cutlets and sauté over moderately high heat until golden brown, about 3 to 4 minutes on each side.

6. Immediately before serving, place a spoonful of chicken allemande sauce or hollandaise sauce over each chicken breast. Garnish each cutlet with a paper frill (optional) and parsley. Serve.

Yield: 8 cutlets, 4 to 8 servings.

Turkey or Chicken Breasts Marsala

MUSHROOMS (OPTIONAL)
2 tablespoons olive oil or
  other vegetable oil
4 ounces mushrooms,
  sliced 1/4-inch thick

1/2 teaspoon lemon juice

TURKEY OR CHICKEN
1 to 1 1/2 pounds sliced
  turkey breast or 4 chicken
  breast halves, skinned and
  boned
2 tablespoons olive oil or
  other vegetable oil

Salt, to taste
Ground white pepper, to taste
2 tablespoons finely grated
  Parmesan cheese (optional)

SAUCE
1 tablespoon finely chopped
  shallots
1/2 cup dry Marsala (see
  Note, next page)

2 tablespoons (1/4 stick)
  butter (no substitute)

GARNISH (OPTIONAL)
Finely chopped parsley

1. Prepare mushrooms: In a heavy, nonreactive, preferably nonstick, 10 to 12-inch skillet, heat the olive oil. Add mushrooms and sprinkle with lemon juice. Sauté over high heat until mushrooms are just tender. Transfer to a bowl and reserve.

2. Prepare turkey or chicken: Dry turkey slices or chicken breasts. Use a mallet or rolling pin to flatten each slice or breast between a folded piece of plastic wrap until about 1/4-inch thick.

3. Heat the oil in the skillet. If using turkey, sauté the slices over moderately high heat for a minute or two on each side. They will not necessarily be brown when done. If using chicken, brown the breasts over moderately high heat, about 2 to 3 minutes on each side. The cooked breasts should be springy to the touch. If a small incision is made in the center of the breast, the meat should be opaque. Do not overcook or the breasts will lose their juices and become tough and stringy.

4. Transfer turkey or chicken to a serving dish. Season with salt and pepper. Sprinkle with Parmesan cheese. Keep warm in a 200° to 250° F oven.

5. Prepare sauce: Pour off all but about a teaspoon of the oil from the skillet. Add shallots and sauté over low heat until tender and light brown.

6. Add Marsala. Boil and stir until a light syrup is formed.

7. Add butter and mushrooms. Heat and stir until the butter is melted and the mushrooms are hot. Season with salt and pepper. Pour over the turkey slices or chicken breasts.

8. Sprinkle with parsley and serve.

Yield: 4 servings.

Note: Dry white wine may be substituted for Marsala.

Chicken and Vegetable Stir-Fry

12 ounces bok choy (celery cabbage or Chinese chard)
1 cup Chicken Broth (p. 42) or canned broth
1/2 cup water
1/2 pound carrots, sliced diagonally into long ovals, 1/8-inch thick
1 1/2 tablespoons cornstarch
2 tablespoons light soy sauce
2 tablespoons dry sherry
7 tablespoons vegetable oil, preferably canola or peanut, divided

8 ounces mushrooms, sliced 1/4-inch thick
1 teaspoon lemon juice
1 medium onion, sliced
1 clove garlic, minced
4 chicken breast halves, skinned, boned, and cut into 2 1/2 x 1/2-inch pieces
1/2 teaspoon salt, or to taste
1/8 teaspoon ground white pepper, or to taste

1. Separate bok choy into ribs. Cut off the leaves and then cut them at an angle into 1 x 1 1/2-inch pieces. Split the stems lengthwise and then cut them at an angle into 2 1/2 x 1/2-inch pieces. Reserve.

2. In a 1 1/2-quart saucepan, bring chicken broth and water to a boil. Add carrot slices and boil gently until barely tender, about 5 minutes. Strain the carrots from the broth and place them in a large bowl. Reserve carrots and broth.

3. In a cup, combine cornstarch, soy sauce, and sherry. Mix until blended. Reserve.

4. Heat a wok or heavy 10 to 12-inch skillet over high heat. Pour in 3 tablespoons of oil. Add mushrooms and sprinkle with lemon juice. Stir-fry until tender and transfer to the large bowl. Reserve.

5. Heat 1 tablespoon of oil in the wok. Add onion and garlic. Stir-fry over moderate heat until just tender but not brown. Add bok choy stems and stir-fry over high heat for 2 minutes. Add leaves and continue to stir-fry for another minute. Transfer to the large bowl. Reserve.

6. In a small bowl, combine chicken with 2 tablespoons of oil. Toss until chicken pieces are evenly coated with oil. Heat the wok and add 1 tablespoon of oil. Add chicken and stir-fry over high heat until chicken is done, about 3 minutes. Transfer to the large bowl and reserve.

7. Add chicken broth to wok. Bring to a boil while scraping loose coagulated juices. Add cornstarch mixture and stir until the liquid is thick. Add chicken and vegetables. Heat and stir until hot. Season with salt and pepper. Serve immediately.

Yield: 6 cups, 4 to 6 servings.

Chicken Meatballs in Sour Cream Sauce

Something new for company or to take to a potluck supper.

MEATBALLS

4 pounds chicken pieces
4 cups water
2 tablespoons (1/4 stick) butter or margarine
1 medium onion, finely chopped
1 clove garlic, minced
1 large egg
3/4 cup fresh bread crumbs from White Bread (p. 210) or firm commercial bread, firmly packed

1/3 cup finely grated Parmesan cheese
1/2 teaspoon dried tarragon
1 teaspoon salt, or to taste
1/4 teaspoon ground white pepper, or to taste

SAUCE

3 tablespoons butter or margarine	1/2 cup sour cream
1/4 cup all-purpose flour	1/8 teaspoon dried tarragon

1. Prepare meatballs: Skin, bone, and grind chicken in a food processor or meat grinder. There should be about 3 cups of ground chicken. Reserve.

2. In a 2-quart saucepan, combine the bones and skin with the water. Bring to a boil, reduce heat, and simmer for 30 to 45 minutes. Reserve.

3. In a heavy 10-inch skillet, melt the butter. Add onion and garlic and sauté over moderate heat until tender but not brown.

4. In a large bowl, lightly beat the egg. Add onion and garlic mixture, ground chicken, bread crumbs, Parmesan cheese, tarragon, salt, and pepper. Mix thoroughly. Form into 20 meatballs, each about 2-inches in diameter. Arrange meatballs in one layer in the skillet.

5. Strain broth. Pour enough broth over the meatballs to cover them. Bring to a boil, reduce heat, and simmer 30 minutes. Turn occasionally.

6. Transfer meatballs to a serving plate. Keep warm. Reserve broth.

7. Prepare sauce: In a 1 1/2-quart saucepan, melt the butter. Whisk in flour until smooth. Stir over low heat for 2 minutes without browning. Add 1 1/2 cups of the reserved broth. Stir over moderate heat until smooth and thick.

8. Add sour cream and tarragon. Stir over low heat until thick.

9. Spoon sauce over meatballs. Serve.

Yield: 20 meatballs, 4 to 5 servings.

Chicken Fricassee

CHICKEN

1/4 cup (1/2 stick) butter or margarine	1/2 cup dry white wine
2 medium carrots, thinly sliced	2 1/2 cups Chicken Broth (p. 42) or canned broth
1 celery rib, finely chopped	1/4 teaspoon dried marjoram or thyme
1 medium onion, chopped	1/2 teaspoon salt, or to taste
1 clove garlic, minced	1/8 teaspoon ground white pepper, or to taste
1 chicken (3 1/2 to 4 pounds), cut into serving pieces	

MUSHROOMS

2 tablespoons (1/4 stick)
butter or margarine
6 ounces mushrooms,
sliced 1/4-inch thick

1 teaspoon lemon juice

SAUCE

1/4 cup (1/2 stick) butter or
margarine
6 tablespoons all-purpose
flour
1 cup milk

Salt, to taste
Ground white pepper, to
taste
1 tablespoon finely chopped
fresh parsley

1. Prepare chicken: In a heavy, nonreactive 4 1/2-quart pot, melt the butter. Add carrots, celery, onion, and garlic. Sauté over low heat until vegetables are tender but not brown, about 7 minutes.

2. Move the vegetables away from the center of the pot. Add half the chicken pieces. Cook and turn over low to moderate heat until the chicken becomes light yellow, but not brown, on all sides. Remove chicken and cook remaining pieces.

3. Return remaining chicken to pot. Pour wine and broth over chicken. There should be enough liquid to just cover the chicken. If needed, add more broth or water. Add marjoram, salt, and pepper. Cover and simmer until the chicken is just tender, about 20 minutes.

4. Transfer the chicken from the broth to a large bowl. Strain broth into a 2-quart saucepan. Reserve the vegetables with the chicken. Skim fat off broth. Boil broth down to 2 cups. Reserve.

5. Prepare mushrooms: Melt the butter in the pot. Add mushrooms and sprinkle with lemon juice. Sauté over high heat until just tender. Transfer mushrooms to the bowl with the chicken and vegetables.

6. Prepare sauce: In the pot, melt the butter. Whisk in flour until smooth. Stir over low heat for 2 minutes without browning. Add the 2 cups of broth and milk. Stir over moderate heat until smooth and thick. Add chicken and vegetables. Season with salt and pepper. Add parsley and mix gently.

7. Reheat and serve.

Yield: 4 servings.

Note: Serve the fricassee with Mashed Potatoes (p.161), noodles, or rice.

Chicken Pot Pie

1 chicken (3 1/2 pounds), cut into serving pieces
4 cups water
1/2 pound (4 medium) carrots, sliced 1/4-inch thick
1 celery rib, finely chopped
1 medium onion, finely chopped
1 clove garlic, minced (optional)
1 bay leaf
1/2 teaspoon salt, or to taste
1/4 teaspoon ground white pepper, or to taste
1 1/2 cups fresh green peas or 1 package (10 ounces) frozen green peas OR 2 cups fresh green beans cut into 1-inch lengths or 1 package (9 ounces) frozen green beans

4 ounces mushrooms, sliced 1/4-inch thick
3/4 pound (2 medium) boiling or all-purpose potatoes, peeled and cut into 1/2 to 3/4-inch cubes
6 tablespoons (3/4 stick) butter or margarine
1/2 cup all-purpose flour
1/2 cup whipping cream, half-and-half, or milk
2 tablespoons finely chopped parsley (optional)
Pie Pastry for a Single Crust 9-inch Pie (p. 316)
1 egg yolk (optional)
1 tablespoon milk (optional)

1. In a heavy 4 1/2-quart pot, combine chicken, water, carrots, celery, onion, garlic, bay leaf, salt, and pepper. Bring to a simmer and skim off any scum. Simmer slowly, uncovered, until the chicken is just tender, about 35 minutes. Do not overcook or the chicken will become stringy.

2. Strain the broth from the chicken and vegetables. Cut chicken into bite-size pieces while discarding the skin and bones. Reserve chicken and vegetables in a large bowl.

3. Skim fat off broth. Bring broth to a boil. Add peas or green beans. Boil until just tender. Strain from broth and add to chicken and vegetables.

4. Bring broth to a boil. Add mushrooms and boil gently for 1 minute. Strain and add to the bowl. Reserve 3 1/2 cups of broth for the sauce. If necessary, add water to equal 3 1/2 cups.

5. Boil potatoes in water until just tender, about 8 minutes. Drain and place in bowl with chicken and other vegetables.

6. In the pot, melt the butter. Whisk in flour until smooth. Stir over low heat for 2 minutes without browning. Add chicken broth and whipping

cream. Stir over moderate heat until smooth and thick. Season with salt and pepper.

7. Add chicken, vegetables, and parsley. Mix gently.

8. Turn mixture into a 12 x 7 1/2-inch rectangular baking dish or a 2 1/2-quart casserole.

9. The warm mixture may be covered with pastry and immediately baked. For a more tender crust and to prepare this dish ahead, chill mixture, cover with pastry, and refrigerate for at least one hour before baking.

— This recipe may be prepared ahead to this point. —

10. Beat the egg yolk and 1 tablespoon of milk together. Brush this glaze over the pastry. Cut several slits in the pastry to let air escape during baking. Bake in a preheated 400° F oven until the crust is golden brown, about 30 minutes. Serve.

Yield: 10 cups, 5 to 6 servings.

Chicken and Mushroom Crêpes

FILLING

1/4 cup (1/2 stick) butter or
  margarine
2 tablespoons finely chopped
  shallots or onion
6 ounces mushrooms
2 teaspoons lemon juice

2 cups chopped cooked
  chicken
Salt, to taste
Ground white pepper, to
  taste

SAUCE

Chicken Allemande Sauce
  (p. 195)

CRÊPES

Crêpes for Entrées (p. 247)

3 tablespoons melted butter
  or margarine

GARNISH

Chopped parsley
  (optional)

1. Prepare filling: In a 10 to 12-inch skillet, melt the butter. Add shallots and sauté over moderate heat until barely tender.

2. Add mushrooms and sprinkle with lemon juice. Sauté over high heat until just tender. Remove from heat and stir in chicken. Stir in 1/2 cup of the chicken allemande sauce. Season to taste with salt and pepper.

3. Place about 1/4 cup of filling on the edge of each crêpe and roll up like a jelly roll. Place crêpes, seam side down, in a buttered baking dish. Brush with melted butter. The crêpes may be refrigerated.

— This recipe may be prepared ahead to this point. —

4. Bake, uncovered, in a 350° F oven until the crêpes are heated through, about 20 to 30 minutes.

5. While the crêpes are baking, heat the remaining sauce over low heat.

6. Spoon sauce over the center of each crêpe. Garnish with parsley and serve.

Yield: 12 crêpes, 4 to 6 servings.

Turkey or Chicken Loaf with Parsley Cream Sauce

A grand way to use leftover turkey or chicken.

TURKEY OR CHICKEN LOAF

3 tablespoons butter or margarine
1/2 cup finely chopped celery
1/2 cup finely chopped onion
1 large egg
2 1/2 cups finely chopped cooked turkey or chicken
1 cup fresh bread crumbs from White Bread (p. 210) or firm commercial bread, firmly packed

1/2 teaspoon dried rubbed sage
1/2 teaspoon salt, or to taste
1/4 teaspoon ground white pepper, or to taste
1/4 cup finely chopped parsley
1/4 cup milk

PARSLEY CREAM SAUCE

3 tablespoons butter or
  margarine
3 tablespoons all-purpose
  flour
1 1/2 cups half-and-half or
  milk

1/4 teaspoon salt, or to taste
1/8 teaspoon ground white
  pepper, or to taste
1 tablespoon finely chopped
  parsley

1. Prepare turkey loaf: Melt butter in a heavy 9 or 10-inch skillet. Add celery and onion and sauté over moderate heat until tender but not brown. Reserve.

2. In a large bowl, lightly beat the egg. Add celery and onion mixture and remaining ingredients. Mix thoroughly.

3. Press the mixture into a buttered 8 1/2 x 4 1/2 x 3-inch glass or metal loaf pan.

4. Bake in a preheated 350° F oven for 40 minutes.

5. Meanwhile, prepare sauce: Melt the butter in a heavy 1 1/2-quart saucepan. Whisk in flour until smooth. Stir over low heat for 2 minutes without browning. Add half-and-half or milk, salt, and pepper. Stir over moderate heat until smooth and thick. Just before serving, stir in parsley.

6. Slice the loaf and serve with the sauce.

Yield: 4 to 5 servings.

Duck à l'Orange

1 duck (4 to 4 1/2 pounds)
1 teaspoon dried tarragon
1 large clove garlic
1/2 medium onion, finely
  chopped
1/2 celery rib, finely chopped
1/2 medium carrot, finely
  chopped
1 1/2 tablespoons cornstarch
1/3 cup dry Marsala wine
1/3 cup orange juice
1 1/2 teaspoons finely grated
  orange rind

2 tablespoons currant jelly
1/2 teaspoon browning sauce
  (optional)
1 teaspoon salt, or to taste
1/4 teaspoon ground white
  pepper, or to taste
2 tablespoons Grand Marnier
  or other orange liqueur
  (optional)
Orange segments from 1 or
  1 1/2 oranges
Parsley for garnish (optional)

1. If the duck has been frozen, be sure it is completely thawed. Wash and dry thoroughly inside and out. Prick the skin all over with a fork. Sprinkle tarragon inside cavity. Place duck, breast side up, on a rack in a roasting pan.

2. Roast, uncovered, in a preheated 375° F oven for 30 minutes. Pour fat out of pan and reserve. Turn duck, breast side down, and roast for 30 minutes. Pour out fat and reserve with other fat. Turn, breast side up, and roast about 30 minutes more until juices are no longer pink when the inside of the thigh is pierced with a fork.

3. While duck is roasting, prepare broth for the sauce: Combine neck, giblets, garlic, onion, celery, and carrot in a 1 1/2-quart saucepan. Cover with water, bring to a boil, reduce heat, and simmer for 1 hour or longer. Strain and discard giblets and vegetables. Boil broth down to 1 cup.

4. Transfer roasted duck to a plate and keep warm. Skim fat off juices in pan. If there are any juices at the bottom of the reserved fat, discard the fat and add the juices to the roasting pan. Add broth to pan. Scrape loose coagulated juices. Strain liquid into a 2-quart saucepan. Bring to a boil.

5. Mix cornstarch and Marsala together until blended. Add to boiling broth. Stir over moderate heat until smooth and thick.

6. Add orange juice, rind, currant jelly, browning sauce, salt, and pepper to sauce. Simmer until sauce reaches desired thickness, about 15 minutes. Reserve.

7. Let the duck rest for at least 15 minutes before carving to help prevent juices from escaping from the meat. Poultry shears may be used

Poultry 125

to cut the duck into two breast and two leg servings. The skin and meat may be removed from the bones using your fingers and a knife. Arrange the duck meat in four portions. Cover each serving with a piece of skin.

— This recipe may be prepared ahead to this point. —

8. The duck may be reheated in a 350° F oven.
9. Reheat sauce. Stir in Grand Marnier and orange segments. Spoon over each serving. Garnish with parsley. Serve.

Yield: 4 servings.

Old-Fashioned Poultry Stuffing

1/2 cup (1 stick) butter or margarine
1 cup chopped celery
1 1/2 cups chopped onion
8 cups bread cubes from White Bread (p. 210) or firm commercial bread, loosely packed
1 1/2 teaspoons dried rubbed sage
1/4 teaspoon dried rubbed thyme
1/4 teaspoon dried marjoram
1/8 teaspoon grated nutmeg
1/2 teaspoon salt, or to taste
1/2 teaspoon ground black pepper, or to taste
1/3 cup Chicken Broth (p. 42) or canned broth

1. In a heavy 4 1/2-quart pot, melt the butter. Add celery and onion. Sauté over moderate heat until tender but not brown. Add remaining ingredients and mix thoroughly.
2. Bake stuffing in a covered baking dish in a 350° F oven for 25 minutes or use to stuff a chicken or turkey.

Yield: 3 cups (after baking). One recipe will stuff a 12 to 16 pound turkey. Use one-half recipe for a 6 to 8 pound turkey. Although one-quarter recipe is enough for a 3 1/2 to 4 pound chicken, I prefer to make at least half the recipe. Use part of the stuffing in the chicken and bake the rest in a covered baking dish.

Cornbread and Sausage Stuffing

1 recipe Skillet Cornbread
(p. 238) (omit sugar)
1/2 pound bulk sausage
1 cup chopped celery
1 1/2 cups chopped onion
3 cups bread cubes from
White Bread (p. 210) or firm
commercial bread, loosely
packed
1/4 cup chopped parsley
2 teaspoons dried rubbed
sage

1/4 teaspoon dried rubbed
thyme
1/4 teaspoon dried marjoram
1/8 teaspoon grated nutmeg
1/2 teaspoon salt, or to taste
1/2 teaspoon ground black
pepper, or to taste
1/2 cup Chicken Broth (p. 42)
or canned broth

1. Crumble cornbread into a large bowl. Reserve.

2. In a heavy 10-inch skillet, stir sausage over moderate heat until it forms brown granules. Use a slotted spoon to transfer sausage to the bowl of cornbread, leaving the fat in the skillet.

3. Add celery and onion to skillet. Sauté over moderate heat until tender but not brown. Add celery, onion, and remaining ingredients to the cornbread and sausage. Mix thoroughly.

4. Bake stuffing in a covered baking dish in a 350° F oven for 25 minutes or use to stuff a turkey or chicken.

Yield: 6 cups (after baking). One recipe will stuff a 12 to 16 pound turkey. Use one-half recipe for a 6 to 8 pound turkey. Although one-quarter recipe is enough for a 3 1/2 to 4 pound chicken, I prefer to make at least half the recipe. Use part of the stuffing in the chicken and bake the rest in a covered baking dish.

Apple and Prune Stuffing

1/2 cup (1 stick) butter or
  margarine
3/4 cup chopped celery
1 cup chopped onion
2 medium apples, peeled,
  cored, and chopped
1/2 cup chopped prunes
1 teaspoon dried rubbed
  sage

2 cups fresh bread crumbs
  from White Bread (p. 210) or
  firm commercial bread,
  firmly packed
3/4 teaspoon salt, or to taste
1/4 teaspoon ground black
  pepper, or to taste

1. In a heavy 4 1/2-quart pot, melt the butter. Add celery and onion. Sauté over moderate heat until tender. Add apple and cook until just tender.

2. Add remaining ingredients and mix thoroughly.

3. Bake stuffing in a covered baking dish in a 350° F oven for 25 minutes or use to stuff a chicken, turkey, or pork roast.

Yield: 3 cups (after baking). Use one recipe for a 6 to 8 pound turkey and 2 recipes for a 12 to 16 pound turkey. One-half recipe will stuff a 3 1/2 to 4 pound chicken.

Apricot and Raisin Stuffing

1/2 cup (1 stick) butter or margarine
1/2 cup finely chopped celery
1/4 cup finely chopped onion
2 cups chopped, peeled apple
6 ounces chopped dried apricots
1/4 cup dark raisins
1/4 cup golden raisins
1/2 teaspoon dried rubbed sage

2 cups fresh bread crumbs from Cornmeal and Honey Bread (p. 218), White Bread (p. 210), or firm commercial bread, firmly packed
3/4 teaspoon salt, or to taste
1/4 teaspoon ground black pepper, or to taste

1. In a heavy 4 1/2-quart pot, melt the butter. Add celery and onion. Sauté over moderate heat until tender. Add apple and cook until just tender.

2. Add remaining ingredients and mix thoroughly.

3. Bake stuffing in a covered baking dish in a 350° F oven for 25 minutes or use to stuff a chicken, turkey, or pork roast.

Yield: 3 cups. One recipe will stuff a 6 to 8 pound turkey. One-half recipe will stuff a 3 1/2 to 4 pound chicken.

Noodle and Mushroom Dressing

1/4 cup (1/2 stick) butter or
 margarine
1/4 cup finely chopped celery
1/4 cup finely chopped carrot
1/4 cup finely chopped onion
1 small clove garlic, minced
4 ounces mushrooms, cut
 into 1/4-inch cubes
1 1/2 teaspoons lemon juice

1/4 cup whipping cream
3/4 teaspoon salt, or to taste
1/8 teaspoon ground white
 pepper, or to taste
8 ounces noodles
1 tablespoon finely chopped
 fresh or frozen chives or
 parsley

1. Melt the butter in a heavy 10-inch skillet. Add celery, carrot, onion, and garlic. Sauté over low heat until tender but not brown.

2. Add mushrooms, sprinkle with lemon juice, and sauté over high heat until just tender.

3. Remove skillet from heat and stir in whipping cream, salt, and pepper. Reserve.

— This recipe may be prepared ahead to this point. —

4. Boil noodles until just tender. Drain and return to pot. Keep warm.

5. Reheat mushroom mixture over low heat. Do not let boil or the cream may separate. Add to noodles. Mix gently.

6. Garnish with chives or parsley. Serve.

Yield: 4 cups, 4 servings.

Note: This dressing is delicious with Roast Chicken (p. 98) and Cream Gravy for Poultry (p. 101).

Beef, Pork, and Lamb

Rib Roast of Beef

1 rib roast of beef (4 to 9
  pounds), at room
  temperature
Ground black pepper, to taste
1 medium carrot, coarsely
  chopped (optional)
1 celery rib, coarsely
  chopped (optional)
1 medium onion, coarsely
  chopped (optional)

Gravy for Poultry or Meat
  Using Cornstarch (Jus Lié)
  (p. 99) (optional)
Yorkshire Pudding (p. 246)
  (optional)
Horseradish Sauce (p. 198)
  (optional)

1. Dry roast with a towel. Place, rib side down, on a wire rack in a lightly oiled roasting pan. Season with pepper.

2. Roast, uncovered, in a preheated 325° F oven. Allow about 15 minutes per pound for a bone-in roast and 22 minutes per pound for a boneless roast. An instant-reading thermometer inserted in the center of the roast will indicate 125° F when medium rare. Check temperature every 8 to 10 minutes during the last half hour of the cooking time. The temperature rises quickly after the meat reaches 115° F and a few minutes difference will greatly affect the doneness of the roast. The meat may also be checked for doneness by turning the roast upside down and making a small deep cut with a sharp-tipped knife between the two center ribs. Twist the knife to enlarge the opening and see the meat. Do not do this more than 2 or 3 times because the meat loses juices each time. Remember that the meat will cook a little more after it is removed from the oven.

3. Add the vegetables to the pan about 1 hour before the roast is done. They will add additional flavor to the gravy.

4. After roasting, cover roast and keep at room temperature for 30 minutes or longer. This will help prevent juices from escaping from the meat when sliced. The beef is best served 30 to 45 minutes after it is removed from the oven.

5. Use the pan drippings to make gravy and Yorkshire pudding.

6. If desired, serve with horseradish sauce.

Yield: A 4 pound bone-in roast will serve 4 to 5; a 9 pound bone-in roast, 9 to 12. A 4 pound boneless roast will serve 6 to 8; a 9 pound boneless roast, 16 to 18.

Sauerbraten

Start this marinated German pot roast 3 to 5 days before you plan to serve it. For my taste, the amount of vinegar given here is perfect, but you may prefer more or less vinegar. Sauerbraten, in my mind, is always better when braised one day and served the next.

2 cups cold water
1 cup dry red wine
1 cup red wine vinegar
1 rump, bottom round, or
  chuck roast of beef (3 to 5
  pounds)
1 large onion, thinly sliced
1 clove garlic, minced
1 medium carrot, thinly sliced
1 celery rib, thinly sliced
1 bay leaf
3 whole cloves
4 juniper berries (optional)
2 teaspoons salt

1/2 teaspoon ground black
  pepper
3 tablespoons bacon fat or
  vegetable oil
1 medium tomato, unpeeled,
  seeded, and coarsely
  chopped
1 1/3 cups Beef Broth (p. 43)
  or 1 can (10 1/2 ounces)
  broth
2/3 cup finely ground
  gingersnap crumbs
1/2 cup sour cream (optional)
Parsley for garnish (optional)

1. In a nonreactive 4-quart casserole, combine the water, wine, and vinegar. Add beef, onion, garlic, carrot, celery, bay leaf, cloves, juniper berries, salt, and pepper. Cover and refrigerate for 3 to 4 days. Turn meat in marinade once daily.

2. Remove beef from marinade and dry well with a towel. Strain marinade reserving both vegetable mixture and marinade.

3. Heat bacon fat in a heavy skillet. Add beef. Brown meat on all sides over moderate heat. Transfer beef to casserole. Add reserved vegetable mixture and tomato.

4. Bring 2 cups of marinade and the beef broth to the boiling point. Pour over beef. Place covered casserole in a preheated 300° F oven. Braise, turning occasionally, until meat is easily pierced with a sharp two-pronged fork, about 1 1/2 to 2 hours. If necessary, adjust oven temperature so casserole contents simmer gently. Do not let the liquid boil and do not cook too long or the beef will become tough and dry.

5. Transfer meat to a serving dish and keep warm. Strain the liquid into a 2-quart saucepan. Discard vegetables. Skim fat off liquid. Spoon some of the liquid over the meat.

6. Bring the liquid to a boil. Add gingersnap crumbs. Simmer and stir

until gravy reaches the desired thickness. The gravy may be blended in a food processor or blender. Stir in sour cream. Season to taste with salt and pepper.

7. Slice the meat across the grain. To serve, overlap the slices on a serving dish. Spoon a ribbon of gravy down the center of the slices. Garnish with parsley.

8. If you plan to serve the sauerbraten the next day, refrigerate the beef and gravy separately. In a 10 to 12-inch skillet, heat and stir the gravy until warm and smooth. Add beef slices and simmer until warm. Garnish with parsley and serve.

Yield: 6 servings.

Note: Serve Sauerbraten with Spiced Red Cabbage (p. 151) and parsleyed boiled new potatoes or Mashed Potatoes (p. 161).

Marinated London Broil

1/4 cup dark soy sauce
2 tablespoons dry sherry
2 tablespoons vegetable oil
1 tablespoon red wine
  vinegar
1 large clove garlic, minced

1 teaspoon grated fresh
  ginger
1/4 teaspoon ground black
  pepper
1 London broil (2 pounds),
  about 1-inch thick

1. In an 11 x 7-inch (2-quart) glass baking dish, combine all ingredients except meat. Add beef and turn to coat all sides with the marinade. Cover and refrigerate for several hours or overnight. Turn meat in marinade several times.

2. Remove meat from marinade and lay it on the oiled rack of a broiler pan. Place pan on a rack about 3-inches below the heating element of a preheated broiler. Broil about 4 minutes on each side. An instant-reading thermometer inserted in the center of the meat will indicate 125° F when the meat is medium rare.

3. Cut meat into thin slices, cutting at an angle and across the grain.

4. The marinade may be heated, strained, and poured over the broiled meat.

Yield: 4 to 6 servings.

Braised Beef in Red Wine

In this recipe, the beef is browned under a broiler instead of in a frying pan. Broiling is easier and more efficient. A dark brown, full-flavored stew is produced. Use a robust red wine for best results.

3 pounds boneless beef for stew (such as chuck), cut into 1 1/2 to 2-inch cubes
2 tablespoons vegetable oil
7 tablespoons butter or margarine, divided
1/2 cup finely chopped carrot
1/4 cup finely chopped celery
3/4 cup chopped onion
1 large clove garlic, minced
1/4 cup all-purpose flour
1 2/3 cups Beef Broth (p. 43) or 1 can (14 1/2 ounces) broth

2 cups dry red wine
1/2 cup unpeeled, seeded, and chopped tomato
1 bay leaf
1/4 teaspoon dried thyme
1/4 teaspoon dried marjoram
1/2 teaspoon salt, or to taste
1/4 teaspoon ground black pepper, or to taste
8 ounces mushrooms, sliced 1/4-inch thick

1. Place beef in a broiling pan with the rack removed or use a similar pan measuring about 14 1/2 x 12 x 1-inches. Pour the oil over the beef. Toss until the pieces of beef are evenly coated with oil.

2. Place pan on a rack 3-inches below the heating element of a broiler. Broil, turning occasionally with a large spoon, until the pieces of beef are brown on all sides, about 15 minutes.

3. Meanwhile, in a nonreactive 4-quart casserole, melt 3 tablespoons of butter. Add carrot, celery, onion, and garlic. Sauté over moderate heat until tender and light brown. Add flour. Stir until smooth.

4. Remove beef from pan and reserve. Skim fat off pan juices. Pour part of the broth into the pan. Scrape pan to loosen browned particles. Add this liquid, remaining broth, and wine to the casserole. Stir until smooth. Add tomato, bay leaf, thyme, marjoram, salt, and pepper. Stir over moderate heat until mixture comes to a boil. Add beef. Cover casserole. Braise in a 325° F oven until beef is tender, about 1 1/2 hours. If necessary, adjust oven temperature so casserole contents simmer gently.

5. Meanwhile, melt 4 tablespoons of butter in a 10-inch skillet. Add mushrooms and sauté over high heat until barely tender. Reserve.

6. When beef is tender, strain meat from liquid. Return beef to casserole. Skim fat off liquid. If desired, boil and stir the liquid until thick. Pour liquid over beef. Add mushrooms and mix gently. Season with salt and pepper. Reheat and serve.

Yield: 6 cups, 5 to 6 servings.

Note: The braised beef may be served over buttered noodles and garnished with chopped parsley.

Old-Fashioned Beef Stew

Here is a streamlined version of an old favorite. Broiling the beef ensures a rich brown sauce and the method is quicker and easier than browning the beef in a skillet.

3 pounds boneless beef for stew (such as chuck), cut into 1 1/2-inch cubes
6 tablespoons vegetable oil, divided
2 medium onions, sliced 1/4-inch thick
2 celery ribs, finely chopped
1/2 cup all-purpose flour
2 2/3 cups Beef Broth (p. 43) or 2 cans (10 1/2 ounces each) broth
2 tablespoons ketchup
1 large clove garlic, minced
1 bay leaf
1/4 teaspoon dried thyme
1/4 teaspoon dried marjoram

1 teaspoon salt, or to taste
1/2 teaspoon ground black pepper, or to taste
1 pound carrots, peeled and sliced 1/4-inch thick
2 pounds boiling or all-purpose potatoes, peeled and cut into 1 1/2-inch cubes
3 tablespoons butter or margarine (optional)
8 ounces mushrooms, sliced 1/4-inch thick (optional)
1 package (10 ounces) frozen green peas, thawed
Chopped parsley for garnish (optional)

1. Place beef in a broiling pan with the rack removed or use a similar pan measuring about 14 1/2 x 12 x 1-inches. Pour 2 tablespoons of oil over the beef. Toss until the pieces of beef are evenly coated with oil.
2. Place pan on a rack 3-inches below the heating element of a broiler. Broil, turning occasionally with a large spoon, until the pieces of beef are brown on all sides, about 15 minutes.

3. Meanwhile, in a nonreactive 4-quart casserole, heat 4 tablespoons of oil. Add onion and celery. Sauté over moderate heat until tender and light brown. Add flour. Stir until smooth.

4. Remove beef from pan and reserve. Skim fat off pan juices. Pour part of the broth into the pan. Scrape the pan to loosen browned particles. Add this liquid, remaining broth, and ketchup to casserole. Stir until smooth. Stir over moderate heat until mixture comes to a boil.

5. Add beef, garlic, bay leaf, thyme, marjoram, salt, and pepper. Mix thoroughly. Cover casserole.

6. Braise in a 325° F oven until beef is tender, about 1 1/4 hours. If necessary, adjust oven temperature so casserole contents simmer gently.

7. Meanwhile, boil carrots until just tender, about 20 minutes. Drain and reserve. Boil potatoes until just tender, about 10 minutes. Drain and reserve.

8. Melt butter in a skillet. Add mushrooms and sauté over high heat until barely tender. Reserve.

9. When beef is tender, skim fat off stew. Add carrots, potatoes, mushrooms, and peas. Mix gently. Season with salt and pepper. Cover and return to oven for 20 minutes.

10. Serve or reheat the next day (my preference). Sprinkle each serving with parsley.

Yield: 12 cups, 4 to 6 servings.

Barbecued Beef Ribs

4 to 4 1/2 pounds beef ribs
2 tablespoons (1/4 stick)
  butter or margarine
1 small onion, finely chopped
2 cloves garlic, minced
1 1/2 cups ketchup
1/4 cup lemon juice
1/4 cup cider vinegar
1/4 cup molasses

1 teaspoon Worcestershire
  sauce
1 teaspoon dry mustard
1/2 teaspoon ground dried
  ginger
1 teaspoon salt, or to taste
1/4 teaspoon cayenne pepper,
  or to taste

1. Cut beef into separate ribs. Arrange in one layer on a rimmed baking sheet brushed with vegetable oil. Roast in a 350° F oven for 30 minutes.

2. Meanwhile, prepare sauce: In a heavy 2-quart saucepan, melt the butter. Add onion and garlic. Sauté over low heat until tender but not brown.

3. Stir in remaining ingredients. Bring to a boil, reduce heat, and simmer, uncovered, for 10 minutes.

4. Brush ribs with sauce. Reduce oven temperature to 325° F and roast until meat is tender, about 1 hour. Turn and baste ribs several times while roasting and immediately before serving.

Yield: 4 to 5 servings.

Beef and Broccoli Stir-Fry

1 to 1 1/4 pounds broccoli
1 1/2 tablespoons cornstarch
2 tablespoons dark soy sauce
2 tablespoons dry sherry
1/4 teaspoon ground dried
  ginger
4 tablespoons vegetable oil,
  preferably canola or peanut,
  divided
1 large onion, sliced

1 large clove garlic, minced
1 red bell pepper, seeded,
  and sliced 1/8-inch thick
1 1/2 pounds boneless tender
  beef steak, cut into 2 x 1/2 x
  1/2-inch strips
1 cup Beef Broth (p. 43) or
  canned broth
Salt and pepper, to taste

1. Cut broccoli into 2 to 2 1/2-inch florets. Save stems for another purpose. Drop florets into boiling water. Boil until barely tender, about 7 minutes. Do not overcook or the broccoli will lose its bright green color. Drain immediately and reserve in a large bowl.

2. In a small bowl, combine cornstarch, soy sauce, sherry, and ginger. Stir until blended. Reserve.

3. Heat a wok or heavy 10 to 12-inch skillet over moderate heat. Pour in 2 tablespoons of oil. Add onion and garlic. Stir-fry until tender but not brown. Add red pepper and continue to stir-fry for a minute or two. Transfer vegetables to the bowl containing the broccoli. Reserve.

4. Add 2 tablespoons of oil to wok. Add beef and stir-fry over high heat until brown but still pink inside. Transfer to bowl with vegetables. Reserve.

5. Pour off any oil remaining in wok. Add broth to wok and bring to a boil while scraping loose the coagulated juices. Add cornstarch mixture and stir until thick. Add beef and vegetables. Heat and stir until hot. Season with salt and pepper. Serve immediately.

Yield: 6 1/2 cups, 4 to 6 servings.

Beef or Beef and Pork Meat Loaf

A favorite from my childhood.

2 tablespoons (1/4 stick)
 butter or margarine
1 medium onion, finely
 chopped
1 clove garlic, minced
1 1/2 pounds ground lean
 beef OR 1 pound ground
 lean beef and 1/2 pound
 ground lean pork
1 large egg
1 teaspoon salt, or to taste
1/4 teaspoon ground black
 pepper, or to taste
2 teaspoons Dijon mustard
1/4 teaspoon dried thyme

1/4 teaspoon dried marjoram
1 cup bread crumbs from
 White Bread (p. 210) or
 firm commercial bread,
 firmly packed
3 tablespoons grated
 Parmesan cheese
1/3 cup Beef Broth (p. 43) or
 canned broth
1/4 cup chopped parsley
 (optional)
1 cup Tomato Sauce (p. 190)
 or 8 ounces canned tomato
 sauce

1. In a 9-inch skillet, melt the butter. Add onion and garlic and sauté over moderate heat until tender but not brown. Transfer to a large bowl.

2. Add all remaining ingredients except tomato sauce. Mix thoroughly.

3. Press mixture into a buttered 8 1/2 x 4 1/2 x 3-inch glass or metal loaf pan.

4. Bake in a 350° F oven for 30 minutes.

5. Pour off fat. Pour tomato sauce over meat loaf. Bake for an additional 15 minutes.

6. Pour off fat, slice, and serve.

Yield: 4 servings.

Swedish Meatballs

These meatballs are browned under the broiler which is easier and more efficient than using a skillet.

MEATBALLS

1 cup fresh bread crumbs
  from White Bread (p. 210) or
  firm commercial bread,
  firmly packed
6 tablespoons milk
2 tablespoons vegetable oil
1 large clove garlic, minced
1 medium onion, finely
  chopped
1 large egg
1 pound ground lean beef

2/3 pound ground lean pork
1/4 teaspoon dried dill weed
1/4 teaspoon salt, or to taste
1/4 teaspoon ground black
  pepper, or to taste
1/4 teaspoon grated nutmeg
1/4 teaspoon ground allspice
1 1/3 cups Beef Broth (p. 43)
  or 1 can (10 1/2 ounces)
  broth

SAUCE

3 tablespoons butter or
  margarine
3 tablespoons all-purpose
  flour

1 1/2 cups half-and-half
1/8 teaspoon dried dill weed
Salt and pepper, to taste

1. Prepare meatballs: In a small bowl, soak bread crumbs in milk. Reserve.

2. In a 10-inch skillet, heat the oil. Add garlic and onion and sauté over moderate heat until tender but not brown. Reserve.

3. In a large bowl, lightly beat the egg. Add bread crumbs and milk, garlic and onion, and all remaining ingredients except broth. Mix thoroughly.

4. Flatten the mixture in the bowl. Divide into 4 parts. Remove one-quarter at a time and divide it into 8 pieces. Shape into balls. On an unbuttered rimmed baking sheet, arrange the 32 meatballs so they are equally spaced.

5. Place baking sheet on a rack 6-inches below the heating element of a broiler. Broil meatballs, without turning, until brown, about 15 minutes.

6. Transfer meatballs to the skillet. Add broth and bring to a boil. Reduce heat, cover, and simmer for 20 minutes. Transfer meatballs to

an 11 x 7-inch or 8-inch square (2-quart) baking dish. Reserve broth for sauce.

7. Prepare sauce: In a heavy 2-quart saucepan, melt the butter. Whisk in flour until smooth. Stir over low heat for 2 minutes without browning. Add half-and-half and 1/2 cup of the reserved broth. Stir over moderate heat until smooth and thick. Stir in dill weed. Season with salt and pepper.

8. Pour sauce over meatballs. Cover the dish with a lid or aluminum foil. The meatballs may be refrigerated until ready to serve.

— This recipe may be prepared ahead to this point. —

9. Bake meatballs, covered, in a 325° F oven until heated through, about 20 to 30 minutes. Serve.

Yield: 32 meatballs, 4 to 6 servings.

Notes:
1. Buttered noodles are a nice accompaniment.
2. This recipe may be used to make excellent appetizers. See Swedish Meatballs for Appetizers (p. 36).

Barbecued Spareribs

3 1/2 to 4 pounds pork
  spareribs
1 to 2 cups Barbecue Sauce
  (p. 196)

Orange slices, cut in half, for
  garnish (optional)
Parsley for garnish (optional)

1. Cut the pork into separate ribs. Drop into a 4 1/2-quart pot one-third full of boiling water. Return water to boiling, and boil ribs for 4 minutes. Drain. This step may be omitted, but it removes some of the fat, allows the pork to better absorb the barbecue sauce, makes the meat more tender, and removes the unpleasant taste that sometimes occurs in pork.

2. On the slotted rack of a broiling pan brushed with vegetable oil, arrange ribs in one layer.

3. Roast in a preheated 350° F oven for 30 minutes. Pour fat out of pan. Return ribs to pan with the rack removed.

4. Brush ribs with 1 cup of barbecue sauce.

5. Roast an additional 30 minutes. Turn and baste ribs several times.

6. Transfer to a serving dish and keep warm.

7. Skim fat off sauce in pan. Spread sauce over ribs.

8. Serve immediately, or refrigerate and reheat in a 350° F oven. The ribs are tastier the next day.

9. The remaining barbecue sauce may be heated and brushed over the ribs.

10. Surround ribs with orange slices. Parsley leaves may be placed in the center of each orange slice. Serve.

Yield: 4 to 5 servings.

Chinese Spareribs

3 1/2 to 4 pounds pork spareribs
1 large clove garlic, minced
1 tablespoon Dijon mustard
1/3 cup ketchup

1/3 cup soy sauce
1/4 cup honey
3 tablespoons cider vinegar
1/4 teaspoon ground dried ginger

1. Cut the pork into separate ribs. Drop into a 4 1/2-quart pot one-third full of boiling water. Return water to boiling, and boil ribs for 4 minutes. Drain. This step may be omitted, but it removes some of the fat, allows the pork to better absorb the sauce, makes the meat more tender, and removes the unpleasant taste that sometimes occurs in pork.

2. On the slotted rack of a broiler pan brushed with vegetable oil, arrange the ribs in one layer.

3. Roast in a preheated 350° F oven for 30 minutes.

4. Meanwhile, in a small bowl, combine the remaining ingredients. Reserve.

5. Pour fat out of pan. Return ribs to pan with the rack removed. Brush sauce on ribs.

6. Roast an additional 30 minutes. Turn and baste ribs several times.

7. Serve immediately, or refrigerate and reheat in a 350° F oven. The ribs are tastier the next day.

Yield: 4 to 5 servings.

Scrapple

Try this for breakfast instead of plain sausage.

3/4 pound (1 1/3 cups) bulk sausage
1/4 teaspoon dried rubbed sage
1/8 teaspoon ground allspice
3 cups water

1 cup cornmeal
1/2 cup whole wheat flour
1/2 teaspoon salt, or to taste
Butter, margarine, or sausage fat for frying

1. In a heavy 10 to 12-inch skillet, stir sausage over moderate heat until it forms brown granules. Pour off fat. The fat may be saved for frying the scrapple.

2. Add sage, allspice, and water. Scrape loose any browned bits of sausage adhering to skillet. Bring to a boil.

3. Add cornmeal and flour all at once. Remove from heat. Stir to a smooth paste. Season with salt.

4. Pack mixture into an 8 1/2 x 4 1/2 x 2 1/2-inch loaf pan. Cover with plastic wrap and refrigerate until chilled.

— This recipe may be prepared ahead to this point. —

5. Unmold the scrapple. Cut into 1/2-inch slices.
6. Fry the slices and serve.

Yield: 16 slices, 8 servings.

Lamb Stew

The delicate taste of lamb combined with colorful vegetables makes this a special delight. In this recipe, the lamb is browned under the broiler. This is easier and more efficient than browning the meat in a frying pan.

3 to 3 1/2 pounds lamb shoulder (bone-in), cut into 1 1/2 to 2-inch cubes
2 tablespoons vegetable oil
6 tablespoons (3/4 stick) butter or margarine, divided
1/4 cup finely chopped carrot
3/4 cup chopped onion
1 large clove garlic, minced
1/4 cup all-purpose flour
1 2/3 cups Chicken Broth (p. 42) or 1 can (14 1/2 ounces) broth
1 cup dry white wine
3/4 cup unpeeled, seeded, and chopped tomato
1/4 teaspoon dried rosemary

1/8 teaspoon dried thyme
1/2 teaspoon salt, or to taste
1/4 teaspoon ground black pepper, or to taste
4 medium carrots, split lengthwise and cut into 2-inch pieces
3/4 pound rutabaga, cut into 3/4-inch cubes (about 2 1/4 cups)
1/2 pound green beans, cut into 1 1/2-inch lengths (about 2 cups)
8 ounces mushrooms, sliced 1/4-inch thick

1. Place lamb in a broiling pan with the rack removed or use a similar pan measuring about 14 1/2 x 12 x 1-inches. Pour the oil over the lamb. Toss lamb until the pieces are evenly coated with oil.

2. Place pan on a rack 3-inches below the heating element of a broiler. Broil, turning occasionally with a large spoon, until the pieces of lamb are brown on all sides, about 15 minutes.

3. Meanwhile, in a nonreactive 4-quart casserole, melt 3 tablespoons of butter. Add finely chopped carrot, onion, and garlic. Sauté over moderate heat until tender and light brown. Add flour. Stir until smooth.

4. Remove lamb from pan and reserve. Skim fat off pan juices. Pour part of the broth into the pan. Scrape pan to loosen browned particles. Add this liquid, remaining broth, and wine to casserole. Stir until smooth. Add tomato, rosemary, thyme, salt, and pepper. Stir over moderate heat until mixture comes to a boil. Add lamb. Cover casserole. Braise in a 325° F oven until lamb is tender, about 1 1/2 hours. If necessary, adjust oven temperature so casserole contents simmer gently.

5. Meanwhile, boil carrots and rutabaga separately until tender. Drain and reserve. Drop beans into boiling water. Boil until barely tender, about 7 minutes. Drain and reserve.

6. Melt 3 tablespoons of butter in a heavy 10-inch skillet. Add mushrooms and sauté over high heat until barely tender. Reserve.

7. When the lamb is tender, strain the stew. Remove bones and return lamb to casserole. Skim fat off liquid. Then pour liquid over lamb. Add all the vegetables and mix gently. Season with salt and pepper. Reheat and serve.

Yield: 8 cups, 4 to 5 servings.

Ham and Turkey or Chicken with Cornbread and Cheddar Cheese Sauce

This recipe may be prepared ahead and is ideal for church suppers and other large gatherings.

4 slices baked ham, preferably Smithfield or Virgina
4 slices cooked turkey or chicken

Skillet Cornbread (p. 238)
Cheddar Cheese Sauce (p. 198)

1. Wrap ham and turkey or chicken in aluminum foil. Warm in a 300° F oven.

2. Divide cornbread into 8 wedges. Split each wedge. Place 2 or 3 pieces on each plate.

3. Arrange ham and turkey or chicken on top of the cornbread. Pour about 1/2 cup of cheese sauce over each serving. Serve.

Yield: 4 to 6 servings.

Vegetables

Baked Acorn or Butternut Squash

Acorn and butternut squash deserve to be more popular. Here's a simple and tasty way to prepare them.

**1 acorn or butternut squash
(1 to 1 1/2 pounds)
Salt, to taste
Pepper, to taste
Ground cinnamon (optional)**

**4 teaspoons dark brown
sugar
2 tablespoons (1/4 stick)
butter or margarine**

1. Using a serrated knife, quarter the squash by cutting from the stem end to the flower end. Use a spoon to scrape out the seeds and stringy material from each quarter.

2. Arrange squash, cut side up, in a buttered 11 x 7-inch baking dish. Sprinkle with salt, pepper, cinnamon, and brown sugar. Dot with butter.

3. Cover dish with a lid or aluminum foil. Bake in a 350° F oven until tender, about 1 hour. Baste squash with its juices once or twice while baking and before serving.

Yield: 4 servings.

Green Beans Amandine

My favorite way to prepare my favorite vegetable.

**1 pound fresh green string
beans
3 tablespoons butter or
margarine
1 tablespoon lemon juice**

**1/4 cup sliced almonds,
toasted
1/2 teaspoon salt, or to taste
1/8 teaspoon ground white
pepper, or to taste**

1. Cut or snap the ends off the beans and pull off any attached strings. Use a knife to split each bean in half lengthwise (French style). Use one of the dark green lines on each side of the bean as a guide. A bean slicer may also be used. There should be about 5 1/2 cups of beans.

2. Drop beans into a 4 1/2-quart pot half full of boiling water. Boil beans until just tender, about 7 minutes. Do not overcook or the beans will lose their bright green color. Drain and keep warm.

— This recipe may be prepared ahead to this point. —

3. Melt the butter in the pot in which the beans were cooked. Add beans, lemon juice, almonds, salt, and pepper.
4. Toss and serve.

Yield: 4 cups, 6 servings.

Bright Green Broccoli

This method produces bright green broccoli with the stems as tender as the florets.

1 to 1 1/4 pounds broccoli
Melted butter or margarine
Salt

Pepper
Finely grated Parmesan or
Romano cheese (optional)

1. Cut broccoli into 4-inch pieces that include a floret and stem. Split each stem lengthwise. This will allow the stems to cook as fast as the attached florets.
2. Drop broccoli into a 4 1/2-quart pot half full of boiling water. Boil until barely tender, about 7 minutes. Do not overcook or the broccoli will lose its bright green color. Drain and keep warm.
3. Brush with melted butter. Season with salt and pepper. Sprinkle with cheese. Serve.

Yield: 4 servings.

Steamed Cabbage

1 medium head (1 1/2 to 2 pounds) green cabbage
1/4 cup (1/2 stick) butter or margarine

3/4 teaspoon salt, or to taste
1/8 teaspoon ground black pepper, or to taste

1. Discard the thick outer leaves of the cabbage. Use a large serrated knife to quarter the cabbage and remove the core from each quarter. Slice cabbage 1/4-inch thick. A food processor is useful for this.

2. Steam cabbage until tender, about 8 minutes. The cabbage may be cooled and reheated.

—This recipe may be prepared ahead to this point.—

3. In a heavy 10-inch skillet, melt the butter. Add cabbage. Heat and toss until cabbage is heated. Season with salt and pepper. Serve.

Yield: 4 cups, 4 to 6 servings.

Steamed Cabbage with Mirepoix

A mirepoix is a mixture of finely diced carrot, onion, and celery.

1/4 cup butter or margarine
1/2 cup finely chopped carrot
1/2 cup finely chopped onion
1/3 cup finely chopped celery
1 clove garlic, minced

Steamed Cabbage (see above) prepared through Step 2
3/4 teaspoon salt, or to taste
1/8 teaspoon ground black pepper, or to taste

1. In a heavy 10-inch skillet, melt the butter. Add carrot, onion, celery, and garlic. Sauté over moderate heat until vegetables are tender but not brown, about 5 minutes.

2. Add cabbage. Heat and toss until cabbage is heated. Season with salt and pepper. Serve.

Yield: 4 cups, 4 to 6 servings.

Steamed Cabbage with Bacon

4 thin slices (3 ounces) bacon
1 medium onion, thinly sliced
Steamed Cabbage (p. 150)
  prepared through Step 2

3/4 teaspoon salt, or to taste
1/8 teaspoon ground black
  pepper, or to taste

1. In a heavy 10-inch skillet, fry the bacon until crisp. Break bacon into small pieces. Reserve.

2. Add onion to fat in skillet. Sauté over moderate heat until tender but not brown.

3. Add cabbage and bacon. Heat and toss until cabbage is heated. Season with salt and pepper. Serve.

Yield: 4 cups, 4 to 6 servings.

Spiced Red Cabbage

2 tablespoons bacon fat or
  2 tablespoons (1/4 stick)
  butter or margarine
2 medium onions,
  coarsely chopped
2 pounds red cabbage,
  sliced 1/4-inch thick
  (about 8 cups)
1 clove garlic, minced
1/4 cup light brown sugar
1 cup Chicken Broth (p. 42) or
  canned broth

1 cup dry red wine
1 cup water
1/3 cup cider or wine vinegar
2 medium apples, peeled,
  cored, and chopped
1/4 teaspoon ground cloves
1/4 teaspoon grated nutmeg
1/4 teaspoon ground allspice
1 teaspoon salt, or to taste
1/4 teaspoon ground black
  pepper, or to taste

1. In a heavy, nonreactive 4 1/2-quart pot, melt the bacon fat. Add onions and sauté over moderate heat until tender but not brown.

2. Add cabbage and remaining ingredients. Mix thoroughly.

3. Cover and boil over moderate heat until cabbage is tender, about 30 minutes. Stir occasionally to prevent scorching.

4. Uncover. Boil off almost all the liquid, stirring frequently. Serve.

Yield: 5 cups, 8 servings.

Glazed Carrots or Parsnips

The carrots or parsnips develop a shiny glaze from the butter; no sugar is added.

1 pound carrots or parsnips, peeled and sliced 1/4-inch thick (about 2 1/2 cups)
1 cup water
2 tablespoons (1/4 stick) butter or margarine

1/2 teaspoon salt, or to taste
1/8 teaspoon ground white pepper, or to taste
Fresh chopped dill, mint, chives, or parsley for garnish (optional)

1. In a heavy 2-quart saucepan, combine carrots, water, butter, salt, and pepper. Bring to a boil. Cover and boil over moderate heat until carrots are tender, about 7 to 10 minutes. Stir occasionally to prevent scorching.
2. Uncover. Boil off almost all the liquid, stirring frequently.
3. Add the herb, toss, and serve.

Yield: 2 cups, 4 servings.

Maple Glazed Carrots or Parsnips

Glazed Carrots or Parsnips (see above) (in Step 1 add a pinch of cinnamon)

2 tablespoons maple syrup

1. Immediately before serving, add maple syrup to carrots.
2. Toss gently over high heat until carrots are glazed.

Yield: 2 cups, 4 servings.

Carrot and Rutabaga Timbales

These colorful timbales are topped with a daisy-shaped decoration made from sliced rutabaga and carrot. The decoration may be omitted (Steps 1 to 3).

1 pound carrots, peeled
and sliced 1/4-inch thick
1 1/2 pounds rutabaga
4 tablespoons (1/2 stick)
butter or margarine, divided
1/2 large onion, sliced
1 large clove garlic, minced

3 large eggs
1/2 cup half-and-half or milk
1/4 teaspoon grated nutmeg
1/4 teaspoon dried basil
1 teaspoon salt, or to taste
1/4 teaspoon black pepper, or
to taste

1. Reserve 8 carrot slices about 5/8-inch in diameter.
2. Peel rutabaga. Use a sharp knife to cut 8 thin slices, about 1/4-thick and 3-inches in diameter. Use a 2 1/4 to 2 1/2-inch daisy-shaped cookie cutter to cut the rutabaga slices into daisy shapes. A few light taps with a mallet on top of the cutter will make cutting the shapes easier.
3. In a 10-inch skillet, melt 2 tablespoons of butter. Add the 8 carrot slices and rutabaga shapes. Sauté over moderate heat until light brown and barely tender, turning once. Butter eight 6-ounce (3/4-cup) soufflé dishes or custard cups. Place a carrot slice in the center of each dish. Top each carrot slice with a rutabaga shape. Reserve.
4. Boil remaining carrot slices until tender, about 15 minutes. Drain and reserve.
5. Cut remaining rutabaga into 1/2-inch cubes and boil until tender, about 20 minutes. Drain and reserve.
6. Meanwhile, add onion and garlic to butter remaining in skillet. Sauté over moderate heat until tender. Transfer to a food processor with a steel blade and purée.
7. Add carrots and rutabaga to the food processor. Process until puréed. Use a rubber spatula or wooden spoon to force mixture through a strainer placed over a 2-quart saucepan.
8. Add 2 tablespoons of butter to the purée. Heat and stir until butter is melted.
9. Meanwhile, in a small bowl, lightly beat eggs with half-and-half.
10. Add egg mixture, nutmeg, basil, salt, and pepper to purée. Mix thoroughly.

11. Fill the dishes with the mixture. Equally space the dishes in a pan measuring about 15 x 11-inches. Place pan on a rack in the middle of a preheated 350° F oven. Pour boiling water into pan until it covers half the depth of the dishes. Bake until a knife inserted in the center comes out clean, about 35 minutes.

12. Unmold and serve.

Yield: 8 servings.

Mashed Rutabaga with Pecan Topping

This underappreciated vegetable is a real treat when prepared as described here.

1 medium rutabaga
  (about 1 1/2 pounds)
1/4 cup chopped pecans
3 tablespoons butter or
  margarine, divided

1/4 cup milk
1/2 teaspoon salt, or to taste
1/8 teaspoon ground black
  pepper, or to taste

1. Peel rutabaga. Use a large serrated knife to cut rutabaga into 1-inch cubes. Cover with water and boil until tender, about 30 minutes. Drain. Purée in a food processor or food mill.

2. Meanwhile, heat pecans in a 350° F oven for a few minutes until they give off a nutty aroma. A toaster oven is useful for this. Do not let the nuts brown or they will taste burned. Melt 1 tablespoon of butter. Add pecans and toss until evenly coated. Reserve.

3. In a 2-quart saucepan, combine the rutabaga, 2 tablespoons of butter, milk, salt, and pepper. Heat and stir with a wooden spatula or spoon to remove excess moisture. Transfer to a serving dish.

4. Sprinkle pecans on top of rutabaga. Serve.

Yield: 2 cups, 4 servings.

Cauliflower with Mornay Sauce

1 medium head cauliflower,
  cut into florets
5 tablespoons butter or
  margarine, divided
3 tablespoons all-purpose
  flour
2 cups milk

1/4 cup finely grated
  Parmesan cheese
1/8 teaspoon grated nutmeg
1 teaspoon Dijon mustard
1/4 teaspoon salt, or to taste
1/4 cup dry bread crumbs

1. Drop cauliflower into boiling water. Boil until barely tender, about 8 to 12 minutes. Drain.

2. Arrange the florets in a buttered 11 x 7-inch or 8-inch square (2-quart) broiler-proof baking dish or pan. Reserve.

3. Melt 3 tablespoons of butter in a heavy 2-quart saucepan. Whisk in flour until smooth. Stir over low heat for 2 minutes without browning. Add milk. Stir over moderate heat until smooth and thick. Add Parmesan cheese, nutmeg, mustard, and salt. Heat and stir until cheese is melted. Pour over cauliflower.

4. Sauté bread crumbs in 2 tablespoons of butter until light golden brown. Sprinkle over cauliflower. The cauliflower may be refrigerated until ready to serve. Let reach room temperature before broiling.

— This recipe may be prepared ahead to this point. —

5. Place dish on a rack 6-inches below the heating element of a broiler. Broil until sauce bubbles and crumbs are golden brown. Serve.

Yield: 6 servings.

Cauliflower with Tomatoes

1 medium head cauliflower,
  cut into florets
2 medium tomatoes,
  unpeeled, seeded, and cut
  into 2 1/2-inch x 1/4-inch
  strips
6 tablespoons (3/4 stick)
  butter or margarine,
  divided

2 teaspoons lemon juice
1/2 teaspoon salt, or to taste
1/8 teaspoon ground white
  pepper, or to taste
1/2 cup grated Swiss cheese
1/4 cup dry bread crumbs

1. Drop cauliflower into boiling water. Boil until barely tender, about 8 to 12 minutes. Drain and reserve.

2. Arrange cauliflower in a buttered 11 x 7-inch or 8-inch square (2-quart) baking dish. Scatter tomato strips over cauliflower.

3. Melt 4 tablespoons of butter. Stir in lemon juice and pour over vegetables. Season with salt and pepper. Sprinkle Swiss cheese over vegetables.

4. Melt 2 tablespoons of butter in a 9-inch skillet. Add bread crumbs and sauté over moderate heat until golden brown. Sprinkle crumbs on top of cheese.

— This recipe may be prepared ahead to this point. —

5. Bake, uncovered, in a preheated 350° F oven until vegetables are hot and cheese is melted, about 20 minutes. Serve.

Yield: 6 1/2 cups, 6 servings.

Confetti Corn

2 tablespoons olive oil or
  other vegetable oil
1 small onion, thinly sliced
1 clove garlic, minced
1/4 green bell pepper, seeded
  and sliced 1/4-inch thick
1 1/2 cups cooked fresh corn
  or 1 can (15 1/4 ounces)
  whole kernel corn, drained

1/2 medium tomato,
  unpeeled, seeded, and cut
  into 1/2-inch squares
1/2 teaspoon salt, or to taste
1/4 teaspoon ground black
  pepper, or to taste

1. In a heavy 10 to 12-inch skillet, heat the oil. Add onion and garlic. Sauté over moderate heat until tender but not brown.

2. Add green pepper and sauté for 1 to 2 minutes. Add corn and tomato. Sauté until hot.

3. Season with salt and pepper. Serve.

Yield: 2 cups, 4 servings.

Fluted Mushroom Caps

Fluted (grooved) mushroom caps are a fascinating garnish and give an elegant appearance to fish, poultry, and meat dishes.

Mushrooms
Lemon juice

Butter or margarine

1. The mushrooms must be very fresh and firm or they will tear apart when the grooves are cut.

2. Professional chefs use a knife but this takes a lot of skill and experience. A single channel zester will produce excellent results with only a little practice. See illustrations, next page. Start at the center of the mushroom cap and use the sharp edge of the zester to cut a groove extending to the edge of the cap in a slightly circular direction (A). Make 4 grooves so the mushroom surface is divided into quarters (B). Then make adjacent grooves in each quarter until the cap is completely grooved (C).

A

B

C

3. When ready to serve, melt enough butter to coat the bottom of a skillet. Add mushrooms. Sprinkle each of the mushrooms with a few drops of lemon juice to prevent them from darkening. Sauté over high heat until the caps are barely tender. Do not overcook or the mushrooms will lose their fresh appearance.

Baked Stuffed Tomatoes

4 tablespoons (1/2 stick)
 butter or margarine,
 divided
1/2 cup chopped onion
4 medium tomatoes
Salt and pepper, to taste
1/2 cup fresh or dry bread
 crumbs from White Bread
 (p. 210) or firm commercial
 bread

1/4 cup finely grated Swiss or
 Parmesan cheese
1/2 teaspoon dried basil
1 tablespoon finely chopped
 parsley

1. Melt 2 tablespoons of butter in a 9-inch skillet. Add onion and sauté over moderate heat until tender but not brown. Reserve.

2. Use a small knife to cut out the tomato stems. Halve the tomatoes. Place halves, cut side up, in an oiled baking dish or pan measuring 13 x 9-inches. Sprinkle with salt and pepper.

3. Spread onion on top of the tomato halves.

4. Combine bread crumbs, cheese, basil, and parsley. Spread over tomatoes. Melt 2 tablespoons of butter and sprinkle over tomatoes.

— This recipe may be prepared ahead to this point. —

5. Bake in a preheated 425° F oven until tomatoes are barely tender, about 15 to 20 minutes. Do not overcook or they will become mushy. If the crumbs are not as brown as you would like, place the tomatoes under a broiler for a minute or two. Serve within 15 minutes.

Yield: 8 tomato halves, 8 servings.

Steamed Yellow Squash, Zucchini, and Carrots with Butter and Wine Sauce

This colorful and delicious vegetable medley is simple to prepare. The vegetables look like they were shaped by a skilled chef but are easy to cut.

1 cup dry white wine
1 1/2 tablespoons finely
  chopped shallots
1 small clove garlic, minced
1/4 cup (1/2 stick) butter
  (no substitute)
1/2 teaspoon salt, or to taste
1/4 teaspoon ground white
  pepper, or to taste

1 medium (1/2 pound) yellow
  summer squash
1 medium (1/2 pound)
  zucchini
2 medium carrots
Finely grated Parmesan
  cheese (optional)

1. In a nonreactive 1/2-quart saucepan, combine wine, shallots, and garlic. Boil gently until reduced by half. Remove from heat. Add butter and stir until melted. Season with salt and pepper. If desired, the sauce may be strained. Reserve.

2. Cut yellow squash and zucchini in half crosswise and then in half lengthwise. Slice each piece lengthwise into 1/4-inch thick strips about 3 to 3 1/2-inches long and 1-inch wide. Reserve.

3. Cut carrots into 2 1/2 x 1/4 x 1/4-inch sticks. Steam carrot sticks for 2 minutes. Add squash and zucchini and continue to steam until barely tender, about 4 to 5 minutes.

4. In a 4 1/2-quart pot, place the vegetables. Pour sauce over vegetables. Heat while tossing gently. Season with salt and pepper. Sprinkle with Parmesan cheese and serve.

Yield: 3 cups, 4 servings.

Mashed Potatoes

No lumps with this method!

**1 3/4 to 2 pounds (1/3 of a
5 pound bag) baking
(Idaho, russet) potatoes
1/2 to 1 cup half-and-half,
milk, or sour cream
3 tablespoons butter or
margarine**

**1/2 teaspoon salt, or to taste
1/4 teaspoon ground black
or white pepper, or to taste
Pinch grated nutmeg
(optional)**

1. Peel potatoes and cut them into 1-inch cubes. They may be peeled hours ahead and covered with cold water to prevent discoloration. Boil until just tender, about 10 to 15 minutes. Use an ice pick or fork to test for doneness. Drain and let the moisture on the potatoes evaporate.

2. Use a food mill or potato ricer to purée the potatoes. If a food mill or ricer is not available, use a fork to mash the potatoes in a strainer placed over a bowl. Then use a wooden spoon or rubber spatula to force the potatoes through the strainer. There should be about 4 cups of potatoes. If the potatoes are to be served later, leave them uncovered. Cooked potatoes should not be covered while hot or they may develop an off flavor.

— This recipe may be prepared ahead to this point. —

3. Return potatoes to pot. Add 1/2 cup of half-and-half and remaining ingredients. Heat over low heat while stirring constantly with a wooden spatula or spoon to prevent scorching. Add additional half-and-half until the desired consistency is reached. Serve immediately.

Yield: 5 cups, 4 to 6 servings.

Duchess Potatoes

Using whole eggs rather than just the yolks makes these potatoes puff a bit and keeps them moist.

Mashed Potatoes (p. 161)
 (use only 1/4 cup of half-
 and-half, milk, or sour
 cream)

2 large eggs
Melted butter or margarine
 (optional)

1. Stir the mashed potatoes over low heat until they are quite thick. Avoid scorching.
2. Remove from heat. Add eggs and beat until blended.
3. Use a 16-inch pastry bag with a 3/4-inch star tip (#9) to pipe 6 or 8 rosettes about 3-inches in diameter onto a buttered baking sheet.
4. Place baking sheet on a rack about 6-inches below the heating element of a broiler. Broil until lightly browned, about 5 minutes.
5. Brush potatoes with melted butter. Serve immediately.

Yield: 6 to 8 servings.

Potato Fingers

Easy to prepare, delectable to eat.

1/4 cup vegetable oil or
 melted margarine
1 1/2 pounds (4 medium)
 baking (Idaho, russet)
 potatoes

Salt and pepper, to taste
1 tablespoon grated
 Parmesan cheese
 (optional)
Paprika (optional)

1. Line a baking sheet with aluminum foil. Brush foil with oil.
2. Scrub the unpeeled potatoes and quarter them lengthwise. Arrange potato quarters, skin side down, on baking sheet. Brush with oil. Season with salt and pepper. Sprinkle with Parmesan cheese and paprika.
3. Bake in a 375° F oven until potatoes are golden brown, about 45 minutes. Baste 2 or 3 times while baking. Serve.

Yield: 16 potato fingers, 4 to 5 servings.

Stuffed Baked Potatoes with Cream Cheese and Bacon

4 baking (Idaho, russet)
   potatoes
1 package (3 ounces) cream
   cheese, at room temperature
5 tablespoons melted butter
   or margarine, divided
6 tablespoons sour cream
5 to 6 ounces bacon, fried
   until crisp and crumbled
   into small pieces, divided

1/2 teaspoon salt, or to taste
1/4 teaspoon pepper, or to
   taste
Fresh or frozen chives
   (optional)

1. Bake potatoes at 425° F until tender, about 1 hour.

2. Cut off the top third of each potato. Scoop out and reserve the pulp. Save the larger bottom shells. (For smaller servings, cut each potato in half to make two shells.)

3. Purée pulp in a food mill or potato ricer. If a food mill or ricer is not available, use a fork to mash the potatoes in a strainer placed over a bowl. Then use a wooden spoon or rubber spatula to force the potatoes through the strainer. Reserve.

4. In an electric mixer, beat the cream cheese until fluffy. Beat in 3 tablespoons of butter and sour cream. Add potato pulp, three-quarters of the bacon, salt, and pepper. Mix thoroughly.

5. Fill shells. Arrange potato halves on a baking sheet. Brush potatoes with remaining butter. The potatoes may be refrigerated until needed.

6. Reheat potatoes, uncovered, in a 425° F oven until heated through and brown on top, about 20 to 25 minutes.

7. Sprinkle with remaining bacon and chives. Serve.

Yield: 4 to 8 servings.

Fan-Tan Roasted Potatoes

During baking, the attached slices separate a bit, giving these potatoes the appearance of fan-tan rolls.

3 pounds (6 to 8 medium) baking (Idaho, russet) potatoes, similar in size and shape
1/2 cup (1 stick) butter or margarine, melted, and 2 tablespoons vegetable oil OR 10 tablespoons vegetable oil

1/2 teaspoon dried rosemary (optional)
Salt and pepper, to taste
Melted butter or margarine to brush the roasted potatoes (optional)
Chopped parsley, chives, or other fresh herb for garnish (optional)

1. Wash, peel, and dry the potatoes. Cut a thin slice off the bottom of each potato so it will not wobble. Cut each potato into 1/4-inch lengthwise or crosswise slices that extend to three-quarters of the depth of the potato (see illustration, below). Be careful not to cut all the way through the potato.

2. Combine butter and vegetable oil. Use part of this mixture to brush a 13 1/2 x 8 1/2-inch baking dish or roasting pan. Arrange potatoes, sliced surface up, in the dish. Brush potatoes with remaining butter and oil. Sprinkle with rosemary. Season with salt and pepper.

3. Roast in a 400° F oven, basting occasionally, until potatoes are tender and the bottom surfaces are browned, about 1 hour.

4. Turn potatoes over and roast until the sliced surfaces are browned, about 10 to 15 minutes.

5. Turn potatoes, sliced side up, brush with melted butter, sprinkle with the herb, and serve. The potatoes may be kept warm in the oven with the heat off.

Yield: 6 to 8 servings.

Roasted New Potatoes with Garlic and Rosemary

2 to 2 1/4 pounds new
potatoes, unpeeled, cut
into 1 1/2-inch chunks
1/4 cup olive oil or other
vegetable oil
1 large clove garlic, minced

2 teaspoons chopped fresh
rosemary
1/2 teaspoon salt, or to taste
1/4 teaspoon ground black
pepper, or to taste

1. Place the potatoes in a 13 1/2 x 8 1/2-inch baking dish. Pour oil over potatoes and toss until potatoes are evenly coated. Sprinkle with garlic, rosemary, salt, and pepper.

2. Roast in a preheated 375° F oven until potatoes are golden brown, about 1 hour. After the first 20 minutes, use a metal spatula or pancake turner to turn the potatoes every 7 to 10 minutes.

3. The potatoes may be garnished with additional rosemary. Serve.

Yield: 4 to 6 servings.

Potatoes Boulangère

2 to 2 1/4 pounds boiling
or all-purpose potatoes
1/4 cup (1/2 stick) butter or
margarine
2 medium onions, sliced
1 clove garlic, minced
1 2/3 cups Chicken Broth
(p. 42) or 1 can (14 1/2
ounces) broth

1/4 teaspoon dried thyme,
marjoram, or rosemary
(optional)
1/4 teaspoon salt, or to taste
1/8 teaspoon ground black
pepper, or to taste

1. Peel potatoes and slice them 1/4-inch thick. A food processor makes this easy. Place in cold water. Reserve.

2. In a 10-inch skillet, melt the butter. Add onions and garlic. Sauté over moderate heat until tender and light brown.

3. Drain potatoes and add to skillet. Toss until slices are evenly coated with butter. Transfer to a buttered 11 x 7-inch (2-quart) baking dish.

4. Add broth, thyme, salt, and pepper to skillet. Bring to a boil and pour over potatoes.

5. Bake, uncovered, in a preheated 425° F oven until potatoes are golden brown, about 1 hour. Serve.

Yield: 6 servings.

Scalloped Potatoes with Cheese

2 to 2 1/4 pounds (6 medium) boiling or all-purpose potatoes, peeled and sliced 1/4-inch thick (a food processor makes this easy)

6 tablespoons (3/4 stick) butter or margarine, divided

1 small onion, finely chopped (optional)

1 large clove garlic, minced (optional)

2 tablespoons all-purpose flour

1 1/2 cups half-and-half or milk

6 to 8 ounces Swiss, sharp Cheddar, or Monterey Jack cheese, grated (1 1/2 to 2 cups, loosely packed)

1 teaspoon Dijon mustard

Pinch grated nutmeg

3/4 teaspoon salt, or to taste

1/4 teaspoon ground white pepper, or to taste

1/2 cup dry bread crumbs

1. Drop potatoes into boiling salted water. Boil gently until barely tender, about 6 to 8 minutes. Drain, rinse under cold water, and reserve.

2. In a heavy 2-quart saucepan, melt 4 tablespoons of butter. Add onion and garlic. Sauté over low heat until tender.

3. Whisk in flour until smooth. Stir over low heat for 2 minutes without browning. Add half-and-half. Stir over moderate heat until smooth and thick.

4. Add cheese. Stir over moderate heat until cheese is melted and sauce is smooth. Stir in mustard, nutmeg, salt, and pepper. Reserve.

5. Cover the bottom of a buttered 11 x 7-inch (2-quart) baking dish with one-third of the potatoes.

6. Pour one-third of the cheese sauce over the potatoes. Layer each remaining third of potatoes and sauce. Reserve.

7. Melt 2 tablespoons of butter. Add bread crumbs. Mix until blended. Sprinkle bread crumbs over potatoes.

8. Bake, uncovered, in a 350° F oven until crumbs are golden brown and potatoes are bubbly, about 30 minutes. Serve.

Yield: 8 cups, 6 servings.

Mashed Sweet Potatoes with Pineapple

3 pounds sweet potatoes
1/4 cup light brown sugar
8 tablespoons (1 stick)
butter or margarine,
divided
1/2 cup sour cream
1/4 teaspoon ground
cinnamon

1/4 teaspoon salt, or to taste
1 can (8 ounces) crushed
pineapple, drained
1/3 cup chopped pecans
(optional)

1. Scrub potatoes in cold water. Bake in a 400° F oven until tender, about 45 to 60 minutes. Cool and peel.

2. In an electric mixer, beat the potatoes until smooth. Add brown sugar, 6 tablespoons of butter, sour cream, cinnamon, and salt. Beat until blended. Mix in pineapple.

3. Turn into a buttered 1 1/2-quart baking dish. Sprinkle with pecans. Dot with 2 tablespoons of butter. Cover with a lid or aluminum foil. The potatoes may be refrigerated until ready to serve.

— This recipe may be prepared ahead to this point. —

4. Bake, covered, in a 350° F oven until heated through, about 20 minutes. Serve.

Yield: 5 1/2 cups, 6 to 8 servings.

Oven Method for White or Brown Rice

This foolproof method produces perfect rice every time.

WHITE RICE
1 cup long-grain white rice,
  preferably parboiled type
1/4 to 1/2 teaspoon salt, or
  to taste

Pinch ground white
  pepper, or to taste
1 3/4 cups water

BROWN RICE
1 cup long-grain brown rice
1/4 to 1/2 teaspoon salt, or
  to taste

Pinch ground black or
  white pepper, or to taste
2 2/3 cups water

1. In a 2-quart covered casserole, combine rice, salt, and pepper.

2. Bring water to a boil and pour over rice. Stir until the grains of rice are separated.

3. Bake, covered, in a preheated 375° F oven until the grains of rice have absorbed all the water, about 25 minutes for white rice and 50 minutes for brown rice. Do not stir while cooking.

4. The rice may be set aside for 30 to 45 minutes before serving.

Yield: 3 cups white rice or 3 1/2 cups brown rice, 4 to 6 servings.

Steamed Brown Rice

Brown rice is unpolished rice and has a delicious nutty flavor. It has a firmer texture and more nutritive value than white rice.

2 cups water
1/2 teaspoon salt, or to taste

1 cup brown rice

1. In a 2-quart saucepan, bring the water and salt to a rapid boil. Pour in rice and stir to separate the grains of rice. Do not stir again or the rice may become gummy.

2. Bring to a boil, cover, reduce heat, and simmer until all the water has been absorbed by the rice, about 25 minutes.

3. Drain in a colander or strainer. Place colander over gently boiling water. Cover colander with a pot lid and steam for 10 minutes.

4. The rice may be kept warm by steaming over simmering water or reheated by steaming over boiling water.

Yield: 3 cups, 4 to 6 servings.

Brown Rice with Mushrooms

Oven Method for White or
  Brown Rice (p. 168) or
  Steamed Brown Rice (p. 168)
3 tablespoons butter or
  margarine
2 tablespoons minced onion
1 clove garlic, minced

4 ounces mushrooms,
  chopped
1/2 teaspoon salt, or to taste
1/4 teaspoon ground black
  pepper, or to taste
2 tablespoons finely chopped
  parsley

1. While rice is cooking, prepare mushroom mixture: In a 10-inch skillet, melt the butter. Add onion and garlic and sauté over low heat until tender but not brown.

2. Add mushrooms and sauté over high heat until tender. Remove from heat. Gently stir in rice, salt, pepper, and parsley.

3. Reheat over low heat. Serve.

Yield: 3 1/2 cups, 4 to 6 servings.

White Rice Pilaf

3 tablespoons butter, margarine, olive oil, or other vegetable oil
1/3 cup finely chopped onion
1/4 cup finely chopped carrot
1/4 cup finely chopped celery
1 1/2 cups long-grain white rice, preferably parboiled type
1 1/3 cups Chicken Broth (p. 42) or Beef Broth (p. 43) or 1 can (10 1/2 ounces) broth
1 1/3 cups water
4 tablespoons finely chopped red or green bell pepper OR 2 tablespoons of each (optional)
1/2 bay leaf (optional)
1/8 teaspoon dried thyme, basil, or tarragon (optional)
1/2 teaspoon salt, or to taste
1/8 teaspoon ground white or black pepper, or to taste
3 tablespoons finely chopped parsley (optional)

1. In a heavy 10-inch skillet, melt the butter. Add onion, carrot, and celery. Sauté over moderate heat until tender.

2. Add rice and stir until all the grains are coated with butter.

3. Stir in remaining ingredients. Bring to a boil and transfer to a 2-quart covered casserole.

4. Bake in a preheated 375° F oven until the liquid has been absorbed by the rice, about 20 to 25 minutes. Do not stir while cooking.

5. Before serving, add parsley. Toss gently with a fork and discard bay leaf. Season to taste with salt and pepper. The rice may be pressed into a 1/2-cup measuring cup or ramekin and unmolded onto each serving plate.

Yield: 4 cups, 6 to 8 servings.

Brown Rice Pilaf

Prepare the above White Rice Pilaf with the following changes:

1. Substitute 1 cup of brown rice for the white rice.
2. Bake the pilaf for about 1 hour.

Yield: 3 cups, 4 to 6 servings.

Brown Rice and Lentil Pilaf

Prepare Brown Rice Pilaf (p. 170), adding 1/3 cup of lentils with the rice in Step 2.

Yield: 3 1/2 cups, 4 to 6 servings.

Barley Pilaf

Give barley a try! This alternative to rice is delicious when prepared as a pilaf.

Prepare White Rice Pilaf (p. 170) with the following changes:

1. Substitute 1 cup of fine or medium barley for the white rice.
2. Bake the pilaf for about 45 minutes.

Yield: 3 1/2 cups, 4 to 6 servings.

Quinoa Pilaf

This grain, pronounced keen-wa, comes from the Andes Mountains in South America where it has been known since ancient times. When cooked, it is light in texture and has a unique and delicious flavor.

Prepare White Rice Pilaf (p. 170) with the following changes:

1. Substitute 1 cup of quinoa for the white rice. Before cooking, place quinoa in a strainer and rinse it thoroughly by running cold water over the grain.
2. Bake the pilaf for 20 to 25 minutes.

Yield: 4 cups, 6 to 8 servings.

Broccoli and Cheese Rice Pilaf

1/4 cup (1/2 stick) butter or margarine
1 1/2 cups long-grain white rice, preferably parboiled type
1 1/3 cups Chicken Broth (p. 42) or 1 can (10 1/2 ounces) broth
1 1/3 cups water
1/8 teaspoon grated nutmeg

1/4 teaspoon salt, or to taste
1/8 teaspoon ground white pepper, or to taste
2 cups tiny broccoli florets or 1 package (10 ounces) frozen chopped broccoli
3 ounces Cheddar cheese, grated (3/4 cup, loosely packed)

1. In a heavy 10-inch skillet, melt the butter. Add rice and stir until all the grains are coated with butter.

2. Stir in chicken broth, water, nutmeg, salt, and pepper. Bring to a boil and transfer to a 2-quart covered casserole.

3. Bake in a preheated 375° F oven until the liquid has been absorbed by the rice, about 20 to 25 minutes. Do not stir while cooking.

4. While rice is cooking, drop broccoli florets into boiling water and boil until just tender, about 3 minutes. Do not overcook or the broccoli will lose its bright green color. Drain. If frozen broccoli is used, cook according to package directions. Reserve.

5. When rice is done, add cheese and broccoli. Toss gently, season to taste with salt and pepper, and serve. The rice may be pressed into a 1/2-cup measuring cup or ramekin and unmolded onto each serving plate.

Yield: 6 cups, 8 servings.

Orange Pecan Rice Pilaf

This rice has an unusual and tempting flavor.

1/4 cup (1/2 stick) butter or margarine
1 1/2 cups long-grain white rice, preferably parboiled type
1 1/3 cups Chicken Broth (p. 42) or 1 can (10 1/2 ounces) broth
1 1/3 cups water
1 1/2 teaspoons finely grated orange rind

1/4 teaspoon salt, or to taste
1/8 teaspoon ground white pepper, or to taste
1/2 bay leaf (optional)
1/3 cup finely chopped pecans
1/4 cup orange juice (optional)

1. In a heavy 10-inch skillet, melt the butter. Add rice and stir until all the grains are coated with butter.
2. Stir in chicken broth, water, orange rind, salt, and pepper. Add bay leaf.
3. Bring to a boil and transfer to a 2-quart covered casserole.
4. Bake in a preheated 375° F oven until the liquid has been absorbed by the rice, about 20 to 25 minutes. Do not stir while cooking.
5. Before serving, add pecans and orange juice. Toss gently until pecans are evenly distributed. Discard bay leaf. Season to taste with salt and pepper. The rice may be pressed into a 1/2-cup measuring cup or ramekin and unmolded onto each serving plate.

Yield: 4 cups, 6 to 8 servings.

Orange Rice Pilaf with Parsley

Follow the above recipe for Orange Pecan Rice Pilaf but substitute 3 tablespoons of finely chopped parsley for the pecans.

Yield: 4 cups, 6 to 8 servings.

Chinese Rice

This rice is similar in taste to fried rice but is easier to prepare.

6 tablespoons (3/4 stick)
  butter or margarine,
  divided
1 1/2 cups long-grain whlte
  rice, preferably parboiled
  type
1 1/3 cups Beef Broth (p. 43)
  or 1 can (10 1/2 ounces)
  broth

1 1/3 cups water
2 to 3 tablespoons soy sauce
2 tablespoons finely chopped
  green onion
2 large eggs
1/3 cup chopped cooked ham
1/2 cup cooked frozen green
  peas

1. In a heavy 10-inch skillet, melt 4 tablespoons of butter. Add rice and stir until all the grains are coated with butter.

2. Stir in beef broth, water, and soy sauce. Bring to a boil and transfer to a 2-quart covered casserole.

3. Bake in a preheated 375° F oven until the liquid has been absorbed by the rice, about 20 to 25 minutes. Do not stir while cooking.

4. Melt 2 tablespoons of butter in the skillet. Add green onion and sauté over low heat until tender but not brown.

5. Break eggs into skillet. Heat and stir with a fork until eggs are scrambled. Stir in ham and peas. Add egg mixture to rice. Toss gently and serve.

Yield: 6 cups, 8 servings.

Pasta

Pasta

If you have children, they will enjoy helping you make pasta, especially rolling and cutting the dough with a pasta machine.

1 1/2 cups unbleached all-purpose flour

2 large eggs
2 teaspoons vegetable oil

DOUGH

1. Place all ingredients in a food processor bowl with a steel blade. Process continuously until crumbs form, about 1 minute. Form the crumbs into a smooth ball.

2. If a food processor is not available, place flour in a bowl and make a well in the center. Put eggs and oil in well. Use a fork to gradually stir eggs and oil into flour. Knead dough until a smooth ball is formed.

3. Divide ball of dough into 3 pieces. Cover with plastic wrap.

4. Flatten one portion of dough. Pass it through the first, or widest, setting of a pasta machine. Fold the strip of dough in half. Roll it through the same machine setting again. Repeat folding and rolling 3 or 4 times until dough is smooth. If dough becomes sticky, dust lightly with flour.

5. Roll dough through each successively thinner setting until the desired thickness is reached. Roll one time for each setting. You will need to determine which setting produces the thickness of pasta you desire. I use the next to the thinnest setting which will make the pasta about 1/16-inch thick. When fully rolled, the pasta strip should be as wide as possible, about 5-inches.

6. Lay the rolled sheet of pasta on a lightly floured board. Cut into one of the shapes described below:

Noodles

1. Flour both sides of the rolled sheet of pasta. This will help prevent the noodles from sticking together after they are cut. Most pasta machines have 2 widths of cutting rollers. Pass the sheet of dough through the cutting rollers of desired width.

2. If the noodles are to be cooked within a short time, spread them on a lightly floured board or baking pan and sprinkle lightly with flour.

3. If the noodles are to be saved for future use, separate them and dry the noodles on a pasta drying rack or over a broomstick supported in a horizontal position. The dried noodles may be frozen in plastic bags.

Yield: One recipe makes 1/2 pound of noodles, 2 to 4 servings.

Lasagna Noodles

1. Cut the 5-inch wide pasta strips in half lengthwise to produce strips 2 1/2-inches wide.

2. Cut the strips into lengths about 1-inch shorter than the baking dish to be used.

Yield: One recipe of this dough, rolled to the next to thinnest setting, will make about 16 lasagna noodles 2 1/2-inches wide and 10-inches long.

Pasta Squares for Cannelloni or Manicotti

Cut the 5-inch wide pasta strips into 5-inch squares.

Yield: One recipe, rolled to the next to thinnest setting, will make about 16 pasta squares.

COOKING PASTA

Noodles

1. Drop one recipe of noodles into a 4 1/2-quart pot two-thirds full of gently boiling water. A tablespoon of vegetable oil added to the water will help prevent the pasta from sticking together. Stir occasionally with a wooden spoon to separate the individual pieces of pasta.

2. Cook the pasta until barely tender. Freshly prepared noodles will be done in only a few minutes. Cook dried noodles until just tender to the bite.

3. Drain immediately after cooking. The noodles may be tossed with melted butter or vegetable oil to prevent sticking.

Lasagna Noodles and Pasta Squares

1. Drop 2 or 3 lasagna noodles or pasta squares at a time into a 4 1/2-quart pot two-thirds full of gently boiling water.

2. Freshly prepared lasagna noodles and pasta squares should be boiled for about 20 seconds. Cook dried pasta until barely tender. Use a small strainer to transfer the lasagna noodles or pasta squares to a bowl of cold water. This will cool them until they can be touched. Then lay the noodles or squares flat on damp cloth towels until used.

SERVING PASTA

Noodles may be served with melted butter, Tomato Sauce (p. 190), Fresh Tomato Sauce (p. 190), Tomato Meat Sauce (p. 191), or Chicken and Tomato Pasta Sauce (p. 192) and sprinkled with grated Parmesan or Romano cheese.

Spinach Pasta

1/4 cup cooked spinach with the liquid pressed out (see Note, below)	1 large egg 1 teaspoon vegetable oil 1 1/3 cups all-purpose flour

1. Combine spinach, egg, and vegetable oil in a food processor with a steel blade. Process until blended.

2. Add flour and continue to process until small crumbs form, about 1 minute. Form the crumbs into a smooth ball.

3. Continue with the directions for Pasta (p. 176), starting with **DOUGH:** Step 3.

Yield: 1/2 pound pasta dough, 2 to 4 servings.

Note: One package (10 ounces) of frozen spinach will yield about 3/4 cup of drained cooked spinach.

Lasagna

Lasagna Noodles (p. 177)
1/4 cup (1/2 stick) butter or margarine
1/4 cup all-purpose flour
2 cups half-and-half
1/2 cup finely grated Parmesan cheese
3 ounces cream cheese (optional)
1 large egg
15 to 16 ounces ricotta cheese
1/8 teaspoon grated nutmeg
1/2 teaspoon salt, or to taste
1/8 teaspoon ground white pepper, or to taste
2 tablespoons finely chopped parsley (optional)
6 to 8 cups Tomato Meat Sauce (p. 191), divided
8 to 16 ounces mozzarella cheese, grated (2 to 4 cups, loosely packed)

1. Prepare lasagna noodles: Boil freshly prepared lasagna noodles for 20 seconds. Boil dried noodles until barely tender. Drop noodles into cold water. Then lay the noodles flat on damp cloth towels.

2. Prepare cheese sauce: In a heavy 2-quart saucepan, melt the butter. Whisk in flour until smooth. Stir over low heat for 2 minutes without browning. Add half-and-half. Stir over moderate heat until

smooth and thick. Add Parmesan cheese. Heat and stir until cheese is melted. Reserve.

3. In an electric mixer, beat cream cheese until soft. Beat in egg, ricotta cheese, nutmeg, salt, and pepper. Add cheese sauce and mix until smooth. Stir in parsley. Reserve.

4. Spread 1 cup of tomato meat sauce on the bottom of a 13 1/2 x 8 1/2-inch baking dish. Arrange 3 to 4 lasagna noodles in one layer on top of the sauce.

5. Spread another 1 cup of tomato meat sauce on top of the noodles. Cover with another layer of 3 to 4 noodles.

6. Spread half the cheese sauce on top of the noodles. Cover with 3 to 4 noodles. Spread the remaining cheese sauce on top of the noodles. Cover with 3 to 4 noodles.

7. Spread 2 cups of tomato meat sauce on top of the noodles.

8. Sprinkle the mozzarella cheese on top. The lasagna may be refrigerated until needed.

— This recipe may be prepared ahead to this point. —

9. Bake, uncovered, in a 350° F oven until the lasagna is lightly browned and heated through, about 30 minutes.

10. Cut into squares and serve with remaining tomato meat sauce.

Yield: 16 cups, 8 servings.

Chicken and Vegetable Lasagna

CHICKEN
3 1/2 pounds chicken pieces
8 cups water
1 pound carrots, sliced into
  rounds, 1/8-inch thick
  (about 3 cups)

1 medium onion, finely
  chopped
1 clove garlic, minced
1 bay leaf
1/2 teaspoon dried basil

VEGETABLES
1 tablespoon butter or
  margarine, melted
2 teaspoons chopped fresh
  or frozen chives
Salt, to taste

Ground white pepper, to taste
2 packages (10 ounces each)
  frozen spinach
1/2 cup water

CHEESE SAUCE

1/2 cup (1 stick) butter or margarine
3/4 cup all-purpose flour
5 1/4 cups milk
1 cup finely grated Parmesan cheese

1/8 teaspoon grated nutmeg
1/2 teaspoon salt, or to taste
1/4 teaspoon ground white pepper, or to taste

NOODLES

16 Lasagna Noodles (p. 177)

CHEESE TOPPING

8 to 16 ounces mozzarella cheese, grated (2 to 4 cups, loosely packed)

TOMATO SAUCE (OPTIONAL)

Fresh Tomato Sauce (p. 190) or
Tomato Sauce (p. 190)

1. Prepare chicken: In a 6-quart pot, combine chicken and other ingredients. Bring to a boil, reduce heat, and simmer 35 minutes.

2. Immediately strain chicken and carrots from broth. Cool chicken and remove skin and bones. Cut chicken into bite-size pieces; there should be about 3 cups. Reserve. Save broth for another purpose.

3. Prepare vegetables: Combine carrots with butter and chives. Season with salt and pepper. Reserve.

4. In a heavy, nonreactive 2-quart saucepan, place the frozen spinach and water. Bring to a boil, breaking up the spinach as it thaws. After spinach is completely thawed, boil it gently for a minute or two until tender. Do not overcook or the spinach will lose its bright green color. Drain and press out the liquid. Season with salt and pepper. Reserve.

5. Prepare cheese sauce: In a heavy 2-quart saucepan, melt the butter. Whisk in flour until smooth. Stir over low heat for 2 minutes without browning. Add milk and stir over moderate heat until smooth and thick. Add Parmesan cheese. Heat and stir until cheese is melted. Stir in nutmeg, salt, and pepper. Reserve.

6. Boil freshly prepared lasagna noodles for 20 seconds. Boil dried noodles until barely tender. Drop noodles into cold water. Then lay the noodles flat on damp cloth towels.

7. Butter two 11 x 7-inch (2-quart) baking dishes. Spread 1/2 cup of cheese sauce in the bottom of each dish. Arrange 2 noodles in one layer on top of the sauce in each dish.

8. Combine spinach with 1/2 cup of the cheese sauce. Spread half the mixture on top of the noodles in each dish. Cover the spinach in each dish with 2 noodles.

9. Combine chicken with 1 cup of cheese sauce. Spread half the mixture on top of the noodles in each dish. Cover the chicken in each dish with 2 noodles.

10. Spread half the carrots on top of the noodles in each dish. Cover the carrots in each dish with 2 noodles.

11. Spread half the remaining cheese sauce over the noodles in each dish. Sprinkle half the mozzarella cheese on top of the lasagna in each dish. The lasagna may be refrigerated until needed.

— This recipe may be prepared ahead to this point. —

12. Bake, uncovered, in a 350° F oven until lasagna is lightly browned and heated through, about 30 minutes. Serve with tomato sauce.

Yield: Two 2-quart dishes, 6 servings per dish.

Seafood Lasagna

LASAGNA

12 to 16 Lasagna Noodles
  (p. 177)
4 cups Tomato Sauce (p.
  190), divided
8 ounces mozzarella cheese,
  grated (2 cups, loosely
  packed)

Finely grated Parmesan
  cheese for garnish
  (optional)
Finely chopped parsley for
  garnish (optional)

SPINACH FILLING

1 package (10 ounces)
  frozen chopped spinach
1/4 cup water
1 tablespoon olive oil
1/4 cup finely chopped
  onion
1 clove garlic, minced
3 ounces cream cheese
  (optional)

1 large egg
15 to 16 ounces ricotta
  cheese
Pinch grated nutmeg
1/4 teaspoon salt, or to taste
1/8 teaspoon ground white
  pepper, or to taste
1/4 cup finely grated
  Parmesan cheese

SEAFOOD MIXTURE

3 to 4 tablespoons olive oil, divided
8 ounces mushrooms, sliced 1/4-inch thick
1 teaspoon lemon juice
1 pound raw shrimp, shelled and deveined (about 2 cups)
1 pound scallops
1 clove garlic, minced
1/2 cup dry white wine
1/4 teaspoon dried basil
1/2 teaspoon salt, or to taste
1/4 teaspoon ground white pepper, or to taste

1. Prepare lasagna noodles: Boil freshly prepared lasagna noodles for 20 seconds. Boil dried noodles until barely tender. Drop noodles into cold water. Then lay the noodles flat on damp cloth towels.

2. Prepare spinach filling: In a heavy, nonreactive 1 1/2-quart saucepan, place the frozen spinach and water. Bring to a boil, breaking up the spinach as it thaws. After spinach is completely thawed, boil it gently for a minute or two until tender. Do not overcook or the spinach will lose its bright green color. Drain and press out the liquid. Reserve.

3. In a heavy, preferably nonstick, 10 to 12-inch skillet, heat 1 tablespoon of olive oil. Add onion and garlic and sauté over low heat until tender but not brown. Reserve.

4. In an electric mixer, beat cream cheese until soft. Add egg, ricotta cheese, nutmeg, salt, and pepper. Beat until smooth. Add spinach, Parmesan cheese, onion, and garlic. Mix thoroughly.

5. Spread 1 cup of tomato sauce on the bottom of a 13 1/2 x 8 1/2-inch baking dish. Arrange 3 or 4 lasagna noodles in one layer on top of the sauce.

6. Spread one-third of the spinach mixture on top of the noodles. Cover with another layer of 3 or 4 noodles.

7. Spread another third of the spinach mixture on top of the noodles. Spread 1 cup of tomato sauce on top of the spinach mixture. Cover with 3 or 4 noodles.

8. Spread the remaining spinach mixture on top of the noodles. Cover with 3 or 4 noodles. Spread 1 cup of tomato sauce on top of the noodles. Sprinkle mozzarella cheese on top.

9. Cover the dish with a lid or aluminum foil. The lasagna may be refrigerated until needed.

10. Prepare seafood mixture: In the skillet, heat 2 tablespoons of oil. Add mushrooms and sprinkle with lemon juice. Sauté over high heat until just tender. Transfer to a large bowl and reserve.

11. In the skillet, heat 1 tablespoon of oil. Add shrimp. Sauté over high heat until pink. Transfer to the large bowl with the mushrooms.

12. Strain scallops reserving their liquid. Add scallops to skillet. Sauté over high heat until scallops release most of their juices. Strain scallops

again, reserving juices with liquid from scallops. Return scallops to skillet and sauté until opaque. If needed, add 1 tablespoon of oil to skillet. Transfer scallops to the large bowl.

13. Add scallop liquid, garlic, and wine to skillet. Boil and stir until syrupy. Add mushrooms, shrimp, scallops, 1 cup of tomato sauce, basil, salt, and pepper. Stir until mixed. The seafood mixture may be refrigerated until needed.

— This recipe may be prepared ahead to this point. —

14. Bake the lasagna, covered, in a 350° F oven until heated through, about 30 minutes. Reheat the seafood mixture. Cut the lasagna into 8 squares. Spoon about 1/2 cup of the seafood mixture over each serving. Garnish with Parmesan cheese and parsley. Serve.

Yield: 8 servings.

Chicken Cannelloni

FILLING
1/2 pound mild bulk sausage
2 tablespoons (1/4 stick) butter or margarine
1 medium onion, finely chopped
1 clove garlic, minced
3 cups cooked, finely chopped chicken (the chicken may be cooked by following the recipe for Chicken Broth, p. 42)
1 large egg, lightly beaten

15 to 16 ounces ricotta cheese
1/4 cup finely grated Parmesan cheese
1/2 teaspoon dried oregano
1/2 teaspoon dried basil
1 tablespoon finely chopped parsley
1/2 teaspoon salt, or to taste
1/4 teaspoon ground white pepper, or to taste

PASTA
14 to 16 Pasta Squares for Cannelloni or Manicotti (p. 177)

SAUCE

1/4 cup (1/2 stick) butter or margarine

6 tablespoons all-purpose flour

1 cup half-and-half and 2 cups milk OR 3 cups milk

1/2 cup finely grated Parmesan cheese

1/8 teaspoon grated nutmeg

1/4 teaspoon salt, or to taste

1/8 teaspoon ground white pepper, or to taste

TOPPING

4 to 8 tablespoons finely grated Parmesan cheese

Finely chopped parsley or paprika (optional)

1. Prepare filling: In a heavy 10-inch skillet, stir sausage over moderate heat until it forms brown granules. Pour off any fat. Transfer sausage to a large bowl.

2. Melt butter in skillet. Add onion and garlic and sauté over moderate heat until tender but not brown. Add to sausage along with remaining filling ingredients. Mix thoroughly and reserve.

3. Prepare pasta: Boil freshly prepared pasta squares for 20 seconds. Boil dried squares until barely tender. Drop squares into cold water. Then lay the squares flat on damp cloth towels. Reserve.

4. Prepare sauce: Melt butter in a heavy 2-quart saucepan. Whisk in flour until smooth. Stir over low heat for 2 minutes without browning. Add half-and-half and milk. Stir over moderate heat until smooth and thick. Add Parmesan cheese. Heat and stir until cheese is melted. Stir in nutmeg, salt, and pepper.

5. Stir 1/2 cup of the cheese sauce into the filling. Spoon filling along one edge of each pasta square and roll up like a jelly roll.

6. Place cannelloni, seam side down, in two buttered 11 x 7-inch (2-quart) baking dishes.

7. Pour half the remaining sauce over the cannelloni in each dish. Use a rubber spatula to separate the cannelloni so the sauce can get between them.

8. Sprinkle each dish with 2 to 4 tablespoons of Parmesan cheese.

9. Cover each dish with a lid or aluminum foil. The cannelloni may be refrigerated until needed.

— This recipe may be prepared ahead to this point. —

10. Bake, covered, in a 350° F oven until the cannelloni are heated through, about 30 minutes. Garnish with parsley or paprika. Serve.

Yield: 14 to 16 cannelloni, 7 to 8 servings.

Spinach Manicotti

8 to 10 Pasta Squares for
  Cannelloni or Manicotti
  (p. 177)
Spinach Filling (p. 181)
3 to 4 cups Fresh Tomato
  Sauce (p. 190) or Tomato
  Sauce (p. 190)

8 ounces mozzarella
  cheese, grated (2 cups,
  loosely packed)
Parsley, finely chopped for
  garnish (optional)

1. Boil freshly prepared pasta squares for 20 seconds. Boil dried squares until barely tender. Drop squares into cold water. Then lay the squares flat on damp cloth towels.

2. Spoon about 1/4 cup of spinach filling along one edge of each pasta square and roll up like a jelly roll.

3. Place manicotti, seam side down, in a buttered or oiled 13 1/2 x 8 1/2-inch baking dish.

4. Pour the tomato sauce over the manicotti. Use a rubber spatula to separate the manicotti so the sauce can get between them. Sprinkle mozzarella cheese on top of manicotti.

5. Cover the dish with a lid or aluminum foil. The manicotti may be refrigerated until needed.

— This recipe may be prepared ahead to this point. —

6. Bake, covered, in a 350° F oven until the manicotti are heated through, about 30 minutes. Garnish with parsley and serve.

Yield: 8 to 10 manicotti, 4 to 5 servings.

Cheese Manicotti

Follow the above recipe for Spinach Manicotti with the following changes:

1. Prepare spinach filling but omit the spinach.
2. Stir 1 tablespoon of finely chopped parsley into the filling.

Yield: 8 to 10 manicotti with sauce, 4 to 5 servings.

Baked Ziti

1/2 pound bulk sausage
1 pound ground lean beef
1 cup milk
8 cups (2 recipes) Tomato
  Sauce (p. 190), divided
15 to 16 ounces ricotta
  cheese
1 large egg

1/4 cup finely grated
  Parmesan cheese
1/4 teaspoon salt, or to taste
1/8 teaspoon ground white
  pepper, or to taste
16 ounces cut ziti
2 tablespoons (1/4 stick)
  butter or margarine

1. In a heavy 10-inch skillet, stir sausage and beef over moderate heat until they form brown granules. Pour off any fat. Add milk and bring to a boil. Cover, reduce heat, and simmer for 30 minutes. Stir in 3 cups of tomato sauce. Reserve.

2. In a bowl, combine ricotta cheese, egg, Parmesan cheese, salt, and pepper. Beat until blended. Reserve.

3. Boil ziti until just tender, about 10 minutes. Drain and toss with butter.

4. Butter a 15 x 10-inch (4-quart) baking dish. Cover bottom of dish with one-third of the ziti. Spread meat mixture over pasta.

5. Cover with another third of the ziti. Spread cheese mixture over ziti. Cover with remaining ziti.

6. Pour remaining tomato sauce over the pasta.

7. Cover dish with a lid or aluminum foil. The ziti may be refrigerated until needed.

— This recipe may be prepared ahead to this point. —

8. Bake, covered, in a 350° F oven until the ziti are heated through, about 40 minutes. Serve.

Yield: 4 quarts, 8 servings.

Chicken Tetrazzini

6 tablespoons (3/4 stick) butter or margarine, divided
1/4 cup all-purpose flour
2 cups Chicken Broth (p. 42) (no substitute)
1 1/2 cups half-and-half or milk
1/2 cup + 2 tablespoons finely grated Parmesan cheese, divided
1 tablespoon + 1 teaspoon lemon juice, divided
2 tablespoons dry sherry
1/8 teaspoon grated nutmeg

1/2 teaspoon salt, or to taste
1/8 teaspoon ground white pepper, or to taste
8 ounces mushrooms, sliced 1/4-inch thick
8 ounces linguine or spaghetti
3 cups cooked chicken in bite-size pieces (chicken may be cooked according to the recipe for Chicken Broth, p. 42)
8 tablespoons toasted slivered or sliced almonds, divided (optional)

1. In a heavy 4 1/2-quart pot, melt 4 tablespoons of butter. Whisk in flour until smooth. Stir over low heat for 2 minutes without browning. Stir in broth and half-and-half. Stir over moderate heat until smooth and thick. Add 1/2 cup of Parmesan cheese. Heat and stir until cheese is melted. Stir in 1 tablespoon of lemon juice, sherry, nutmeg, salt, and pepper. Reserve.

2. In a heavy 10-inch skillet, melt 2 tablespoons of butter. Add mushrooms and sprinkle with 1 teaspoon of lemon juice. Sauté over high heat until barely tender. Reserve.

3. Boil linguine until just tender. Drain. Add linguine, mushrooms, chicken, and 6 tablespoons of almonds to sauce. Mix gently.

4. Place in a buttered 11 x 7-inch or 8-inch square (2-quart) baking dish. Sprinkle with 2 tablespoons of Parmesan cheese and then 2 tablespoons of almonds. Cover with a lid or aluminum foil. The dish may be refrigerated until ready to serve.

— This recipe may be prepared ahead to this point. —

5. Bake the covered dish in a preheated 350° F oven for 30 minutes. Uncover and continue to bake until heated through, about 10 minutes. Serve.

Yield: 8 cups, 4 servings.

Macaroni and Cheese

8 ounces elbow macaroni
5 tablespoons butter or
  margarine, divided
3 tablespoons all-purpose
  flour
3 cups milk
11 slices (8 ounces) American
  cheese or 8 ounces sharp
  Cheddar cheese, grated
  (2 cups, loosely packed)
1/4 teaspoon paprika

2 teaspoons Dijon mustard
1/2 teaspoon Worcestershire
  sauce
Pinch grated nutmeg
3/4 teaspoon salt, or to taste
1/4 teaspoon ground white
  pepper
1/2 cup fresh or dried bread
  crumbs from White Bread
  (p. 210) or firm commercial
  bread

1. Boil macaroni until just tender, about 8 minutes. Drain and toss with 1 tablespoon of butter. Reserve.

2. In a heavy 4 1/2-quart pot, melt 2 tablespoons of butter. Whisk in flour until smooth. Stir over low heat for 2 minutes without browning. Add milk. Stir over moderate heat until smooth and the thickness of cream.

3. Add the slices of American cheese or grated Cheddar cheese, paprika, mustard, Worcestershire sauce, nutmeg, salt, and pepper. Heat and stir until smooth.

4. Add macaroni, mix gently, and turn into a buttered 11 x 7-inch or 8-inch square (2-quart) baking dish.

5. Cover dish with a lid or aluminum foil. Bake in a preheated 350° F oven for 20 minutes.

6. Meanwhile, in a 9-inch skillet, melt 2 tablespoons of butter. Add bread crumbs and sauté over moderate heat until golden brown.

7. Uncover, sprinkle with bread crumbs, and serve.

Yield: 8 cups, 6 servings.

Sauces

Tomato Sauce

2 tablespoons (1/4 stick) butter, margarine, or olive oil
1 medium onion, finely chopped
2 cloves garlic, minced
1 can (28 ounces) whole tomatoes, preferably Italian plum, undrained and coarsely chopped
1 can (6 ounces) tomato paste
1/4 teaspoon dried basil
1/4 teaspoon dried oregano
1/2 teaspoon salt, or to taste
1/4 teaspoon ground black pepper, or to taste
1/2 cup dry white wine (optional)
1/2 teaspoon granulated sugar (optional)

1. In a heavy, nonreactive 2-quart saucepan, melt the butter. Add onion and garlic. Sauté over moderate heat until tender but not brown.

2. Add remaining ingredients. Bring to a boil, reduce heat, and simmer, uncovered, for 20 minutes. Stir occasionally.

Yield: 4 cups.

Fresh Tomato Sauce

Use only very ripe and delicious tomatoes for this recipe.

2 tablespoons (1/4 stick) butter, margarine, or olive oil
1/2 cup finely chopped onion
2 cloves garlic, minced
2 pounds fresh, ripe tomatoes, peeled, seeded, and coarsely chopped (about 4 cups)
3/4 teaspoon chopped fresh basil or 1/4 teaspoon dried basil
1/2 teaspoon salt, or to taste
1/4 teaspoon ground black or white pepper, or to taste

1. In a heavy, nonreactive 10-inch skillet, melt the butter. Add onion and garlic and sauté over low heat until tender but not brown.

2. Add tomatoes and remaining ingredients. Heat and stir until tomatoes are slightly softened. Serve.

Yield: 3 cups, 4 servings.

Notes:

1. Serve this sauce over pasta. The sauce may be sprinkled with Parmesan cheese.

2. For a quick delicious meal, prepare 1/4 pound of spaghetti or other pasta for each person. Spoon Fresh Tomato Sauce (p. 190) over each serving of pasta and sprinkle with Parmesan cheese. Equally space 4 small clumps of buttered cooked spinach around the sauced pasta. Arrange sautéed shrimp and/or scallops or slices of sautéed chicken breast and/or sausage between the clumps of spinach.

Tomato Meat Sauce

3 tablespoons butter, margarine, or olive oil
1 large onion, chopped (about 3/4 cup)
2 cloves garlic, minced
2 pounds ground lean beef
2 cans (28 ounces each) crushed or whole tomatoes, undrained and coarsely chopped

1 can (12 ounces) tomato paste
1 teaspoon dried basil
1 teaspoon dried oregano
2 teaspoons salt, or to taste
1/2 teaspoon ground black pepper, or to taste
1 cup dry red wine
4 to 6 ounces mushrooms, chopped (optional)

1. In a heavy, nonreactive 4 1/2-quart pot, melt the butter. Add onion and garlic and sauté over moderate heat until tender but not brown.

2. Add beef and stir over moderate heat until it forms brown granules. Pour off any fat.

3. Add remaining ingredients. Bring to a boil, reduce heat, and simmer, uncovered, for 2 hours. Stir occasionally.

Yield: 10 cups.

Chicken and Tomato Pasta Sauce

Try this tasty pasta sauce made with chicken as a refreshing change from sauces with beef.

6 tablespoons (3/4 stick) butter, margarine, or olive oil
1 large carrot, finely chopped
1 celery rib, finely chopped
1 medium onion, finely chopped
2 cloves garlic, minced
4 chicken breast halves, skinned and boned
2/3 cup dry white wine
2 cans (28 ounces each) tomatoes, preferably Italian plum, undrained and coarsely chopped

1 can (6 ounces) tomato paste
1/2 teaspoon dried basil
1/2 teaspoon dried oregano
1/8 teaspoon grated nutmeg
1 1/2 teaspoons salt, or to taste
1/4 teaspoon ground black pepper, or to taste

1. In a heavy, nonreactive 4 1/2-quart pot, melt the butter. Add carrot, celery, onion, and garlic. Sauté over moderate heat until tender but not brown.

2. Grind chicken in a food processor or meat grinder. Add the chicken to the pot with the vegetables. Sauté over moderate heat until the chicken forms white granules with no trace of pink. Stir in remaining ingredients.

3. Bring to a boil, reduce heat, and simmer, uncovered, for 1 hour and 15 minutes. Stir occasionally.

Yield: 8 cups, 8 to 10 servings.

Note: Serve this sauce over linguine, fettuccine, penne, mostaccioli rigati, or other pasta. Use 1 to 1 1/2 pounds of pasta for 6 to 8 servings. Garnish with chopped parsley.

Hollandaise Sauce

Don't be nervous. With a little care, your sauce will be a great success.

FOR 1 1/4 CUPS

3 egg yolks
2 tablespoons cold water
3/4 cup (1 1/2 sticks) butter
  (no substitute), preferably
  unsalted, melted
1 to 3 teaspoons lemon juice,
  to taste

Pinch salt, or to taste
Pinch ground white pepper,
  or to taste
Pinch grated nutmeg
  (optional)

FOR 3/4 CUP

2 egg yolks
4 teaspoons cold water
1/2 cup (1 stick) butter
  (no substitute), preferably
  unsalted, melted
3/4 to 2 teaspoons lemon
  juice, to taste

Pinch salt, or to taste
Pinch ground white pepper,
  or to taste
Pinch grated nutmeg
  (optional)

1. In a nonreactive 1 1/2-quart saucepan, beat the egg yolks and water together with a whisk until foamy.

2. Whisk over low heat until mixture becomes very warm and slightly thickened. At this point, a wisp of steam will rise from the surface. Do not overcook or the yolks will scramble. Immediately, remove from heat.

3. Add 1 tablespoon of the butter, drop by drop, while beating constantly. Continue to beat while adding remaining butter in a fine stream. Be sure to cover the entire surface of the bottom of the pan with the whisk. If salted butter is used, do not add the milky residue or the sauce may become too salty. The sauce should have the consistency of heavy cream. If the sauce is not thick enough, whisk over low heat until thick. Do not overcook or the sauce will separate.

4. Beat in lemon juice, salt, pepper, and nutmeg.

5. Serve immediately or keep warm by covering the saucepan and placing it in a pan of lukewarm, not hot, water. Stir occasionally.

6. Serve sauce within 30 minutes of preparation to prevent growth of harmful bacteria.

Note: Serve this sauce with vegetables such as Bright Green Broccoli (p. 149) or asparagus, Broiled or Baked Fish with Wine (p. 80 or p. 82), sautéed chicken breasts, Chicken Cordon Bleu (p. 113), or Chicken Cutlets Tarragon (p. 114).

Mustard Hollandaise

Add 1 1/2 to 2 tablespoons of Dijon mustard to 1 1/4 cups of Hollandaise Sauce (p. 193) or add 3 to 4 teaspoons to 3/4 cup.

Lemon Butter Sauce (Beurre Blanc)

This heavenly sauce is easy to make. However, be sure to use low heat in Step 2 or the sauce will separate. It is safer to use too little heat than too much.

1/4 cup whipping cream
1/2 cup (1 stick) unsalted
  butter (no substitute),
  chilled and divided into 8
  pieces

1 teaspoon lemon juice, or
  to taste
Pinch salt, or to taste
Pinch ground white pepper,
  or to taste

1. In a heavy 1 1/2-quart saucepan, boil cream, stirring constantly, until reduced to 2 tablespoons.
2. Reduce heat to low. Add butter, one piece at a time, whisking constantly until each piece is melted before adding the next one. The sauce should become smooth and have the thickness of heavy cream. Season to taste with lemon juice, salt, and pepper.
3. Remove from heat and keep at room temperature until ready to serve but no longer than 15 minutes. Reheat by stirring over low heat until warm. Do not overheat or the sauce will separate. Serve immediately.

Yield: 1/2 cup, 4 servings.

Note: This sauce is especially good with broiled, grilled, or baked fish or poultry.

Orange Butter Sauce (Beurre Blanc)

Prepare Lemon Butter Sauce (Beurre Blanc) (p. 194) and stir in 1/2 teaspoon of finely grated orange rind.

Yield: 1/2 cup, 4 servings.

Chicken Allemande Sauce

This rich velvety sauce is the perfect touch for sautéed chicken breasts, Chicken Cordon Bleu (p. 113), or Chicken Cutlets Tarragon (p. 114). The sauce may also be used to make Chicken and Mushroom Crêpes (p. 122). Use full-flavored chicken broth for superb results.

1 large egg yolk
1 cup (1/2 pint) whipping
  cream, divided
4 tablespoons (1/2 stick)
  butter (no substitute),
  divided
2 tablespoons all-purpose
  flour

1 cup Chicken Broth (p. 42)
  (no substitute)
1 teaspoon lemon juice
Pinch grated nutmeg
  (optional)
1/4 teaspoon salt, or to taste
1/8 teaspoon ground white
  pepper, or to taste

1. Place egg yolk in a small bowl. Add 2 tablespoons of cream. Whisk until blended. Reserve.

2. In a 1 1/2-quart saucepan, gently boil remaining cream, stirring occasionally, until reduced to about 1/2 cup. Remove from heat and reserve.

3. In a 1 1/2-quart saucepan, melt 2 tablespoons of butter. Whisk in flour until smooth. Stir over low heat for 2 minutes without browning.

4. Add chicken broth. Stir over moderate heat until smooth and thick. Stir in boiled cream.

5. Add about a third of the sauce to the yolk and cream. Whisk until smooth. Return mixture to saucepan. Stir constantly over moderate heat until sauce is thick.

6. Reduce heat to low. Add remaining butter and whisk until melted.

7. Remove from heat. Season sauce with lemon juice, nutmeg, salt, and pepper.

8. When ready to serve, heat and stir sauce over low heat until warm. The sauce may be refrigerated and reheated.

Yield: 1 2/3 cups.

Barbecue Sauce

2 tablespoons (1/4 stick)
 butter, margarine, olive oil,
 or other vegetable oil
1 medium onion, finely
 chopped
2 cloves garlic, minced
1 1/2 cups ketchup
2 tablespoons dark soy sauce
1 teaspoon Dijon mustard
2 tablespoons lemon juice
2 tablespoons red wine
 vinegar

1/4 cup molasses or honey,
 or 2 tablespoons of each
1/2 teaspoon salt, or to taste
1/4 teaspoon ground black
 pepper, or to taste
1/8 teaspoon cayenne pepper,
 or to taste
1/2 teaspoon liquid smoke
 (optional)

1. In a heavy 2-quart saucepan, melt the butter. Add onion and garlic. Sauté over moderate heat until tender but not brown.
2. Stir in remaining ingredients. Bring to a boil, reduce heat, and simmer, uncovered, for 30 minutes.
3. If desired, strain the sauce.

Yield: 2 cups.

Note: Use for Barbecued Spareribs (p. 142) or Barbecued Chicken (p. 108).

Sour Cream and Mustard Sauce

2 tablespoons (1/4 stick)
  butter or margarine
1/2 cup sour cream
2 teaspoons Dijon mustard

1/8 teaspoon salt, or to taste
Pinch ground white pepper,
  or to taste

1. In a heavy, nonreactive 1/2-quart saucepan, melt the butter. Remove from heat and whisk in remaining ingredients.
2. When ready to serve, reheat over low heat until warm. Do not overheat or the sauce may separate.

Yield: 1/2 cup, 4 servings.

Note: This sauce may be served with Broiled Fish with Wine (p. 80), Baked Fish with Wine (p. 82), Roast Chicken (p. 98), Broiled Chicken with Wine (p. 104), Baked Chicken with Wine (p. 106), or pork.

Sour Cream and Shallot Sauce

2 tablespoons (1/4 stick)
  butter or margarine
1 to 2 tablespoons finely
  chopped shallots
1/2 cup sour cream

1/4 teaspoon salt, or to taste
1/8 teaspoon ground white
  pepper, or to taste
1/4 teaspoon dried tarragon
  (optional)

1. In a heavy, nonreactive 1/2-quart saucepan, melt the butter. Add shallots and sauté over low heat until tender but not brown.
2. Remove from heat. Stir in remaining ingredients.
3. When ready to serve, reheat over low heat until warm. Do not overheat or the sauce may separate.

Yield: 1/2 cup, 4 servings.

Note: This sauce may be served with Broiled Fish with Wine (p. 80), Baked Fish with Wine (p. 82), Roast Chicken (p. 98), Broiled Chicken with Wine (p. 104), Baked Chicken with Wine (p. 106), or pork.

Horseradish Sauce

1 cup Mayonnaise (p. 75)   1/4 cup prepared horseradish
1/2 cup sour cream

Stir all ingredients together until smooth. Refrigerate until served.

Yield: 1 3/4 cups.

Note: Serve this sauce with Rib Roast of Beef (p. 132) or as a dip with corn chips or vegetables.

Cheddar Cheese Sauce

3 tablespoons butter or   1/4 teaspoon Worcestershire
  margarine   sauce
1/4 cup all-purpose flour   1 teaspoon Dijon mustard
2 cups milk   Pinch grated nutmeg
4 ounces Cheddar cheese   1/8 teaspoon cayenne pepper,
  (preferably extra sharp),   or to taste
  grated (1 cup, loosely   1/4 teaspoon salt, or to taste
  packed)

1. In a heavy 2-quart saucepan, melt the butter. Add flour. Stir over low heat for 2 minutes without browning. Add milk. Stir over moderate heat until smooth and thick.

2. Add cheese. Heat and stir until melted and smooth. Mix in remaining ingredients.

Yield: 2 1/2 cups.

Note: Use this sauce to prepare Ham and Turkey or Chicken with Cornbread and Cheddar Cheese Sauce (p. 146), or serve it on toast with sliced tomato and crisp bacon or on vegetables such as Bright Green Broccoli (p. 149) or cauliflower.

Cranberry Orange Sauce

This traditional accompaniment to the Thanksgiving turkey is also perfect with chicken and duck.

3/4 cup fresh orange juice
1 cup granulated sugar
12 ounces (3 cups) fresh
** or frozen cranberries**

2 teaspoons finely grated
** orange rind**

1. In a heavy, nonreactive 2-quart saucepan, combine orange juice and sugar. Heat and stir until sugar dissolves.

2. Add cranberries and bring to a boil. Cook over moderate heat until cranberries pop and soften, about 5 minutes.

3. Stir in orange rind.

4. Serve chilled or at room temperature.

Yield: 2 1/2 cups.

Cranberry Relish

This relish is a welcome gift. Present it in a clear jar to show off its bright crimson color. For best flavor, prepare the relish several days before serving.

24 ounces (6 cups) fresh or frozen cranberries
1 tablespoon finely grated orange rind
2 cups orange sections, seeded and cut in half crosswise
1 cup orange juice
2 1/2 cups granulated sugar
2 cups chopped, peeled apple

3/4 cup raisins
3/4 cup chopped walnuts or pecans
2 tablespoons cider vinegar
1/2 teaspoon ground cinnamon
1/2 teaspoon ground dried ginger
1/4 teaspoon ground allspice

1. In a heavy, nonreactive 4 1/2-quart pot, combine all ingredients.
2. Stir over high heat until cranberries pop and soften, about 5 minutes.
3. Chill before serving.

Yield: 7 cups.

Yeast Breads

*S*top! Before you pass over the yeast dough recipes and on to the quick breads, please take a moment to let me encourage you to try recipes using yeast. You may be afraid your first attempt will be a disaster. However, if you follow these directions, your first try will be a fabulous success. Bread does take time to rise but you are free to do other things while it rises. You may stay in the kitchen and prepare other recipes or leave and return only at the necessary times. Creating a loaf of bread from raw ingredients will satisfy a strong creative urge and always delight you. Once you have enjoyed the aroma of bread baking in your own kitchen and tasted it warm from the oven, you will eagerly look forward to your next bread baking session. The quality and healthiness of homemade breads far surpass store-bought products. The variety of breads that can be created are endless. I invite you to join me in this homey and relaxing pursuit.

Advice on Yeast Baking

YEAST

There are two commonly available forms of active dry yeast: regular and fast-rising. They are produced in package and bulk forms. A package of regular yeast contains a scant tablespoon whereas a package of fast-rising yeast contains 2 1/4 teaspoons. Each package (regular or fast-rising) contains 1/4 ounce (7 grams).

Fast-rising yeast reduces rising times up to 50%. Although you may be tempted to use only fast-rising yeast, I have found the slower action of regular yeast gives most breads more flavor and a better texture than the fast-rising form. However, fast-rising yeast is quite useful for doughs that derive most of their flavor from a high content of butter and sugar. These ingredients inhibit the action of yeast. Doughs rich in butter and sugar will rise much faster if fast-rising yeast is used instead of regular yeast. The form of yeast I prefer for each bread is given in the recipe.

EGGS

Eggs should be warmed before adding them to dough. Otherwise, they will slow the action of the yeast and prolong the rising time. Warm eggs by breaking them into a stainless steel bowl and placing the bowl over hot water. Stir occasionally until the eggs are warm.

FLOUR

I prefer to use bread flour because it gives bread more volume than all-purpose flour. If all-purpose flour is used, unbleached flour will produce more volume than bleached flour.

Since flours vary so much in moisture content, it is impossible to specify the exact amount needed for each recipe. Amounts of flour listed in the recipes are only guidelines. Enough flour must be added so the kneaded dough becomes a smooth and elastic ball that is not sticky. Avoid adding too much flour or the bread will become heavy.

MILK

Whole, low fat, or skim milk can be used in the recipes in this chapter.

MEASURING

Although all ingredients should be measured carefully, be especially accurate in measuring liquid ingredients. Even a small change in the amount of liquid added will result in a major change in the total amount of flour used. This may significantly alter the quality as well as the quantity of the final product.

KNEADING

Although this part of breadmaking is considered to be relaxing and therapeutic by many home bakers, an electric mixer with a dough hook handles the job beautifully. All recipes in this book recommend using a mixer for the kneading process. If you have always avoided making bread because you hate to knead by hand, you no longer have an excuse! Be sure to use a mixer that has enough power to knead bread. I use a KitchenAid mixer. Although many people use a food processor to knead bread, I prefer the slower kneading of a mixer which I believe produces a better quality bread. Also, when using a mixer, flour may be added slowly until just the right amount is used. If a food processor is used, adding the right amount of flour is more difficult.

If you do not have a mixer, the dough may be mixed and kneaded by hand. Make a batter by beating the first amount of flour(s) listed in the recipe with the liquid ingredients. Instead of using the paddle attachment of a mixer, use a wooden spoon to beat the batter until it is smooth. If butter is to be added, beat it in at this time. Then, instead of using a dough hook to knead the dough, gradually add the remaining flour and work it into the batter with a wooden spoon until the mixture begins to form a dough.

Turn mixture out onto a lightly floured work surface. The work surface should not absorb heat from the dough or the cooled dough will be slow to rise. A wooden or plastic board or a plastic laminate surface are ideal work surfaces for kneading since they do not absorb heat. Marble, granite, and the new solid surface products for counters will quickly cool a dough and should not be used.

Use a pastry scraper to help knead dough in the early stages. Scrape about half of the dough up from the work surface and fold it over the remaining dough. Press the top half of the dough into the bottom half. If dough is sticky, sprinkle it lightly with additional flour. Repeat the folding process until dough begins to come together.

Now start to knead the dough with your hands. Fold the dough in half by bringing the half that is away from you toward you. Use the heels of your hands to press the top half of dough into the bottom half in a direction that is downward and away from you. Turn dough a quarter of a turn. Repeat folding, pressing, and turning process until dough becomes very elastic and forms a smooth ball. Sprinkle dough with additional flour as needed. Although enough flour should be used so dough forms an elastic ball that is not sticky, do not add any more than necessary or the bread will become heavy. Kneading by hand usually takes about 8 to 10 minutes. It is far better to knead for too long a time than to stop too soon.

RISING

After dough is kneaded, place it in a lightly buttered heavy ceramic or glass bowl that has been warmed by filling it with hot water. Cover the bowl with plastic wrap to prevent the dough from drying out. If the plastic wrap is lightly oiled, it is less likely to stick to the dough. Place dough in a warm, draft-free place to rise. Avoid temperature fluctuations.

The ideal range of temperature for rising doughs using regular active dry yeast is 75° - 80° F. If dough rises at a temperature above 85° F, the bread may develop an unpleasant fermented taste. It is far better to let dough rise at too low a temperature than to risk ruin at too high a temperature. If the fast-rising form is used, dough should rise at 80° - 85° F.

A warming oven is the best place for bread to rise because the temperature can be accurately controlled. Dough rises evenly and rising times are predictable. If the warming oven does not have a calibrated thermostat, place a thermometer in the warming oven and adjust the control dial until the desired temperature is reached. Mark the control dial so you will know where to set it the next time you bake bread. Place bowl on a pot holder or towel if there is a hot spot in the bottom of the warming oven.

If a warming oven is not available, a regular oven can be used. Turn the oven on at 250° F for about 1 minute. This will usually provide enough heat for one rising period. Place a thermometer in the oven to be sure the temperature is within the correct range.

Dough may also rise in a warm room but keep the bowl at least several feet away from the heat source.

If dough rises higher than directed during the last rise, punch it down, reshape, and let rise again.

BRAIDING

Braid dough as shown in the following illustrations:

Fold the left strip of dough (1) over the middle strip (2) as shown in A and B.

Then fold the right strip (3) over the middle strip (1) as shown in B and C.

Repeat these two steps until the loaf is completely braided as shown in D.

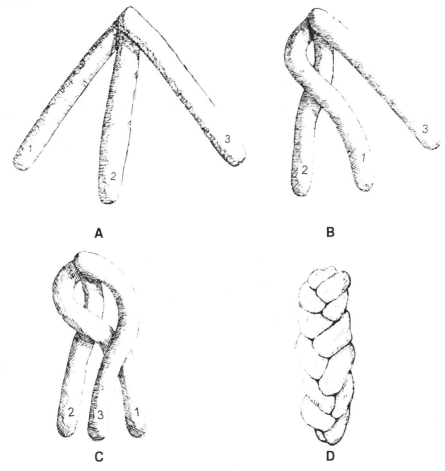

A

B

C

D

SHAPING A LOAF OF BREAD

Press dough into an 8-inch square (A). Fold each of the two short edges inward about 1-inch (B). Then fold the long edges (C) until they meet in the center of the loaf (D). Pinch the seams to seal. Place the loaf, seam side down, in a buttered loaf pan (E).

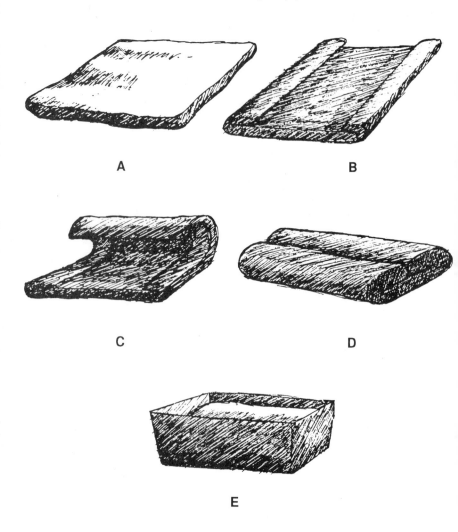

A

B

C

D

E

SHAPING ROLLS

Bread dough can be made into a variety of rolls of different sizes and shapes.

Use a pastry scraper or knife to cut dough into the desired number of pieces. First halve the dough and then cut each half in half. Continue to halve each piece until the desired number of pieces of dough is made. This method ensures all pieces will be the same size.

Round rolls

Hold the piece of dough so that the fingers of one hand are along one top edge and the thumb is on the bottom of the dough. Place fingers and thumb of the other hand on the opposite side of the dough. Pull edges downward (A, B) and press them together at the bottom of the dough to seal (C). In a similar manner, pull the remaining two edges downward (D). The piece of dough should now be a smooth ball (E). If not, repeat this process until the surface is smooth and rounded.

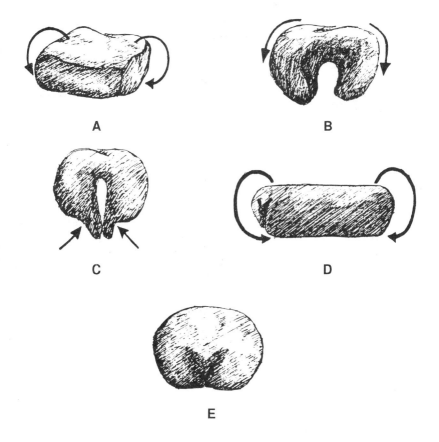

A

B

C

D

E

Oval rolls

Flatten a piece of dough into an oval shape. Fold the oval in half lengthwise. Press edges together using the heel of your hand. On the work surface, roll the dough forward and backward under the palms of your hands using greater pressure at the ends to create an oval roll.

Single-Knot Rolls

On the work surface, roll the piece of dough forward and backward under the palms of your hands to form a smooth rope of dough about 8-inches long. Tie into a knot with one end protruding through the center (A,B). Tuck the other end under the roll (C).

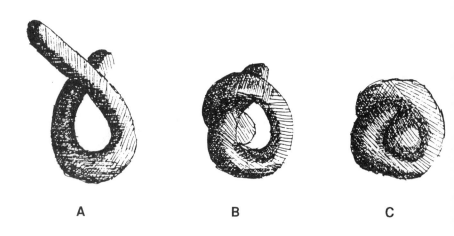

A   B   C

Split Rolls

Shape pieces of dough into round rolls (p. 207). Sprinkle each roll with rye or whole wheat flour. Then firmly press the floured handle of a wooden spoon, 1/2 to 3/4-inch in diameter, against the center of the roll until it reaches the work surface. After lifting the handle, the roll will be oval and have an attractive split in the middle. Invert the rolls and let them rise on a lightly oiled baking sheet that has been sprinkled with rye or whole wheat flour. When the rolls have almost doubled, carefully turn them right side up without deflating them. Let rise until they have finished doubling in size, about 15 minutes.

Braided Rolls

Use a pastry scraper or knife to cut a piece of dough into 3 equal strips, leaving them attached at one end. Stretch each strip. Then braid them together (p. 205). Firmly pinch strips together at each end to prevent them from separating while rising.

Crescent Rolls

Divide the dough for Dinner Rolls (p. 221) into 4 pieces. Roll each piece of dough into a 9-inch circle. The dough will be about 1/4-inch thick. Let dough rest for 4 minutes. Cut into 8 wedges. Starting at the middle of the curved edge of each wedge, make a 1/2-inch cut toward the center of the circle. Stretch the side with the cut (the cut causes this side to stretch easily) while rolling up the wedge toward the tip. This will prevent the roll from becoming too thick in the center. Place on a buttered baking sheet. Curve roll, twist ends, and bring ends toward each other to form a crescent.

ELECTRIC SLICER

This appliance is a useful investment if you bake a lot of bread. It produces even slices of desired thickness which are not easily achieved with a knife.

FREEZING BREAD

Bread freezes well. Be sure bread is cooled completely before it is frozen. Wrap in plastic wrap or place in good quality plastic bags. For maximum protection, cover the wrapped bread with aluminum foil. Bread may be sliced before freezing and the individual slices used as needed.

White Bread

1 package regular active
 dry yeast
1/4 cup warm water
 (105° - 115° F)
About 7 1/2 cups bread
 flour or all-purpose flour
3/4 cup milk

1 1/4 cups water
3 tablespoons maple syrup,
 honey, or granulated sugar
2 1/2 teaspoons salt
3 tablespoons butter or
 margarine, at room
 temperature

1. In a small bowl, dissolve yeast in warm water. Reserve. In an electric mixer bowl, place 4 cups of flour. Reserve.

2. In a 1 1/2-quart saucepan, combine milk, water, maple syrup, and salt. Heat and stir until warm (105° - 115° F).

3. Pour liquid ingredients and yeast into the mixer bowl with the flour. Beat at low speed with a paddle attachment, if available, until the flour is moistened. Increase speed to medium, drop in butter divided into small pieces, and continue to beat for 2 minutes.

4. Stop mixer and add 2 1/2 cups of flour. Using a dough hook at low speed, begin to knead the dough. Gradually add up to 1 cup of flour, in 2 to 3 tablespoon amounts, until the dough gathers on the dough hook and completely cleans the bottom and sides of the bowl, about 3 to 4 minutes. Then knead the dough for an additional 9 minutes. If the dough begins to stick to the bottom of the bowl, add flour as needed.

5. Turn dough onto a lightly floured work surface. Knead by hand until it becomes elastic and forms a smooth ball, about 1 minute. Place in a large lightly buttered bowl.

6. Cover bowl with plastic wrap and let rise in a warm place (75° - 80° F) until doubled in bulk, about 1 hour.

7. Punch dough down to deflate it. Fold the edges inward to form a ball and turn over. Let rise until doubled in bulk, about 45 minutes. This second rise may be omitted but the flavor and texture of the bread will not be as good.

8. Turn dough onto an unfloured work surface. Press down to remove any air bubbles. Cut dough in half.

9. Press each half of dough into an 8-inch square. Fold each of the two short edges inward about 1-inch and then fold the long edges until they meet in the center of the loaf. Pinch seams to seal. Place each loaf, seam side down, in a buttered 8 1/2 x 4 1/2-inch pan.

10. Cover each pan loosely with plastic wrap. Let rise until the dough extends about 1-inch above the rim of each pan, about 1 hour. Be careful that the loaves do not rise too much.

11. Bake in a preheated 400° F oven for 10 minutes. Reduce oven temperature to 350° F and bake until loaves are golden brown and sound hollow when tapped, about 25 minutes. Immediately remove loaves from pans. Cool on wire racks.

12. For a soft and shiny crust, brush the top of the warm loaves with butter or margarine.

Yield: 2 loaves.

White Bread - Sponge Method

This method takes a little more effort and time than the previous recipe but produces loaves with more flavor and a wonderful light texture. A sponge is a mixture of yeast, water, and flour allowed to rise until "spongy." A sponge is usually made the night before its intended use. On the day of use, the sponge is mixed with additional ingredients to produce a dough.

SPONGE

1 package regular active dry yeast	2 cups bread flour or all-purpose flour
1 cup water, at room temperature (70° - 75° F)	

DOUGH

3/4 cup milk	About 5 1/2 cups bread flour or all-purpose flour
1/2 cup water	
3 tablespoons maple syrup, honey, or granulated sugar	3 tablespoons butter or margarine, at room temperature
2 1/2 teaspoons salt	

1. Prepare the sponge the night before it is intended to be used: In an electric mixer bowl, dissolve the yeast in the water. Add flour. Use a paddle attachment, if available, and beat at medium speed for 2 minutes. Use a rubber spatula to scrape down sides of bowl and form mixture into one mass. Cover bowl tightly with plastic wrap. Let sponge rise at room temperature (70° - 75° F) during the night, about 10 to 12 hours.

2. The next morning, prepare the dough: In a 1 1/2-quart saucepan, combine milk, water, maple syrup, and salt. Heat and stir until warm (105° - 115° F).

3. Add half the liquid ingredients and 1 cup of flour to the sponge. Use a paddle attachment, if available, and beat at low speed until flour is moistened. Add remaining liquid ingredients and 1 cup of flour. Beat until flour is moistened. Increase speed to medium, drop in butter divided into small pieces, and beat for 2 minutes.

4. Stop mixer and add 2 1/2 cups of flour. Using a dough hook at low speed, begin to knead the dough. Gradually add up to 1 cup of flour, in 2 to 3 tablespoon amounts, until the dough gathers on the dough hook and completely cleans the bottom and sides of the bowl, about 3 to 4 minutes. Then knead the dough for an additional 9 minutes. If the dough begins to stick to the bottom of the bowl, add flour as needed.

5. Turn dough onto a lightly floured work surface. Knead by hand until it becomes elastic and forms a smooth ball, about 1 minute. Place in a large lightly buttered bowl.

6. Cover bowl with plastic wrap and let rise in a warm place (75° - 80° F) until doubled in bulk, about 1 hour.

7. Turn dough onto an unfloured work surface. Press down to remove any air bubbles. Cut dough in half.

8. Press each half of dough into an 8-inch square. Fold each of the two short edges inward about 1-inch and then fold the long edges until they meet in the center of the loaf. Pinch seams to seal. Place each loaf, seam side down, in a buttered 8 1/2 x 4 1/2-inch pan.

9. Cover each pan loosely with plastic wrap. Let rise until the dough extends about 1-inch above the rim of each pan, about 1 hour. Be careful that the loaves do not rise too much.

10. Bake in a preheated 400° F oven for 10 minutes. Reduce oven temperature to 350° F and bake until loaves are golden brown and sound hollow when tapped, about 25 minutes. Immediately remove loaves from pans. Cool on wire racks.

11. For a soft and shiny crust, brush the top of the warm loaves with butter or margarine.

Yield: 2 loaves.

Pain de Mie (Sandwich Bread)

This recipe produces bread with a thin crust, firm texture, and rectangular shape which is ideal for canapés and elegant sandwiches.

Follow the recipe for White Bread (p. 210) or White Bread – Sponge Method (p. 211) with the following changes:

1. Use loaf pans measuring 9 1/4 x 5 1/4-inches instead of 8 1/2 x 4 1/2-inches.

2. During the last rise, let the dough rise until it is 3/4-inch below the rim of each pan, about 40 minutes. Watch this rise very carefully. If the dough rises higher than it should, punch it down, reshape loaves, and let rise to the proper height.

3. Place loaves on the middle rack of a preheated 375° F oven. Invert a buttered baking sheet over the two loaf pans with the buttered side facing the dough. Place two weights such as cast iron skillets or bricks on top of the baking sheet making sure a weight is over each loaf pan.

4. Bake bread for 20 minutes. Remove weights and baking sheet, and continue to bake until loaves are golden brown and sound hollow when tapped, about 5 minutes. Immediately remove loaves from pans. Cool on wire racks.

5. Use an electric slicer or serrated knife to cut the bread into thin slices.

Yield: 2 loaves.

Melba Toast

1. Slice the above Pain de Mie (Sandwich Bread) 1/8-inch thick.

2. Bake bread on unbuttered baking sheets in a 300° F oven until crisp and light brown, about 12 to 14 minutes.

3. Store in airtight containers.

Note: For herb toast, prepare the above Melba Toast but brush the bread with garlic butter and season with salt, pepper, dried basil, dried oregano, and grated Parmesan cheese before baking.

Cinnamon Swirl Raisin Bread

DOUGH

2 packages regular active
dry yeast
1/3 cup warm water
(105° - 115° F)
1 teaspoon salt
1/2 cup granulated sugar
About 7 1/2 cups bread
flour or all-purpose flour

1 1/4 cups warm milk
(105° - 115° F)
2 large eggs, warmed (p. 202)
6 tablespoons (3/4 stick)
butter or margarine, at
room temperature

FILLING

3 teaspoons water, divided
1 tablespoon ground
cinnamon

3 tablespoons granulated
sugar
1 1/3 cups raisins, divided

1. In a small bowl, dissolve yeast in water. Reserve. In an electric mixer bowl, combine salt, sugar, and 3 cups of flour.

2. Add milk, yeast, and eggs. Beat at low speed with a paddle attachment, if available, until the flour is moistened. Increase speed to medium, drop in butter divided into small pieces, and continue to beat for 2 minutes.

3. Stop mixer and add 3 1/2 cups of flour. Using a dough hook at low speed, begin to knead the dough. Gradually add up to 1 cup of flour, in 2 to 3 tablespoon amounts, until the dough gathers on the dough hook and completely cleans the bottom and sides of the bowl, about 3 to 4 minutes. Then knead the dough for an additional 9 minutes. If the dough begins to stick to the bottom of the bowl, add flour as needed.

4. Turn dough onto a lightly floured work surface. Knead by hand until it becomes elastic and forms a smooth ball, about 1 minute. Place in a large lightly buttered bowl.

5. Cover bowl with plastic wrap and let rise in a warm place (75° - 80° F) until doubled in bulk, about 1 hour.

6. Turn dough onto an unfloured work surface. Press down to remove any air bubbles. Cut dough in half.

7. Roll each half of dough into a rectangle about 20 x 8-inches. Brush each rectangle with 1 1/2 teaspoons of water. Stir cinnamon and sugar together. Sprinkle half the mixture over each half of dough. Spread 2/3 cup of raisins over each rectangle.

8. Starting at a short end, tightly roll each piece of dough like a jelly roll. Pinch bottom seam to seal. At the end of each loaf, push the center inward while bringing the dough at the outer edge toward the center. Pinch seam to seal. This will eliminate the spiral seams at the ends. Place each loaf, seam side down, in a buttered 8 1/2 x 4 1/2-inch pan.

9. Cover each pan loosely with plastic wrap. Let rise until the dough extends about 1 1/2-inches above the rim of each pan, about 45 minutes. Be careful that the loaves do not rise too much.

10. Bake in a preheated 375° F oven for 10 minutes. Reduce oven temperature to 325° F and bake until loaves are golden brown and sound hollow when tapped, about 20 to 25 minutes. Immediately remove loaves from pans.

11. For a soft and shiny crust, brush the top of the warm loaves with butter or margarine. Cool on wire racks.

Yield: 2 loaves.

Whole Wheat Bread

2 packages regular active
  dry yeast
1/2 cup warm water
  (105° - 115° F)
2 cups whole wheat flour
About 5 1/2 cups bread
  flour or all-purpose flour
3/4 cup milk
1 cup water

1/4 cup molasses, honey,
  maple syrup, barley malt
  (available in health food
  stores), or brown sugar
2 1/2 teaspoons salt
3 tablespoons butter or
  margarine, at room
  temperature

1. In a small bowl, dissolve yeast in warm water. Reserve. In an electric mixer bowl, place the whole wheat flour and 2 cups of bread flour. Reserve.

2. In a 1 1/2-quart saucepan, combine milk, water, molasses, and salt. Heat and stir until warm (105° - 115° F).

3. Pour liquid ingredients and yeast into the mixer bowl with the flour. Beat at low speed with a paddle attachment, if available, until the flour is moistened. Increase speed to medium, drop in butter divided into small pieces, and continue to beat for 2 minutes.

4. Stop mixer and add 2 1/2 cups of bread flour. Using a dough hook at low speed, begin to knead the dough. Gradually add up to 1 cup of

flour, in 2 to 3 tablespoon amounts, until the dough gathers on the dough hook and completely cleans the bottom and sides of the bowl, about 3 to 4 minutes. Then knead the dough for an additional 9 minutes. If the dough begins to stick to the bottom of the bowl, add flour as needed.

5. Turn dough onto a lightly floured work surface. Knead by hand until it becomes elastic and forms a smooth ball, about 1 minute. Place in a large lightly buttered bowl.

6. Cover bowl with plastic wrap and let rise in a warm place (75° - 80° F) until doubled in bulk, about 1 hour.

7. Punch dough down to deflate it. Fold the edges inward to form a ball and turn over. Let rise until doubled in bulk, about 1 hour. This second rise may be omitted but the flavor and texture of the bread will not be as good.

8. Turn dough onto an unfloured work surface. Press down to remove any air bubbles. Cut dough in half.

9. Press each half of dough into an 8-inch square. Fold each of the two short edges inward about 1-inch and then fold the long edges until they meet in the center of the loaf. Pinch seams to seal. Place each loaf, seam side down, in a buttered 8 1/2 x 4 1/2-inch pan.

10. Cover each pan loosely with plastic wrap. Let rise until the dough extends about 1-inch above the rim of each pan, about 1 hour. Be careful that the loaves do not rise too much.

11. Bake in a preheated 400° F oven for 10 minutes. Reduce oven temperature to 350° F and bake until loaves are golden brown and sound hollow when tapped, about 25 minutes. Immediately remove loaves from pans. Cool on wire racks.

12. For a soft and shiny crust, brush the top of the warm loaves with butter or margarine.

Yield: 2 loaves.

Whole Wheat Raisin Bread

Follow recipe for Whole Wheat Bread (p. 215) with these changes:

1. Stir 1 tablespoon of ground cinnamon into the flour in Step 1 (optional).

2. Gradually knead 1 1/3 to 1 3/4 cups of raisins into the dough toward the end of Step 4.

Yield: 2 loaves.

Whole Wheat Braid

1. Follow the recipe for Whole Wheat Raisin Bread (p. 216) until the dough is ready to be shaped into loaves.
2. Divide the dough into 3 equal pieces. Cut each piece into thirds and form into strips about 12-inches long.
3. Braid each set of 3 strips together to form a loaf (p. 205). Firmly pinch the strips together at each end to prevent them from separating while rising.
4. Let the braids rise on a buttered baking sheet until doubled in bulk, about 1 hour at 75° - 80° F.
5. Bake in a preheated 375° F oven until loaves are golden brown and sound hollow when tapped, about 30 to 35 minutes.
6. For a soft and shiny crust, brush the top of the loaves with butter or margarine while warm. Cool on wire racks.

Yield: 3 loaves.

Rye Bread

1. Follow the recipe for Whole Wheat Bread (p. 215) but substitute rye flour for the whole wheat flour.
2. I prefer to use molasses as the sweetening agent.
3. One tablespoon of caraway seeds may be added with the rye flour.
4. An additional 1/2 to 3/4 cup of flour may be needed when the bread is kneaded.

Yield: 2 loaves.

Whole Wheat or Rye Rolls

1. Prepare either Whole Wheat Bread (p. 215), or Rye Bread (see above) until it is ready to be shaped.
2. Instead of making 2 loaves of bread, shape each half of dough into 12 to 16 round, oval, single-knot or braided rolls (pp. 207 - 209). If you

would like the rolls to have a floured appearance after baking, press the top of each roll into whole wheat or rye flour.

3. Place rolls on lightly buttered baking sheets. Cover loosely with plastic wrap. Let rise until doubled in bulk, about 45 minutes.

4. If the tops of the rolls have not been pressed into flour, they may be brushed with glaze immediately before baking. For the glaze, beat an egg yolk with 1 tablespoon of milk. Try not to get any of the glaze on the baking sheet or it will burn while baking. The glazed rolls may be sprinkled with sesame seeds.

5. Bake rolls in a preheated 375° F oven until they are golden brown and sound hollow when tapped, about 18 minutes.

6. If the rolls have not been pressed into flour or glazed, they may be brushed with butter or margarine while still warm.

Yield: 24 to 32 rolls.

Cornmeal and Honey Bread

Cornmeal gives this bread unusual texture and character.

1 package regular active
 dry yeast
1/4 cup warm water
 (105° - 115° F)
About 6 1/2 cups bread
 flour or all-purpose flour
1 3/4 cups cornmeal

3/4 cup milk
1 1/4 cups water
3 tablespoons honey
2 1/2 teaspoons salt
3 tablespoons butter or
 margarine, at room
 temperature

1. In a small bowl, dissolve yeast in warm water. Reserve. In an electric mixer bowl, place 3 cups of flour and cornmeal. Reserve.

2. In a 1 1/2-quart saucepan, combine milk, water, honey, and salt. Heat and stir until warm (105° - 115° F).

3. Pour liquid ingredients and yeast into the mixer bowl with the flour and cornmeal. Beat at low speed with a paddle attachment, if available, until the flour is moistened. Increase speed to medium, drop in butter divided into small pieces, and continue to beat for 2 minutes.

4. Stop mixer and add 2 1/2 cups of flour. Using a dough hook at low speed, begin to knead the dough. Gradually add up to 1 cup of flour, in 2 to 3 tablespoon amounts, until the dough gathers on the dough hook and completely cleans the bottom and sides of the bowl, about 3 to 4

minutes. Then knead the dough for an additional 9 minutes. If the dough begins to stick to the bottom of the bowl, add flour as needed.

5. Turn dough onto a lightly floured work surface. Knead by hand until it becomes elastic and forms a smooth ball, about 1 minute. Place in a large lightly buttered bowl.

6. Cover bowl with plastic wrap and let rise in a warm place (75° - 80° F) until doubled in bulk, about 1 hour.

7. Punch dough down to deflate it. Fold the edges inward to form a ball and turn over. Let rise until doubled in bulk, about 1 hour. This second rise may be omitted but the flavor and texture of the bread will not be as good.

8. Turn dough onto an unfloured work surface. Press down to remove any air bubbles. Cut dough in half.

9. Press each half of dough into an 8-inch square. Fold each of the two short edges inward about 1-inch and then fold the long edges until they meet in the center of the loaf. Pinch seams to seal. Place each loaf, seam side down, in a buttered 8 1/2 x 4 1/2-inch pan.

10. Cover each pan loosely with plastic wrap. Let rise until the dough extends about 1-inch above the rim of each pan, about 1 hour. Be careful that the loaves do not rise too much.

11. Bake in a preheated 400° F oven for 10 minutes. Reduce oven temperature to 350° F and bake until loaves are golden brown and sound hollow when tapped, about 25 minutes. Immediately remove loaves from pans. Cool on wire racks.

12. For a soft and shiny crust, brush the top of the warm loaves with butter or margarine.

Yield: 2 loaves.

Challah (Egg Bread)

A light fine-grained bread with a beautiful shiny golden brown crust.

2 packages regular active
 dry yeast
1 1/4 cups warm water
 (105° - 115° F)
2 tablespoons honey, maple
 syrup, or granulated sugar
3 large eggs, warmed (p. 202)

2 teaspoons salt
About 6 cups bread flour
 or all-purpose flour
1/4 cup (1/2 stick) butter or
 margarine, at room
 temperature

1 large egg yolk
1 tablespoon milk or water

**Poppy or sesame seeds
(optional)**

1. In an electric mixer bowl, dissolve yeast in water.

2. Add honey, eggs, salt, and 3 cups of flour. Use a paddle attachment, if available, and beat at medium speed until blended, about 1 minute.

3. Add butter, divided into small pieces, and continue to beat until blended, about 2 minutes.

4. Stop mixer and add 2 cups of flour. Using a dough hook at low speed, begin to knead the dough. Gradually add up to 1 cup of flour, in 2 to 3 tablespoon amounts, until the dough gathers on the dough hook and completely cleans the bottom and sides of the bowl, about 3 to 4 minutes. Then knead the dough for an additional 9 minutes. If the dough begins to stick to the bottom of the bowl, add flour as needed.

5. Turn dough onto a lightly floured work surface. Knead by hand until it becomes elastic and forms a smooth ball, about 1 minute. Place in a large lightly buttered bowl.

6. Cover bowl with plastic wrap and let rise in a warm place (75° - 80° F) until doubled in bulk, about 1 hour.

7. Punch dough down to deflate it. Fold the edges inward to form a ball and turn over. Let rise until doubled in bulk, about 1 hour. This second rise may be omitted but the flavor and texture of the bread will not be as good.

8. Turn dough onto an unfloured work surface. Press down to remove any air bubbles.

9. Divide dough into 2 or 3 pieces. Cut each piece into thirds and form these into strips about 12-inches long. Braid each set of 3 strips together to form 2 or 3 loaves (p. 205). Firmly pinch strips together at each end to prevent them from separating while rising.

10. Place loaves on a buttered baking sheet. Cover loosely with plastic wrap and let rise until doubled in bulk, about 45 minutes.

11. Beat egg yolk and milk together. Brush loaves with this glaze. Avoid getting any glaze on the baking sheet or it will burn while baking. The loaves may be sprinkled with poppy or sesame seeds.

12. Bake in a preheated 375° F oven until loaves are golden brown and sound hollow when tapped, about 25 minutes. Cool on wire racks.

Yield: 2 or 3 loaves.

Note: This dough may be used to form 24 braided rolls (p. 209).

Dinner Rolls

1 package regular active
  dry yeast
1/4 cup warm water
  (105° - 115° F)
2 tablespoons granulated
  sugar
2 teaspoons salt
About 5 1/2 cups bread
  flour or all-purpose flour
1 1/4 cups warm milk
  (105° - 115° F)
1 large egg, warmed (p. 202)
  or an additional 1/3 cup milk

3 tablespoons butter or
  margarine, at room
  temperature
1/4 cup (1/2 stick) butter or
  margarine, melted
  (optional)
1 large egg yolk (optional)
1 tablespoon milk (optional)
Sesame or poppy seeds
  for garnish (optional)

1. In a small bowl, dissolve yeast in water. Reserve.

2. In an electric mixer bowl, combine sugar, salt, and 3 cups of flour. Add milk, egg, and yeast.

3. Use a paddle attachment, if available, and beat at medium speed until blended, about 1 minute. Add butter, divided into small pieces, and continue to beat until blended, about 2 minutes.

4. Stop mixer and add 1 1/2 cups of flour. Using a dough hook at low speed, begin to knead the dough. Gradually add up to 1 cup of flour, in 2 to 3 tablespoon amounts, until the dough gathers on the dough hook and completely cleans the bottom and sides of the bowl, about 3 to 4 minutes. Then knead the dough for an additional 9 minutes. If the dough begins to stick to the bottom of the bowl, add flour as needed.

5. Turn dough onto a lightly floured work surface. Knead by hand until it becomes elastic and forms a smooth ball, about 1 minute. Place in a large lightly buttered bowl.

6. Cover bowl with plastic wrap and let rise in a warm place (75° - 80° F) until doubled in bulk, about 1 hour.

7. Turn dough onto an unfloured work surface. Press down to remove any air bubbles. Cut dough into 24 equal pieces.

8. Shape each piece of dough into round, oval, single-knot, crescent, or braided rolls (pp. 207 - 209). Place on buttered baking sheets. Cover loosely with plastic wrap. Let rise until doubled in bulk, about 1 hour.

9. Immediately before baking, the rolls may be brushed with melted butter or glaze. Make glaze by beating the egg yolk and milk together.

Avoid getting any glaze on the baking sheets or it will burn while baking. Glazed rolls may be sprinkled with sesame or poppy seeds.

10. Bake in a preheated 400° F oven until rolls are golden brown and sound hollow when tapped, about 12 to 15 minutes. If rolls were brushed with butter before baking, brush them again. Cool on a wire rack.

Yield: 24 rolls.

French Bread

SPONGE
1/2 teaspoon regular active
  dry yeast
1 cup water, at room
  temperature (70° - 75° F)

2 cups bread flour

DOUGH
1/2 teaspoon regular active
  dry yeast
1 1/3 cups water, at room
  temperature (70° - 75° F),
  divided
About 5 cups bread flour,
  divided

1 tablespoon salt
Cornmeal, for dusting baking
  pans
1 large egg white
1 tablespoon water

1. Prepare the sponge the night before it is intended to be used: In an electric mixer bowl, dissolve the yeast in the water. Add flour. Use a paddle attachment, if available, and beat at medium speed for 2 minutes. Use a rubber spatula to scrape down sides of bowl and form mixture into one mass. Cover bowl with plastic wrap. Let sponge rise at room temperature (70° - 75° F) during the night, about 10 to 12 hours.

2. Prepare the dough the next morning: Dissolve the yeast in 1 cup of water. Add to sponge. Use a paddle attachment, if available, and beat at low speed for a few seconds. Add 2 cups of flour and beat until the flour is moistened.

3. Add salt to 1/3 cup of water. Stir until most of the salt has dissolved. Add salt solution and 1 cup of bread flour to dough. Beat at medium speed for 2 minutes.

4. Stop mixer and add 1 cup of flour. Using a dough hook at low speed, begin to knead the dough. Gradually add up to 1 cup of flour, in 2

to 3 tablespoon amounts, until the dough gathers on the dough hook and completely cleans the bottom and sides of the bowl, about 3 to 4 minutes. Then knead the dough for an additional 9 minutes. If the dough begins to stick to the bottom of the bowl, add flour as needed.

5. Turn dough onto a lightly floured work surface. Knead by hand until it becomes elastic and forms a smooth ball, about 1 minute. Place in a large lightly oiled bowl.

6. Cover the bowl with plastic wrap and let rise at room temperature (70° - 75° F) until about 2 1/2 times in bulk, about 2 1/2 hours.

7. Turn dough onto an unfloured work surface. Press down to remove any air bubbles.

8. Shape dough into loaves as described below. If dough becomes sticky, sprinkle it lightly with flour. Use as little flour as possible.

Long Loaves

Use a French bread pan measuring about 17 x 5 1/2 x 2-inches and molded with two 2 1/2-inch wide and 2-inch deep troughs (see illustration, below). Lightly coat the troughs with vegetable oil and sprinkle them with cornmeal. Baking sheets may be used in place of French bread pans but the baked loaves will be flatter. Divide dough in half. Press and lengthen each piece of dough until it measures about three-quarters of the length of the pan. Fold the dough in half lengthwise. Press the edges together with the heel of your hand. Use the side of your hand to press a groove in the center of the dough along its entire length. Bring the two long edges together at the center. Pinch the edges to seal. Roll the dough forward and backward under the palms of your hands to make a loaf of even diameter and desired length. When placed in the pan, seam side down, the loaf should be about 1-inch shorter than the pan at each end. Practice is needed to make well-shaped cylindrical loaves with a smooth surface but do not become overly concerned since rising will improve their appearance.

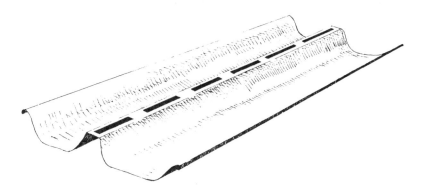

Long Thin Loaves

Follow the directions for long loaves (p. 223) but use two French bread pans each measuring 16 1/2 x 8 1/2 x 1-inches and molded with three 2 1/4-inch wide and 1-inch deep troughs. Divide dough into 6 equal pieces.

Round Loaves

Divide dough into 3 pieces. Flatten each piece of dough. With the dough resting on the work surface, pull an edge upward and press it into the center of the dough. Repeat this until the bottom and sides of the ball are round and smooth. Invert the loaves onto a lightly oiled baking sheet that has been sprinkled with cornmeal.

9. Cover dough loosely with plastic wrap and let rise until about 2 1/2 times in bulk, about 1 1/2 to 2 hours.

10. Meanwhile, place a heavy pan, such as a cast iron skillet, on the lowest rack in the oven. Place the other rack in the middle of the oven. Preheat oven to 450° F 15 to 20 minutes before the bread is ready to be baked.

11. In a small bowl, lightly beat the egg white and water. Immediately before baking, brush loaves with egg white mixture. Slash loaves with a single edge razor blade or a very sharp knife. Long loaves or long thin loaves may be slashed with diagonal cuts placed along the length of the loaves. Round loaves may be slashed with a single slash, 2 slashes like a cross, or multiple slashes like a tick-tack-toe design (see illustration, above). The slashes should be a little more than 1/4-inch deep.

12. Put 1/2 cup of water into a long-handled ladle. Pour the water into the heated pan. Be careful not to be burned by the steam. Immediately place the bread pans on the rack in the middle of the oven.

13. Bake loaves until they are golden brown and have a hollow sound when tapped, about 30 minutes for long loaves and 20 minutes for long

thin loaves. Bake round loaves for 15 minutes, reduce temperature to 400° F, and bake for about 10 minutes. Cool on wire racks.

14. If the crust becomes soft, reheat the bread in a 350° F oven to restore crispness.

Yield: 2 long loaves, 6 long thin loaves, or 3 round loaves.

Whole Wheat French Bread

Follow the recipe for French Bread (p. 222) except substitute 2 cups of whole wheat flour for 2 cups of bread flour in Step 2.

Yield: 2 long loaves, 6 long thin loaves, or 3 round loaves.

Italian Bread

Follow the recipe for French Bread (p. 222) with the following changes:

1. In Step 2, substitute 1 cup of skim or low fat milk for the water.
2. Dissolve 1 tablespoon of barley malt (available in health food stores) or molasses in the milk before adding the yeast.

Yield: 2 long loaves, 6 long thin loaves, or 3 round loaves.

Crusty Rolls

1. Prepare French Bread (p. 222) or Italian Bread (see above) through Step 7.
2. Cut dough into 24 or 32 pieces.
3. Shape dough into round, oval, or split rolls (pp. 207 - 209). The dough may also be shaped into small loaves as described in the French Bread recipe.
4. Place rolls on baking sheets that have been lightly oiled and sprinkled with cornmeal, rye, or whole wheat flour. If the dough has been

shaped into small loaves, several can be placed in each trough of a French bread pan that has been lightly oiled and sprinkled with cornmeal.

5. Cover loosely with plastic wrap and let rise until doubled in bulk, about 1 hour.

6. Immediately before baking, the rolls may be slashed with a single edge razor blade. Single slashes, two slashes like a cross, or diagonal slashes may be used. The slashes should be a little more than 1/4-inch deep.

7. Bake rolls as described in the French Bread recipe (Steps 10 - 13, p. 224). The rolls will be done in about 12 to 15 minutes.

8. If the rolls become soft, reheat them in a 350° F oven to restore crispness.

Yield: 24 to 32 rolls.

Sweet Dough

Breads made with sweet dough should have a light texture. To ensure this, measure all ingredients accurately.

This dough requires only a short kneading period since strong gluten development is not needed.

Sweet dough is rich in sugar and butter which inhibit the action of yeast. However, this dough will rise about twice as fast if fast-rising yeast is used instead of regular yeast. If regular yeast is used, the milk should be 105° - 115° F.

1/2 cup granulated sugar	**1 1/2 cups hot milk**
1 teaspoon salt	**(125° - 130° F)**
2 packages fast-rising active	**2 large eggs, warmed (p. 202)**
dry yeast	**6 tablespoons (3/4 stick)**
7 cups sifted bread flour	**butter or margarine, at**
or all-purpose flour,	**room temperature**
divided	

1. In an electric mixer bowl, combine sugar, salt, yeast, and 4 cups of flour. Use a paddle attachment, if available, and mix thoroughly.

2. Pour in milk and beat at medium speed until blended, about 1 minute. Add eggs and beat until smooth, about 1 minute. Add butter,

divided into small pieces, and continue to beat until blended, about 2 minutes.

3. Stop mixer and add 2 cups of flour. Using a dough hook at low speed, begin to knead the dough. Gradually add up to 1 cup of flour, in 2 to 3 tablespoon amounts, until the dough gathers on the dough hook and completely cleans the bottom and sides of the bowl, about 3 to 4 minutes. Then knead the dough for an additional 3 minutes.

4. Turn dough onto a lightly floured work surface. Knead by hand until it becomes elastic and forms a smooth ball, about 1 minute. If the dough is sticky, knead in an additional tablespoon of flour. Do not use any more flour than necessary.

5. Place dough in a large lightly buttered bowl. Cover bowl with plastic wrap and let rise in a warm place (80° - 85° F) until doubled in bulk, about 1 hour.

6. Turn dough onto an unfloured work surface. Use dough as directed in Pecan Caramel Buns (see below), Cinnamon Raisin Buns (p. 228), and Hot Cross Buns (p. 229).

Pecan Caramel Buns

Sweet Dough (p. 226)
1 cup light brown sugar,
** firmly packed**
3/4 cup (1 1/2 sticks)
** melted butter or**
** margarine, divided**
4 teaspoons water

1 1/3 cups pecan halves or
** pieces**
1/2 cup granulated sugar
4 teaspoons ground
** cinnamon**
1 cup raisins

1. While the dough is rising, prepare four 8-inch round layer cake pans. Place 1/4 cup of brown sugar, 2 tablespoons of melted butter, and 1 teaspoon of water in each pan. Stir the ingredients into a smooth syrup. Sprinkle 1/3 cup of pecans over the syrup in each pan.

2. Cut dough in half. Roll or press each half into a 20 x 12-inch rectangle. Brush remaining butter over the rectangles.

3. In a small bowl, mix granulated sugar and cinnamon together. Sprinkle half the mixture over each piece of dough. Spread half the raisins over each rectangle.

4. Starting at a long end, tightly roll each piece of dough like a jelly roll. Pinch seam to seal. Shape each roll so that it is about 18-inches long. Cut each roll into 16 slices. Arrange 8 slices in each prepared pan.

Place one slice in the center and evenly space the others around the center one. Flatten the slices until their edges touch each other.

5. Cover each pan with plastic wrap. Let rise in a warm place (80° - 85° F) until the buns reach 1/4-inch below the rim of each pan, about 1 hour.

6. Bake in a preheated 375° F oven until buns are golden brown, about 20 minutes.

7. Immediately turn buns out onto serving plates or wire racks.

8. Serve warm or at room temperature. If not served immediately, store buns in an airtight container.

Yield: 32 buns.

Cinnamon Raisin Buns

BUNS
6 tablespoons (3/4 stick) butter or margarine, melted
Sweet Dough (p. 226)

1/2 cup granulated sugar
4 teaspoons ground cinnamon
1 1/3 cups raisins

FROSTING
1 cup confectioners' sugar
2 tablespoons milk

1/4 teaspoon vanilla extract

1. Brush four 8-inch round layer cake pans with part of the melted butter. Reserve.

2. Cut dough in half. Roll or press each half into a 20 x 12-inch rectangle. Brush remaining butter over the two rectangles.

3. In a small bowl, mix granulated sugar and cinnamon together. Sprinkle half the mixture over each piece of dough. Spread half the raisins over each rectangle.

4. Starting at a long end, tightly roll each piece of dough like a jelly roll. Pinch seam to seal. Shape each roll so that it is about 18-inches long. Cut each roll into 16 slices. Arrange 8 slices in each prepared pan. Place one slice in the center and evenly space the others around the center one. Flatten the slices until their edges touch each other.

5. Cover each pan with plastic wrap. Let rise at 80° - 85° F until the buns reach 1/4-inch below the rim of each pan, about 1 hour.

6. Bake in a preheated 375° F oven until buns are golden brown, about 20 minutes.

7. Immediately turn buns out onto serving plates or wire racks.

8. Prepare frosting: Combine all ingredients in a small bowl. Beat until smooth. Drizzle over warm buns.

9. Serve warm or at room temperature. If not served immediately, store buns in an airtight container.

Yield: 32 buns.

Hot Cross Buns

DOUGH
Prepare **Sweet Dough (p. 226)** with the following additions:

1. In Step 1, add these spices to the mixer bowl:

1 1/2 teaspoons ground cinnamon

3/4 teaspoon grated nutmeg
1/4 teaspoon ground cloves

2. After Step 3 is completed, knead in the following fruits until evenly distributed

1/3 cup (2 ounces) finely chopped candied lemon rind, citron, or mixed candied fruit

3/4 cup dried currants or chopped raisins

GLAZE
1 large egg yolk

2 tablespoons cold water

FROSTING
2 tablespoons (1/4 stick) butter or margarine, at room temperature
1 cup confectioners' sugar

1/8 teaspoon vanilla extract
4 teaspoons milk

1. Cut dough into 32 pieces. Shape each piece into a round roll (p. 207).

2. Arrange buns about 1 1/2-inches apart on 2 buttered baking sheets. Cover loosely with plastic wrap. Let rise in a warm place (80° - 85° F) until doubled in bulk, about 1 hour.

3. Beat egg yolk and water together. Brush over buns.

4. Bake buns, one sheet at a time, in a preheated 375° F oven until golden brown, about 20 minutes. Cool on wire racks.

5. Prepare frosting: Combine all ingredients in a small bowl. Beat until smooth.

6. Use a pastry bag with a 1/4-inch plain round tip or a narrow knife to make a cross of frosting on top of each bun.

7. If buns are not served immediately, store in an airtight container.

Yield: 32 buns.

Kugelhopf (Austrian Sweet Bread)

This impressive bread is baked in a crown (fluted tube) pan (see illustration, next page).

1 package regular active
 dry yeast
1/4 cup warm water
 (105° - 115° F)
3 large eggs, warmed (p. 202)
1/4 cup granulated sugar
2 cups sifted all-purpose
 flour
8 tablespoons (1 stick) butter,
 at room temperature,
 divided

Finely grated rind of a lemon
1/3 cup raisins
1/2 cup finely chopped mixed
 candied fruits
1/2 cup slivered or chopped
 almonds, toasted
1/2 teaspoon vanilla extract
Confectioners' sugar for
 dusting

1. In a small bowl, dissolve yeast in water. Reserve.

2. In an electric mixer, using a whisk attachment, if available, beat eggs and sugar at high speed until smooth and light in color.

3. Add yeast and flour. Use a paddle attachment, if available, and beat at medium speed until blended, about 3 minutes.

4. Cover bowl with plastic wrap. Let rise in a warm place (80° - 85° F) for 30 minutes.

5. While dough is rising, whip 6 tablespoons of butter in an electric mixer. Stir in lemon rind, raisins, candied fruit, almonds, and vanilla.

6. After dough has risen, add butter mixture. Use a rubber spatula to mix thoroughly.

7. Butter an 8-inch (8-cup) crown pan using a full 2 tablespoons of butter. Turn dough into mold.

8. Cover mold with plastic wrap. Let rise almost to the top of the mold, about 1 1/2 hours.

9. Bake in a preheated 375° F oven until golden brown, about 20 to 25 minutes.

10. Immediately loosen the bread from the mold with a sharp-tipped knife. Turn out onto a wire rack to cool.

11. Lightly dust the kugelhopf with confectioners' sugar before serving. It may be cut into slices and reassembled before dusting with confectioners' sugar. This bread is best when served warm with whipped sweet butter. Kugelhopf freezes well.

Yield: One 8-inch tube loaf, 8 to 12 servings.

Crumb Cake

This crumb cake is a perfect coffee cake.

CAKE

1 package fast-rising active
   dry yeast
3 tablespoons granulated
   sugar
1/4 teaspoon salt
2 1/3 cups sifted all-
   purpose flour, divided

1/2 cup warm milk
   (125° - 130° F)
1 large egg yolk
2 tablespoons (1/4 stick)
   butter or margarine, at
   room temperature

CRUMBS

2 cups all-purpose flour
1/2 cup granulated sugar
1/4 cup light brown sugar
1 teaspoon baking powder
1 teaspoon ground
  cinnamon
1/4 teaspoon grated nutmeg

3/4 cup (1 1/2 sticks) butter or
  margarine, at room
  temperature
Finely grated rind of a
  medium lemon
1 large egg

CHEESE FILLING (OPTIONAL)

8 ounces Neufchâtel or
  cream cheese
1/4 cup granulated sugar
2 tablespoons all-purpose
  flour

1 tablespoon sour cream
1/2 teaspoon vanilla
  extract
1/2 teaspoon finely grated
  lemon rind

NUTS (OPTIONAL)

1/2 cup sliced almonds

TOPPING (OPTIONAL)

1/2 cup confectioners' sugar

ICING (OPTIONAL)

1 cup confectioners' sugar   2 tablespoons milk

1. In an electric mixer, combine yeast, sugar, salt, and 1 1/3 cups of flour. Use a paddle attachment, if available, and mix thoroughly.

2. Pour in milk and beat at medium speed until blended, about 1 minute. Add egg yolk and beat until smooth, about 1 minute. Add butter, divided into small pieces, and continue to beat until blended, about 1 minute.

3. Stop mixer and add 1/2 cup of flour. Using a dough hook at low speed, begin to knead the dough. Gradually add up to 1/2 cup of flour, in 2 to 3 tablespoon amounts, until the dough gathers on the dough hook and completely cleans the bottom and sides of the bowl, about 3 to 4 minutes. Since there is only a small amount of dough, stop the mixer at times and use a rubber spatula to push the dough to the center of the bowl so it can gather on the dough hook. Knead the dough for 3 additional minutes.

4. Turn dough onto a lightly floured work surface. Knead by hand until it becomes elastic and forms a smooth ball, about 1 minute. If the dough is sticky, knead in an additional tablespoon or so of flour. Do not use any more flour than necessary.

5. Place dough in a large lightly buttered bowl. Cover bowl with plastic wrap and let rise in a warm place (80° - 85° F) until doubled in bulk, about 35 minutes.

6. Butter a jelly roll pan measuring 15 x 11 x 1-inches. Press the dough in the pan until the bottom of the pan is covered and the dough extends halfway up the sides.

7. Cover pan loosely with plastic wrap. Let rise until doubled in bulk, about 20 minutes.

8. Meanwhile, prepare crumbs: Place flour, granulated sugar, brown sugar, baking powder, cinnamon, and nutmeg in a food processor with a steel blade. Process until ingredients are mixed. Add butter, divided into small pieces, and lemon rind. Process until mixture resembles cornmeal. Add egg and process until crumbs form. If a food processor is not available, combine dry ingredients in a bowl. Add butter and lemon rind. Use a pastry blender to cut in butter until mixture resembles cornmeal. Add egg and stir until crumbs form. Reserve.

9. Prepare cheese filling: In an electric mixer, cream the Neufchâtel cheese. Beat in sugar and then remaining ingredients. Reserve.

10. Place two lengthwise, parallel, and equally-spaced bands of cheese filling on the risen dough.

11. Spread crumbs evenly on top of dough but only partially cover the bands of cheese filling.

12. Sprinkle with nuts.

13. Bake in a preheated 375° F oven until the crumbs are light brown, about 18 minutes.

14. Cool in pan for 5 minutes. Turn out onto a baking sheet. Invert onto a serving dish or wire rack.

15. Use a small strainer to sift confectioners' sugar over cake. Alternatively, prepare icing by beating confectioners' sugar and milk together until smooth and drizzle on top of cake.

16. Serve warm or at room temperature. If the crumb cake is not served immediately, store in an airtight container.

Yield: One 15 x 11-inch cake, 8 servings.

Stollen (German Christmas Bread)

This full-flavored fruit bread makes an impressive Christmas present.

About 6 1/2 cups bread
flour or all-purpose flour
1/3 cup granulated sugar
1 teaspoon salt
2 packages fast-rising active
dry yeast
1/2 teaspoon ground
cinnamon
1/4 teaspoon grated nutmeg
1 1/3 cups milk
1 teaspoon finely grated
lemon rind
1 teaspoon finely grated
orange rind
2 tablespoons rum, brandy,
or Grand Marnier
1 teaspoon vanilla extract
2 large eggs, warmed (p. 202)
3/4 cup (1 1/2 sticks) butter or
margarine, at room
temperature, and 5
tablespoons butter or
margarine, melted

8 ounces (1 cup) chopped
mixed candied fruit
4 ounces (1/2 cup) candied
cherries, cut in halves
1 cup raisins
1 1/4 cups slivered or
coarsely chopped
almonds, toasted
2 tablespoons granulated
sugar (optional)
1/4 teaspoon ground
cinnamon (optional)
Confectioners' sugar for
dusting
Candied cherries for garnish
(optional)

1. In an electric mixer bowl, combine 3 1/2 cups of flour, 1/3 cup of granulated sugar, salt, yeast, 1/2 teaspoon of cinnamon, and nutmeg. Use a paddle attachment, if available, and mix thoroughly. Reserve.

2. In a 1 1/2-quart saucepan, combine milk, lemon and orange rinds, rum, and vanilla extract. Heat until 125° - 130° F. Add milk mixture and eggs to mixer bowl. Beat at medium speed until smooth, about 1 minute.

3. Add 3/4 cup of butter, divided into small pieces, and beat until blended, about 2 minutes.

4. Stop mixer and add 2 1/4 cups of flour. Using a dough hook at low speed, begin to knead the dough. Gradually add up to 3/4 cup of flour in 2 to 3 tablespoon amounts until the dough gathers on the dough hook and completely cleans the bottom and sides of the bowl, about 3 to 4

minutes. Then knead the dough for an additional 3 minutes. If the dough begins to stick to the bottom of the bowl, add flour as necessary.

5. After dough has been kneaded, gradually add candied fruit, cherries, raisins, and almonds to mixer and continue to knead until fruit and nuts are evenly distributed throughout dough, about 2 to 3 minutes. If the dough seems sticky, knead in additional flour by tablespoon amounts. Approximately 1/4 cup will be needed. Instead of using a mixer, the fruit and nuts can be kneaded in by hand.

6. Turn dough onto a lightly floured work surface. Knead by hand until it becomes elastic and forms a smooth ball, about 1 minute. Place in a large lightly buttered bowl. Cover bowl with plastic wrap. Let rise in a warm place (80° - 85° F) until doubled in bulk, about 1 hour.

7. Turn dough onto an unfloured work surface. Cut dough in half. Flatten each half into an oval measuring about 16 x 9-inches. Brush the ovals with part of the melted butter. Combine 2 tablespoons of sugar with 1/4 teaspoon of cinnamon. Sprinkle over loaves. Fold each oval in half lengthwise so that about two-thirds of the bottom half is covered (see illustration, below).

8. Place loaves on a 17 x 12-inch buttered baking sheet. Reserve 1 tablespoon of butter for brushing the loaves after baking. Brush top of loaves with remaining butter. Cover loosely with plastic wrap. Let rise until doubled in bulk, about 45 minutes.

9. Bake in a preheated 375° F oven until loaves are golden brown and sound hollow when tapped, about 30 minutes. Brush the warm loaves with butter. Cool on wire racks.

10. Sprinkle loaves with confectioners' sugar. Halved candied cherries may be placed along the center of each loaf. Stollen may be sliced, frozen, and then toasted when desired.

Yield: 2 loaves.

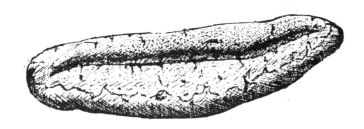

Maple or Honey Butter

1/2 cup (1 stick) butter or
 margarine
2 tablespoons maple
 syrup or honey

1/2 teaspoon ground
 cinnamon

1. In an electric mixer, cream the butter. Add remaining ingredients and beat until light and fluffy.
2. Refrigerate until served.

Yield: 1/2 cup.

Note: This spread is delicious on bread and pancakes.

Whipped Cream Cheese with Maple Syrup

8 ounces cream cheese

2 tablespoons maple
 syrup

1. In an electric mixer, beat the cream cheese. Add maple syrup and beat until light and fluffy.
2. Refrigerate until served.

Yield: 1 cup.

Note: Try this spread on Banana Nut Bread (p. 240).

Quick Breads

Skillet Cornbread

A cast iron skillet gives this bread a delightfully crisp brown crust.

1 cup all-purpose flour
1 1/2 cups cornmeal
1 tablespoon baking powder
1 teaspoon salt
2 tablespoons granulated
  sugar (see Note, below)

2 large eggs
1 3/4 cups milk
4 tablespoons (1/2 stick)
  butter or margarine

1. Sift flour, cornmeal, baking powder, salt, and sugar (if using) into a large bowl. Mix thoroughly. Reserve.

2. In a small bowl, use a whisk to beat the eggs until foamy. Stir in milk. Reserve.

3. In a 10-inch cast iron skillet on top of the stove, melt the butter. Swirl the skillet to coat the bottom and lower inch of the sides of the skillet. Pour the butter into the liquid ingredients leaving enough to coat the skillet.

4. Pour liquid ingredients into flour mixture. Mix with a fork until flour is completely moistened. Do not overmix.

5. Spread batter in skillet. Immediately place in a preheated 375° F oven. Bake until cornbread is browned around the edges, about 25 minutes.

6. Turn out onto a wooden board or serve directly from the skillet as soon as possible.

Yield: One 10-inch cornbread, 6 to 8 servings.

Note: If the cornbread will be used in poultry stuffing, omit the sugar.

Blueberry Orange Bread

6 tablespoons (3/4 stick)
 butter or margarine
1 cup granulated sugar
2 large eggs, at room
 temperature
1 1/2 tablespoons finely
 grated orange rind
1/2 cup orange juice

1 tablespoon lemon juice
2 1/4 cups sifted all-purpose
 flour
1 1/2 teaspoons baking
 powder
1/4 teaspoon salt
1 to 1 1/4 cups blueberries

1. In an electric mixer, cream the butter. Add sugar and beat until fluffy. Add eggs and orange rind. Beat until smooth and light.

2. Combine orange juice with lemon juice. Reserve.

3. Sift flour, baking powder, and salt together. Add one-third of the dry ingredients to the mixer alternately with half of the combined juices. Start and end with the flour mixture. Be sure ingredients are mixed thoroughly after each addition but no more than necessary. Use a rubber spatula to scrape sides of bowl as needed.

4. Fold in blueberries using only a few strokes.

5. Spread batter evenly in a buttered 8 1/2 x 4 1/2-inch loaf pan.

6. Bake in a preheated 325° F oven until a cake tester comes out clean, about 1 hour and 10 minutes.

7. Cool cake in pan for 5 minutes before turning out onto a wire rack.

8. Serve warm or at room temperature.

Yield: One loaf.

Banana Nut Bread

A fine use for ripe bananas.

2 medium ripe bananas
1/2 cup (1 stick) butter or
  margarine, at room
  temperature
1 cup light brown sugar,
  firmly packed
2 large eggs, at room
  temperature

1/4 cup milk, at room
  temperature
2 cups sifted all-purpose
  flour
1 teaspoon baking soda
1/2 cup coarsely chopped
  walnuts or pecans

1. In an electric mixer, beat bananas until mashed. Transfer to a measuring cup; there should be 1 cup. Reserve.

2. Cream butter in mixer bowl. Add brown sugar and beat until fluffy. Add eggs and beat until smooth. Add bananas and milk. Mix until smooth.

3. Sift flour and baking soda together. Add to mixer. Mix at low speed just until flour is completely moistened. Do not overmix.

4. Stir in nuts.

5. Spread mixture evenly in a buttered 8 1/2 x 4 1/2-inch loaf pan.

6. Bake in a preheated 350° F oven until a cake tester comes out clean, about 1 hour. Cool on a wire rack.

Yield: One loaf.

Note: Tasty sandwiches may be made with this bread and Whipped Cream Cheese with Maple Syrup (p. 236).

Streusel Nut Coffee Cake

CRUMBS

1 cup all-purpose flour
1 cup light brown sugar,
  firmly packed
1 1/2 teaspoons ground
  cinnamon

1/2 cup (1 stick) butter or
  margarine, chilled
1 1/3 cups chopped pecans
  or sliced or slivered
  almonds

CAKE

3/4 cup (1 1/2 sticks)
  butter or margarine, at
  room temperature
3/4 cup granulated sugar
3 large eggs, at room
  temperature
2 1/4 cups sifted all-
  purpose flour

2 teaspoons baking powder
1 teaspoon baking soda
3/4 cup sour cream, at
  room temperature
1 teaspoon vanilla extract

1. Prepare crumbs: In a food processor bowl with a steel blade, combine flour, brown sugar, and cinnamon. Process for a few seconds until mixed. Add butter, divided into small pieces, and process until crumbs form. If a food processor is not available, combine dry ingredients in a bowl and use a pastry blender to cut in the butter. Stir in nuts. Reserve.

2. Prepare cake batter: In an electric mixer, cream the butter. Add sugar and beat until fluffy. Add eggs and beat until smooth.

3. Sift flour, baking powder, and baking soda together. Add to mixer. Mix only until blended.

4. Add sour cream and vanilla. Mix only until blended.

5. Spread batter in a buttered and floured 13 x 9 x 2-inch pan.

6. Sprinkle crumbs over cake.

7. Bake in a preheated 350° F oven until a cake tester comes out clean, about 35 minutes.

8. Cool cake in pan for 5 minutes before turning out onto a wire rack or plate.

9. Serve warm or at room temperature.

Yield: One 13 x 9-inch cake, 8 to 12 servings.

Blueberry Muffins

6 tablespoons (3/4 stick)
 butter or margarine, at
 room temperature
2/3 cup granulated sugar
2 large eggs, at room
 temperature
2 cups sifted all-purpose
 flour

2 teaspoons baking powder
1/2 teaspoon salt
2/3 cup milk, at room
 temperature
1 cup blueberries
1 tablespoon granulated
 sugar (optional)

1. In an electric mixer, cream the butter. Add 2/3 cup of sugar and beat until fluffy. Add eggs, one at a time, beating until smooth.

2. Sift flour, baking powder, and salt together. Add one-third of the dry ingredients to the mixer alternately with half of the milk. Start and end with the flour mixture. Be sure the ingredients are mixed thoroughly after each addition but no more than necessary. Use a rubber spatula to scrape sides of bowl as needed.

3. Fold in blueberries using only a few strokes.

4. Place 2 1/2-inch paper baking cups in a 12 cup muffin pan. Fill cups with batter. Sprinkle muffins with 1 tablespoon of sugar.

5. Bake in a preheated 400° F oven until muffins are lightly browned and a cake tester comes out clean, about 20 minutes.

6. These muffins are best served warm.

Yield: 12 muffins.

Banana Pecan Muffins

2 medium bananas
1/2 cup light brown sugar,
 firmly packed
1 large egg
1/4 cup milk

1/4 cup vegetable oil
2 cups sifted all-purpose
 flour
2 teaspoons baking powder
1/2 cup chopped pecans

1. In an electric mixer, beat bananas until mashed. Transfer to a measuring cup; there should be 1 cup.

2. Return banana to mixer bowl. Add brown sugar, egg, milk, and vegetable oil. Beat until smooth.

3. Sift flour and baking powder together. Add to banana mixture. Mix with a rubber spatula until flour is completely moistened. Do not overmix or the muffins will have a coarse texture.

4. Fold in pecans using only a few strokes.

5. Place 2 1/2-inch paper baking cups in a 12 cup muffin pan. Fill cups with batter.

6. Bake in a preheated 400° F oven until muffins are brown around the edges and a cake tester comes out clean, about 15 minutes.

Yield: 12 muffins.

Pumpkin Raisin Muffins

1 cup dark brown sugar,
 firmly packed
1 large egg
3/4 cup canned pumpkin
1/4 cup milk
1/4 cup vegetable oil
1 3/4 cups sifted all-purpose
 flour

2 teaspoons baking powder
1/2 teaspoon ground
 cinnamon
1/4 teaspoon grated nutmeg
1/8 teaspoon ground cloves
1/2 cup raisins

1. In a large bowl, combine brown sugar, egg, pumpkin, milk, and vegetable oil. Whisk until smooth.

2. Sift together flour, baking powder, cinnamon, nutmeg, and cloves. Add to pumpkin mixture. Mix with a rubber spatula until flour is completely moistened. Do not overmix or the muffins will have a coarse texture.

3. Fold in raisins using only a few strokes.

4. Place 2 1/2-inch paper baking cups in a 12 cup muffin pan. Fill cups with batter.

5. Bake in a preheated 400° F oven until a cake tester comes out clean, about 20 minutes.

Yield: 12 muffins.

Scones

These rich biscuits are favorite tea cakes in Great Britain.

2 cups all-purpose flour
4 teaspoons baking powder
2 tablespoons granulated
  sugar
1/4 teaspoon salt
6 tablespoons (3/4 stick)
  butter or margarine, chilled

7 tablespoons milk, divided
1 large egg
1/4 cup dried currants or
  raisins

1. Place flour, baking powder, sugar, and salt in a food processor with a steel blade. Process for a few seconds to mix ingredients.

2. Cut butter into 1/2-inch cubes. Add to processor. Process with a pulsing action until the mixture resembles cornmeal. Transfer to a large bowl. If a food processor is not available, combine dry ingredients in a large bowl and use a pastry blender to cut in the butter.

3. In a small bowl, beat 1 tablespoon of milk with the egg until frothy. Pour three-quarters of the egg mixture over the flour mixture. Reserve the other quarter to use as a glaze.

4. Pour 6 tablespoons of milk over the flour mixture. Stir with a fork until a dough begins to form.

5. Sprinkle raisins over mixture.

6. Use one hand in a clawing motion to blend the ingredients but do not overwork the dough. If the dough seems dry, add a little more egg mixture. Form dough into a ball.

7. Place dough on a lightly floured surface. Flatten slightly. Roll dough until it is 1/2-inch thick. Cut into rounds with a 2 to 3-inch cutter. Gently knead the scraps together, reroll, and cut. The last piece of dough may be pressed inside the cutter (resting on the work surface) until it assumes the circular shape of the cutter.

8. Place the rounds on a buttered baking sheet. Brush the tops with the reserved egg glaze being careful not to get any on the baking sheet.

9. Bake scones in a preheated 450° F oven until golden brown, about 12 minutes.

10. Serve warm with butter or Devonshire cream and preserves.

Yield: 8 (3-inch) or 15 (2-inch) scones.

Whole Wheat Pancakes

These pancakes have character. Rather than drown them in syrup, serve them with fresh fruit such as sliced peaches, strawberries, blueberries, or Spiced Apple Slices (p. 366). Top each serving with a dollop of sour cream.

1 1/4 cups whole wheat
  flour
1/3 cup wheat germ
1 1/2 teaspoons baking
  powder
1/2 teaspoon salt

1 large egg
1 tablespoon maple syrup
1 1/2 cups milk
3 tablespoons butter or
  margarine, melted

1. In a large bowl, mix flour, wheat germ, baking powder, and salt together.

2. In a small bowl, beat the egg. Stir in maple syrup, milk, and butter. Pour into flour mixture. Stir until flour is moistened. Do not overmix or the pancakes will be tough.

3. Cook pancakes on a lightly buttered griddle or in a heavy skillet. Use about 2 tablespoons of batter for each pancake. Turn each pancake only once.

Yield: 16 pancakes, 3 1/2 to 4-inches in diameter, 4 servings.

Popovers

Popovers are always a spectacular surprise and are easy to make.

3 large eggs
1 cup milk
4 tablespoons (1/2 stick)
  melted butter or
  margarine, divided

1 cup sifted all-purpose flour
1/4 teaspoon salt

1. In a small bowl, combine eggs, milk, and 2 tablespoons of melted butter. Beat until blended.

2. In a large bowl, combine flour and salt. Gradually add liquid ingredients while stirring until smooth.

3. Strain batter twice. Use a rubber spatula to force any lumps through the strainer.

4. Pour batter into a liquid measuring cup or other pitcher. Cover and refrigerate until needed.

— This recipe may be prepared ahead to this point. —

5. Place a 6 cup popover pan on the middle rack of an oven preheated to 375° F. Alternatively, use 6 custard cups, each holding 6-ounces (3/4-cup), equally spaced on a baking sheet. Preheat the pan or cups for 2 minutes or longer.

6. Brush the cups with 2 tablespoons of butter. Gently stir the batter and pour into the cups.

7. Bake until the popovers are dark brown, about 35 to 40 minutes Do not open the oven door until the popovers are almost completely baked. About 5 minutes before they are done, use a sharp knife to cut a slit in each popover to allow steam to escape.

8. If needed, use a sharp narrow knife to remove the popovers from the cups.

9. Serve immediately.

Yield: 6 popovers, 6 servings.

Yorkshire Pudding

The perfect accompaniment for Rib Roast of Beef (p. 132).

Follow the recipe for Popovers (p. 245) with the following changes:

1. Use 3 tablespoons of roast beef drippings instead of the butter.

2. In Step 5, preheat a 9-inch square baking pan in a 400° F oven. A popover pan or custard cups may also be used (preheat oven to 375° F).

3. After the square pan is heated, pour in the roast beef drippings. If a popover pan or custard cups are used, brush them with the drippings.

4. Pour batter into pan or cups. Bake until pudding is dark brown, about 35 minutes.

5. Serve immediately.

Yield: 6 servings.

Crêpes for Entrées

An infinite variety of fillings may be wrapped in these paper-thin pancakes. See Chicken and Mushroom Crêpes (p. 122) and Crab and Mushroom Crêpes (p. 95).

2 large eggs
1 1/4 cups milk
1 cup sifted all-purpose flour

Butter or margarine to brush crêpe pan or skillet

1. In a small bowl, combine eggs and milk. Whisk until foamy.
2. Place flour in a large bowl. Gradually add liquid ingredients while stirring until smooth.
3. Strain the mixture into a liquid measuring cup or other pitcher. Use a rubber spatula to force any lumps through the strainer.
4. Brush a 6 to 7-inch crêpe pan or skillet with butter or margarine. A partially unwrapped stick of butter can be used.
5. Heat pan over moderately high heat until butter sizzles.
6. Meanwhile, stir batter and pour about 3 tablespoons into a 1/4-cup measuring cup.
7. Remove pan from heat and pour batter, all at once, into the center of the pan. Tilt pan to swirl batter into a thin film that coats the pan. Return to heat.
8. As the crêpe begins to brown, use a long narrow spatula to loosen the edges of the crêpe from the pan. The crêpe may also be loosened by banging the edge of the pan on a pot holder or towel placed on the work surface. When the crêpe has browned, about 1 minute, using your fingers and the spatula placed completely under the diameter of the crêpe, turn it over. Brown the other side, about 1/2 minute, then invert crêpe onto a plate.
9. Repeat Steps 4 to 8 until all the crêpes are made. The crêpes may be piled on top of each other. They may be covered with plastic wrap and refrigerated for a day before using.
10. When the crêpes are filled, the side that was browned first is usually the most attractive and should be on the outside of the rolled crêpe.

Yield: 12 crêpes.

Crêpes for Desserts

Prepare Crêpes for Entrées (p. 247) but stir the following ingredients into the eggs and milk in Step 1:

1 1/2 teaspoons granulated sugar
1/4 teaspoon vanilla extract

Yield: 12 crêpes.

Cakes

*P*lease do not reach for a box of cake mix! A "from scratch" cake is always more delicious. Many of the cakes in this book may be made quickly with just a little more effort than required for a mix. Try the Yellow Layer Cake (p. 252), Butter Sponge (Génoise) Cake (p. 260), and Butter Sponge (Génoise) Cake Roll (p. 266) with their variations for superb flavor, texture, and ease of preparation. Once you do, I doubt you will ever settle for a box cake mix again.

Advice on Frosting Cakes

Be sure the cake is completely cool before frosting or the frosting will melt.

For easy handling or if you plan to put chopped nuts on the sides of a cake (p. 251), place the cake on a piece of cardboard of the same size and shape. The removable bottom of a tart pan or springform pan may also be used.

A wax paper shape made to fit the bottom of a cake will prevent a metal serving plate from being scratched when the cake is cut. Invert the pan used to bake the cake over a piece of wax paper. Then use the tip of a sharp knife or an ice pick to trace around the pan and score the paper. Pull the circular section apart from the rest of the wax paper or use scissors, if necessary.

Strips of wax paper will protect a serving dish from frosting spills. First, place the wax paper shape in the center of the serving plate. Then arrange three strips of wax paper so they form a triangle, cover the outer edges of the serving plate, and overlap the wax paper shape. Place cake on wax paper and frost the cake. Remove each paper strip by carefully pulling it away while holding the side of a spatula at the bottom of the cake to prevent frosting from pulling away from the cake.

If crumbs form easily when the cake is frosted, frost cake with a thin layer of frosting to hold the crumbs in place. Then apply the final layer of frosting.

To frost the top of a cake as smoothly as possible, keep as much of the length of the spatula edge as possible in contact with the frosting while it is spread.

The top of a cake may be attractively decorated using a spatula with a rounded tip. Start at one edge and draw the tip of the spatula back and forth across the top, creating parallel lines. After this is done, some of the frosting will extend over the edges. Use the spatula, pointing straight downward, to blend the overhanging frosting into the frosting on the sides of the cake.

ROSETTES

If desired, reserve some frosting for decorating the cake using a pastry bag and tip (tube). You need not spend a lot of time learning elaborate decorative techniques. Even if you only learn to make rosettes, you will produce elegant looking cakes. If the tops of the rosettes are not perfect, a piece of fruit, nut, or candy will cover any irregular places. I like to use a 12-inch pastry bag for piping frostings. The two tips I use most often for making rosettes are 1/2-inch in diameter, have fluted openings, and are known as rosette or star tips. One has wide teeth (#5) and the other narrow teeth (#5B).

To fill the pastry bag, place the wide end between your thumb and fingers with the tip end pointed downward. Open bag until about half of it is folded back and covers your hand. Use a rubber spatula to fill the bag no more than half full. Avoid getting any filling on the inside of the upper half of the bag.

Twist the top of the pastry bag to cover the filling. Avoid enclosing any air pockets. Hold the twisted part between the thumb and index finger of your writing hand. This will prevent filling from coming out of the top. For best results, use your writing hand to force the filling from the bag. Your non-writing hand should only guide the tip and not be used to force the filling from the bag. Before piping, place the tip close to the surface of the cake. Twist top of bag as needed to maintain pressure on the filling.

To make a rosette, pipe a circle and then continue to pipe a smaller circle on top of the first one. Move the tip to the center of the rosette, release pressure on the bag, and then with one quick motion pull tip up to separate it from the rosette.

Rosettes are usually placed around the edge on top of the cake. A large rosette may be placed in the center.

NUTS

Chopped pecans, walnuts, or almonds may be pressed on the sides of a frosted cake. Use about 1/2 cup of chopped nuts for a 9-inch, 2 or 3-layer cake. Use one hand to hold the cake (on a cardboard circle or the bottom of a removable tart or springform pan) over a pie pan containing the nuts. Use your other hand to sprinkle the nuts on the cake. Nuts that do not adhere will fall into the pan to be reused.

Pecan or walnut halves may be evenly spaced around the top edge of a frosted cake.

CHERRIES (CANDIED OR MARASCHINO)

Whole or halved cherries may be alternated with nut halves around the top edge of a cake. Whole cherries can be used as candle holders. Insert the candles into the holes made where the pits were removed.

Yellow Layer Cake

A moist cake with a fine and even texture.

FOR ONE, 1 1/2-INCH HIGH, 9-INCH ROUND LAYER CAKE

2 large eggs
1 teaspoon vanilla extract
3/4 cup granulated sugar
1/4 cup (1/2 stick) butter, preferably unsalted, or margarine

1/2 cup milk
1 cup sifted cake flour
1 teaspoon baking powder
1/8 teaspoon salt

FOR TWO, 1 1/2-INCH HIGH, OR THREE, 1-INCH HIGH, 9-INCH ROUND LAYER CAKES

4 large eggs
1 1/2 teaspoons vanilla extract
1 2/3 cups granulated sugar
1/2 cup (1 stick) butter, preferably unsalted, or margarine

1 cup milk
2 cups sifted cake flour
2 1/2 teaspoons baking powder
1/4 teaspoon salt

1. Break eggs into an electric mixer bowl. Place bowl over hot water. Stir occasionally until eggs are warm. Add vanilla.

2. Use a wire whisk attachment, if available, to beat eggs at high speed for 20 seconds. Pour in sugar and continue to beat until light yellow and thick, about 5 to 7 minutes.

3. While the eggs are beating, heat butter and milk in a 1 1/2-quart saucepan until butter melts and milk scalds. Keep hot until needed.

4. Sift flour, baking powder, and salt together. Add to beaten eggs. Mix only until blended. Use a rubber spatula to clean the sides of the bowl as needed. The batter will be quite thick.

5. Add the hot milk mixture and mix only until blended. The batter will be liquid.

6. Immediately pour batter into buttered and floured layer cake pan(s). Drop pan(s) twice from about 2-inches above the work surface to remove any large bubbles.

7. Place pan(s) on a rack in the middle of a preheated 350° F oven. Bake until golden brown and a cake tester comes out clean, about 18 to 20 minutes for 1 1/2-inch high cakes and 15 to 18 minutes for 1-inch high cakes.

8. Cool in pan(s) for 5 minutes before turning out onto a wire rack(s).

9. Cool completely before frosting.

Notes:

1. The layer cake(s) may be used to make Coconut Layer Cake (p. 255), Coconut Pineapple (or Lemon) Layer Cake (p. 255), Boston Cream Pie (p. 258), or Easter Bunny Cake (p. 258).

2. The cakes may be frosted with any of the frostings listed in the index.

3. The layers may be moistened with Rum or Liqueur Syrup (p. 287) before frosting.

4. The bottom layer may be spread with raspberry jam before the cake is frosted.

5. Chopped nuts may be pressed on the sides of the frosted cake (p. 251).

Lemon Layer Cake

FOR TWO, 1 1/2-INCH HIGH, OR THREE, 1-INCH HIGH, 9-INCH ROUND LAYER CAKES

Follow the recipe for Yellow Layer Cake (p. 252) with the following changes:

1. Reduce vanilla extract to 1/2 teaspoon.

2. In Step 3, stir 1 teaspoon of finely grated lemon rind into the milk and butter mixture.

Notes:

1. The layer cakes may be filled and frosted with Marshmallow Frosting (p. 292). They may also be filled with Lemon Cake Filling (p. 287) and frosted with Lemon Buttercream (p. 291) or Marshmallow Frosting (p. 292).

2. Sliced or chopped toasted almonds (1/2 cup) may be pressed on the sides of the frosted cake (p. 251).

Orange Layer Cake

**FOR TWO, 1 1/2-INCH HIGH, OR THREE, 1-INCH HIGH,
9-INCH ROUND LAYER CAKES**

Follow the recipe for Lemon Layer Cake (p. 253) but substitute the finely grated rind of a large orange (about 2 1/2 teaspoons) for the lemon rind.

Note: The cakes may be frosted with Orange Buttercream (p. 291) or Marshmallow Frosting (p. 292).

Spice Layer Cake

**FOR TWO, 1 1/2-INCH HIGH, OR THREE, 1-INCH HIGH,
9-INCH ROUND LAYER CAKES**

Follow the recipe for Yellow Layer Cake (p. 252) with the following changes:

1. Reduce vanilla extract to 1 teaspoon.
2. Use 1 cup of granulated sugar and 2/3 cup of light brown sugar, firmly packed, instead of 1 2/3 cups of granulated sugar.
3. In Step 4, sift flour and baking powder with the following spices:

1 teaspoon ground cinnamon   **1/4 teaspoon grated nutmeg**
1/2 teaspoon ground allspice   **1/4 teaspoon ground cloves**

Notes:
1. Frost the cakes with Brown Sugar Marshmallow Frosting (p. 292).
2. Coarsely chopped walnuts or pecans (1 1/4 cups) may be sprinkled on the sides of the cake (p. 251).

Coconut Layer Cake

1 2/3 cups (7 ounces) grated
fresh, frozen, or packaged
coconut (p. 16)
Yellow Layer Cake (p. 252)
(three, 1-inch high, 9-inch
round layers)

7 cups Marshmallow Frosting
(p. 292)

1. The coconut may be toasted by stirring it frequently on a rimmed baking sheet in a 350° F oven.
2. Frost one layer and sprinkle with 1/3 cup of coconut. Cover with second layer, frost, and sprinkle with 1/3 cup of coconut. Place third layer on top and finish frosting cake.
3. Sprinkle remaining coconut on top and sides of cake.

Yield: One 9-inch (3-layer) cake, 12 servings.

Coconut Pineapple (or lemon) Layer Cake

Yellow Layer Cake (p. 252)
(three, 1-inch high, 9-inch
round layers)
Pineapple Cake Filling
(p. 288) or Lemon Cake
Filling (p. 287)

1 2/3 cups (7 ounces) grated
fresh, frozen, or packaged
coconut (p. 16)
3 cups Marshmallow Frosting
(p. 292)

1. Spread one layer with half the filling. Sprinkle with 1/3 cup of coconut. Cover with second layer and spread with remaining filling. Sprinkle with 1/3 cup of coconut. Top with third layer.
2. Frost cake and sprinkle remaining coconut on top and sides of cake.

Yield: One 9-inch (3-layer) cake, 12 servings.

Chocolate Layer Cake

**FOR TWO, 1 1/2-INCH HIGH, OR THREE, 1-INCH HIGH,
9-INCH ROUND LAYER CAKES**

2/3 cup unsweetened cocoa
1 cup water
3/4 cup (1 1/2 sticks)
  butter or margarine, at
  room temperature
2 cups granulated sugar
3 large eggs, at room
  temperature

1 1/2 teaspoons vanilla
  extract
2 1/2 cups sifted cake flour
1 teaspoon baking soda
1/4 teaspoon salt

1. Place cocoa in a small bowl. Bring water to a boil and pour over cocoa. Stir until blended. Cool to room temperature and reserve.

2. In an electric mixer, cream the butter. Add sugar and beat until fluffy.

3. Beat in eggs, one at a time, until smooth and light in color. Stir in vanilla.

4. Sift flour, baking soda, and salt together. Add flour mixture to mixer alternately with cocoa mixture. Start and end with flour mixture using about one-quarter each time. Add one-third of the cocoa mixture each time. Be sure ingredients are mixed thoroughly after each addition but no more than necessary. Use a rubber spatula to scrape sides of bowl as needed.

5. Pour batter into buttered and floured layer cake pans.

6. Bake in a preheated 350° F oven until a cake tester comes out clean, about 30 minutes for 1 1/2-inch high cakes and 20 minutes for 1-inch high cakes. Cool cakes in pans for 5 minutes before turning out onto wire racks.

Notes:

1. The layer cakes may be frosted with Marshmallow Frosting (p. 292), Chocolate Frosting (p. 293), Chocolate, Chocolate Mocha or Coffee Buttercream (p. 290), Quick Chocolate Buttercream (p. 291), or Penuche Frosting (p. 296).

2. The layers may be moistened with Rum or Liqueur Syrup (p. 287) before frosting.

3. The bottom layer cake may be spread with raspberry jam before the cake is frosted.

4. Chopped nuts may be pressed on the sides of the cake (p. 251).

Devil's Food Cake

Blame the devil if you eat too much of this temptation!

3 large eggs
1 teaspoon vanilla extract
1 cup granulated sugar
3/4 cup light brown sugar,
  firmly packed
1/2 cup (1 stick) butter or
  margarine

4 ounces (4 squares)
  unsweetened chocolate
1 1/4 cups milk
2 1/4 cups sifted cake flour
1 1/4 teaspoons baking soda
7 cups Marshmallow Frosting
  (p. 292) (optional)

1. Break eggs into an electric mixer bowl. Place bowl over hot water and stir occasionally until eggs are warm. Add vanilla.

2. Use a wire whisk attachment, if available, to beat eggs at high speed for 1 minute. Gradually beat in granulated and brown sugar and continue to beat until light yellow and thick, about 5 to 7 minutes.

3. While eggs are beating, combine butter and chocolate in a heavy 1 1/2-quart saucepan. Stir over moderate heat until melted. Add milk. Heat and stir until smooth. Remove from heat. Reserve.

4. Sift flour and baking soda together. Add to beaten egg mixture. Mix only until smooth. The batter will be quite thick. Use a rubber spatula to scrape sides of bowl as needed.

5. Add chocolate mixture. Mix only until blended.

6. Pour batter into 2 buttered and floured 9-inch round layer cake pans.

8. Drop each pan twice from about 2-inches above the work surface to remove any large bubbles.

9. Bake in a preheated 350° F oven until a cake tester comes out clean, about 25 to 30 minutes. Cool cakes in pans for 5 minutes before turning out onto wire racks.

10. Cool completely before frosting with Marshmallow Frosting or another frosting.

Yield: One 9-inch layer cake, 10 to 12 servings.

Boston Cream Pie

Yellow Layer Cake (p. 252)
(one, 1 1/2-inch high, 9-inch
round layer)
Cream Filling for Pastries
(Crème Pâtissière) (p. 350)

Chocolate Glaze (p. 297)

1. Split cake into two layers.
2. Spread cream filling on the bottom layer to within 1/2-inch of the edge. Top with other layer.
3. Spread glaze on top of cake.
4. Refrigerate until served.

Yield: One 9-inch cake, 6 to 8 servings.

Easter Bunny Cake

This delightful cake is fun and easy to decorate yet looks like a professional cake decorator made it. Make it for adults as well as children!

Yellow Layer Cake (p. 252),
Lemon Layer Cake (p. 253),
Orange Layer Cake (p. 254),
Chocolate Layer Cake
(p. 256), or Devil's Food
Cake (p. 257) (two, 1 1/2-inch
high, 9-inch round layers)
7 cups Marshmallow Frosting
(p. 292)

1 2/3 cups (7 ounces) grated
fresh, frozen, or packaged
coconut (p. 16)
2 drops red food coloring
2 drops green food coloring
18 jelly beans (assorted
colors)
Licorice sticks, red or black

1. See illustration, next page. Cover a tray or baking sheet with wax paper. Cut one of the cakes into ears and a bow tie using the edge of a cake pan as a guide. Arrange cakes on tray as shown. Place pieces of wax paper under edges of cake. These will prevent frosting from getting on tray and will be removed after cake is frosted.
2. Frost cake with marshmallow frosting.

3. In a small bowl, combine about 1/2 cup of the coconut, red food coloring, and 1/2 teaspoon of water. Mix thoroughly until coconut is colored pink. Arange some of this coconut lengthwise down the center of each ear and use the remainder to cover the bow tie.

4. In a similar manner, color another 1/2 cup of coconut green. Reserve.

5. Sprinkle the remaining coconut over the rest of the cake. Remove wax paper strips.

6. Use 2 blue or purple jelly beans for the eyes and a pink or yellow jelly bean for the nose. Arrange remaining jelly beans on the bow tie. Place pieces of licorice sticks for eyebrows, mouth, and whiskers.

7. Cover the tray surrounding the cake with the green coconut.

Yield: 12 servings.

Butter Sponge (Génoise) Cake

This cake is a snap to make. An electric mixer does all the work.

FOR ONE 9-INCH ROUND LAYER CAKE

3 large eggs
1 teaspoon vanilla extract
1/2 cup granulated sugar
3/4 cup sifted cake flour

1/8 teaspoon salt
2 tablespoons (1/4 stick) butter (no substitute), preferably unsalted, melted

**FOR TWO 9-INCH ROUND LAYER CAKES OR
ONE 10-INCH ROUND LAYER CAKE**

6 large eggs
1 1/2 teaspoons vanilla extract
3/4 cup + 2 tablespoons granulated sugar

1 1/2 cups sifted cake flour
1/4 teaspoon salt
5 tablespoons butter (no substitute), preferably unsalted, melted

FOR ONE 9-INCH SQUARE LAYER CAKE

5 large eggs
1 1/2 teaspoons vanilla extract
3/4 cup granulated sugar
1 1/4 cups sifted cake flour

1/4 teaspoon salt
1/4 cup (1/2 stick) butter (no substitute), preferably unsalted, melted

1. Break eggs into an electric mixer bowl. Place bowl over hot water. Stir occasionally until eggs are warm. Add vanilla.

2. Use a wire whisk attachment, if available, to beat eggs at high speed for 20 seconds. Pour in sugar and continue to beat until light yellow and thick, about 5 to 7 minutes.

3. Sift flour and salt together. After eggs are beaten, use a strainer to sift a third of the flour over the egg mixture. Fold in with a large rubber spatula until partially blended. Repeat with each remaining third of flour. Continue to fold until mixture is thoroughly blended but no more than necessary.

4. Pour butter over batter. Fold in thoroughly but use as few strokes as possible.

5. Pour batter into buttered and floured pan(s). Drop pan(s) twice from about 2-inches above the work surface to remove any large bubbles.

6. Bake in a preheated 350° F oven until a cake tester comes out clean, about 20 to 25 minutes. Cool cake(s) in pan(s) for 5 minutes before turning out onto a wire rack(s).

7. Cool completely before frosting.

Notes:

1. The cake(s) may be used to make Strawberry and Other Fruit Shortcakes (p. 262), Lemon Almond Cake (p. 263), or Chocolate Buttercream Cake (p. 265).

2. The cakes may be frosted with any of the Buttercreams (pp. 290 - 291).

3. The layers may be moistened with Rum or Liqueur Syrup (p. 287) before frosting.

4. The bottom layer may be spread with raspberry jam before the cake is frosted.

5. Chopped nuts may be pressed on the sides of the frosted cake (p. 251).

6. The cake(s) may be served plain or sprinkled with confectioners' sugar.

Strawberry and Other Fruit Shortcakes

This is a delectable dessert to make for a few people or a large crowd. Since the cake can be made quickly, enough shortcake may be prepared in a few hours to serve 100 or more guests.

FOR 8 SERVINGS
Butter Sponge (Génoise)
Cake (p. 260) (one 9-inch
round or square layer)
Whipped Cream for Desserts
(p. 371)

1 pint strawberries or other
fruit (sliced or whole),
sugared

FOR 12 SERVINGS
Butter Sponge (Génoise)
Cake (p. 260) (one 10-inch
round layer)
2 recipes Whipped Cream
for Desserts (p. 371)

2 pints strawberries or other
fruit (sliced or whole),
sugared

FOR A CROWD (12 TO 16 SERVINGS PER RECIPE)
Butter Sponge (Génoise)
Cake (p. 260) (batter for one
10-inch round layer,
prepared through Step 4)
1/4 cup confectioners'
sugar

2 recipes Whipped Cream
for Desserts (p. 371)
2 pints strawberries or
other fruit (sliced or
whole), sugared

FOR 8 OR 12 SERVINGS
1. Cut the 9-inch cake into 8 pieces or the 10-inch cake into 12 pieces.

2. Split each piece of cake into 2 or 3 layers.

3. Immediately before serving, place a spoonful of whipped cream and strawberries between the layers and on top of each portion.

FOR A CROWD (12 TO 16 SERVINGS PER RECIPE)

1. Butter an 18 x 13 x 1-inch baking sheet which is known as a half-bun pan in the restaurant supply trade. Line pan with wax paper. The paper should extend about 1-inch over each of the short ends of the pan. Butter wax paper.

2. Spread batter in prepared pan. Drop pan twice from about 2-inches above the work surface to remove any large bubbles.

3. Bake cake in a preheated 375° F oven until a cake tester comes out clean, about 10 minutes. Do not overbake.

4. While cake is baking, sift confectioners' sugar over a towel slightly larger than the pan.

5. When cake is done, immediately invert pan onto towel. Lift pan off cake. Peel off wax paper.

6. After cake is cool, cut into 12 to 16 pieces.

7. Immediately before serving, top each portion with a spoonful of whipped cream and strawberries.

Lemon Almond Cake

An elegant cake for special occasions.

Butter Sponge (Génoise)
  Cake (p. 260) (one 10-inch
  round layer)
Lemon Cake Filling (p. 287)

Lemon Buttercream (p. 291)
1/2 cup sliced almonds,
  toasted

1. Split cake into 3 layers. Spread lemon filling between layers.

2. Frost top and sides of cake with buttercream. Use a spatula to make parallel lines on top of the cake (p. 250).

3. Use a pastry bag with a 1/2-inch star tip (#5 or 5B) to pipe 32 rosettes around the edge on top of the cake. The rosettes should just touch each other.

4. Insert an almond slice between each of the rosettes. Press remaining almond slices on the sides of the cake.

5. Refrigerate. Let reach room temperature before serving.

Yield: One 10-inch round layer cake, 12 to 16 servings.

Chocolate Butter Sponge (Génoise) Cake

FOR TWO 9-INCH ROUND LAYER CAKES OR
ONE 10-INCH ROUND LAYER CAKE

6 large eggs
1 teaspoon vanilla extract
1 cup granulated sugar
6 tablespoons sifted
  unsweetened cocoa (use
  a tea strainer to sift)

1 1/4 cups sifted cake flour
1/4 teaspoon salt
1/4 cup (1/2 stick) butter
  (no substitute), preferably
  unsalted, melted

1. Follow the recipe for Butter Sponge (Génoise) Cake (p. 260) using ingredients listed above.

2. In Step 3, sift the cocoa with the flour and salt, stir together, and sift over beaten eggs as described.

Notes:

1. The cakes may be frosted with Vanilla, Chocolate, Chocolate Mocha, or Coffee Buttercream (p. 290) or Quick Chocolate Buttercream (p. 291).

2. The 10-inch cake may be used to make Chocolate Buttercream Cake (p. 265).

3. The layers may be moistened with Rum or Liqueur Syrup (p. 287) before frosting.

4. The bottom layer may be spread with raspberry jam before the cake is frosted.

5. Chopped nuts may be pressed on the sides of the frosted cake (p. 251).

6. The cake(s) may be served plain or sprinkled with confectioners' sugar.

Chocolate Buttercream Cake

This classy cake has a variety of flavors that blend together beautifully.

2 recipes Buttercream (p. 289) (prepared through Step 4)

2 teaspoons vanilla extract or rum OR 1 tablespoon instant coffee granules dissolved in 2 teaspoons hot water

4 ounces (4 squares) semisweet chocolate, melted and cooled to room temperature

1 pound (4 sticks) butter (no substitute), preferably unsalted (to complete buttercream)

Chocolate Butter Sponge (Génoise) Cake (p. 264) or Butter Sponge (Génoise) Cake (p. 260) (one 10-inch round layer)

Rum or Liqueur Syrup (p. 287) (optional)

1/3 cup raspberry jam (optional)

16 maraschino or candied cherry halves and 1 whole cherry (optional)

3 ounces (3 squares) semisweet chocolate, melted (for making chocolate circles) (optional)

1/2 cup sliced almonds, toasted (optional)

1. Divide buttercream mixture in half. Add vanilla, rum, or coffee to one half. Beat until blended. Reserve. Add chocolate to remaining buttercream. Beat until blended. Reserve.

2. In an electric mixer with a paddle attachment, if available, whip the butter. Replace paddle attachment with a wire whisk attachment, if available. Beat half the butter, 2 tablespoons at a time, into each buttercream until smooth and light. Reserve.

3. Split cake into 3 layers. Use a pastry brush to brush bottom layer with a third of the rum syrup. Spread the layer with raspberry jam.

4. If the chocolate butter sponge cake is used, use the vanilla, rum, or coffee buttercream to spread between the layers and, if desired, reserve some for rosettes. Use the chocolate buttercream to frost the cake. If the butter sponge cake is used, either one of the buttercreams may be used to fill the cake and make rosettes. Use the other buttercream to frost the cake.

5. Spread a thin layer of the desired buttercream on top of the jam. Place the middle cake layer on top. Brush with a third of the rum syrup. Spread a thin layer of buttercream on the layer.

6. Place last layer on top. Brush with rum syrup. Any remaining syrup may be brushed on the sides of the cake. Frost top and sides of cake with the other buttercream.

7. Decorate cake as desired.

One suggestion: Use a pastry bag with a 1/2-inch star tip (#5 or 5B) to pipe 16 rosettes around the top edge of the cake and a larger one in the center. Place half a cherry on top of each rosette at the edge of the cake. Place a whole cherry on the large rosette. Cut nine or ten 2-inch circles out of wax paper. Spread chocolate over shapes. Refrigerate shapes until firm. Peel off wax paper and press chocolate circles on frosting on sides of cake.

Another suggestion: Decorate the cake with rosettes and cherries as described above. Omit chocolate circles and press sliced almonds on the sides of the cake.

8. Refrigerate. Let reach room temperature before serving.

Yield: One 10-inch cake, 12 to 16 servings.

Butter Sponge (Génoise) Cake Roll

Cake rolls are great fun and the ideal solution for a fast yet sensational dessert.

3 large eggs
1 teaspoon vanilla extract
1/2 cup granulated sugar
3/4 cup sifted cake flour
1/8 teaspoon salt

2 tablespoons (1/4 stick)
   butter (no substitute),
   preferably unsalted, melted
2 tablespoons confectioners'
   sugar

1. Break eggs into an electric mixer bowl. Place bowl over hot water. Stir occasionally until eggs are warm. Add vanilla.

2. Use a wire whisk attachment, if available, to beat eggs at high speed for 20 seconds. Pour in sugar and continue to beat until light yellow and thick, about 5 to 7 minutes.

3. Meanwhile, butter a 15 x 11 x 1-inch rimmed baking sheet. Line pan with wax paper. The paper should extend about 1-inch over each of the short ends of the pan. Butter the wax paper.

4. Sift flour and salt together. After eggs are beaten, use a strainer to sift a third of the flour over the egg mixture. Fold in with a large rubber spatula until partially blended. Repeat with each remaining third of flour. Continue to fold until mixture is thoroughly blended but no more than necessary.

5. Pour butter over batter. Fold in thoroughly but use as few strokes as possible.

6. Spread batter in prepared pan. Drop pan twice from about 2-inches above the work surface to remove any large bubbles.

7. Bake in a preheated 375° F oven until a cake tester comes out clean, about 8 to 10 minutes. Do not overbake.

8. While cake is baking, sift confectioners' sugar over a cloth towel slightly larger than the pan.

9. When cake is done, immediately invert pan onto towel. Lift pan off cake. Peel off wax paper.

10. Starting at a short side, roll up the cake and towel together to form a smooth roll. Cool on a wire rack.

11. When completely cool, unroll cake, spread with desired filling, and roll up.

Yield: One cake roll, 8 to 10 servings.

Lemon or Pineapple Cake Roll

1. Fill a Butter Sponge (Génoise) Cake Roll (p. 266) with Lemon Cake Filling (p. 287) or Pineapple Cake Filling (p. 288).

2. Frost with Marshmallow Frosting (p. 292) and sprinkle with 1/2 cup of coconut or toasted sliced almonds. Alternatively, the frosting may be omitted and the cake roll sprinkled with confectioners' sugar.

Yield: One cake roll, 8 to 10 servings.

Jelly Roll

1. Fill a Butter Sponge (Génoise) Cake Roll (p. 266) with 1 cup of your favorite jelly or jam. I like raspberry or currant.
2. Sprinkle with confectioners' sugar or frost with Marshmallow Frosting (p. 292).

Yield: One cake roll, 8 to 10 servings.

Strawberry Cake Roll

1 pint fresh strawberries
1 1/2 tablespoons granulated
  sugar
1 teaspoon unflavored gelatin
4 teaspoons cold water
1 cup (1/2 pint) whipping
  cream

6 tablespoons confectioners'
  sugar, divided
1/4 teaspoon vanilla extract
Butter Sponge (Génoise)
  Cake Roll (p. 266)

1. Remove stems from strawberries. Reserve 8 berries to garnish the top. Slice remaining berries, toss with granulated sugar, and reserve.
2. In a heatproof custard cup or small bowl, dissolve gelatin in water. Reserve.
3. In an electric mixer, combine cream, 4 tablespoons of confectioners' sugar, and vanilla. Use a wire whisk attachment, if available, and beat at moderate speed until the cream holds the impressions made by the beater and is thick enough to retain its shape. Do not overbeat or the cream will become grainy and separate.
4. If an electric mixer is not available, use a large whisk and a stainless steel bowl placed over cold water and ice cubes.
5. Place the cup containing the gelatin in a saucepan of hot water. Heat and stir until gelatin is completely dissolved. Fold into whipped cream.
6. Unroll cooled cake roll and spread with cream.
7. Drain sugared strawberries and distribute them evenly over the whipped cream. Roll up cake roll.
8. Sift 2 tablespoons of confectioners' sugar on the top of the cake roll.

9. Arrange the reserved strawberries (either whole or sliced and overlapping) down the center of the cake roll.

10. Refrigerate until served. Serve as soon as possible.

Yield: One cake roll, 8 to 10 servings.

Note: A long layer cake may be made instead of a cake roll. Cool the cake without rolling it. Cut the cake lengthwise into two strips. Spread one strip with whipped cream and sprinkle with sliced strawberries. Cover with other strip. Sprinkle with confectioners' sugar and garnish with reserved strawberries.

Chocolate Butter Sponge (Génoise) Cake Roll

3 large eggs
1/2 teaspoon vanilla extract
1/2 cup granulated sugar
3 tablespoons sifted
  unsweetened cocoa (use
  a tea strainer to sift)
1/2 cup + 2 tablespoons
  sifted cake flour

1/8 teaspoon salt
2 tablespoons (1/4 stick)
  butter (no substitute),
  preferably unsalted, melted
2 tablespoons confectioners'
  sugar

1. Follow the recipe for Butter Sponge (Génoise) Cake Roll (p. 266) using the above ingredients.

2. In Step 4, sift the cocoa with the flour and salt, stir together, and sift over the beaten eggs as described.

Yield: One cake roll, 8 to 10 servings.

Note: This cake roll may be filled with Whipped Cream for Desserts (p. 371), sprinkled with confectioners' sugar, and served with Chocolate Sauce (p. 373) or Chocolate Fudge Sauce (p. 373). The cake roll may be filled and frosted with Vanilla, Chocolate, Chocolate Mocha, or Coffee Buttercream (p. 290). The cake roll may also be used to prepare Chocolate Cake Roll (p. 270).

Chocolate Cake Roll

CAKE
Chocolate Butter Sponge (Génoise) Cake Roll (p. 269)

WHIPPED CREAM FILLING
1 cup (1/2 pint) whipping
  cream
2 tablespoons confectioners'
  sugar

1 teaspoon vanilla or almond
  extract

CHOCOLATE GLAZE
2 ounces (2 squares)
  semisweet chocolate

1/2 cup whipping cream

1. When cake is cool, combine filling ingredients in an electric mixer bowl. Beat at medium speed, using a wire whisk attachment, if available, until the cream holds the impressions made by the beater and is thick enough to retain its shape. Do not overbeat or the cream will become grainy and separate.

2. Unroll cake, spread with filling, and roll up. Refrigerate while preparing glaze.

3. In a heavy 1/2-quart saucepan, combine chocolate and whipping cream. Stir over low heat until chocolate is melted and mixture is smooth. Cool to room temperature. Spread over chilled cake.

4. Refrigerate until served.

Yield: One cake roll, 8 to 10 servings.

Bûche de Noël (Yule Log Cake)

Time-consuming but lots of fun. Children love to make the marzipan figures and help decorate the cake. You will want to use this cake as a centerpiece for your Christmas dinner table. See illustration, next page.

CAKE ROLL

4 large eggs
1/2 teaspoon vanilla extract
2/3 cup granulated sugar
1/4 cup sifted unsweetened cocoa (use a tea strainer to sift)
3/4 cup sifted cake flour

1/8 teaspoon salt
3 tablespoons butter (no substitute), preferably unsalted, melted
2 tablespoons confectioners' sugar

BUTTERCREAM

Coffee Buttercream (p. 290)

3 ounces (3 squares) semisweet chocolate, melted

DECORATIONS

Meringue Mushrooms (p. 298) (optional)
Holly leaves, berries, and snowmen made from Marzipan (p. 299) (optional)

Confectioners' sugar for dusting (optional)

1. Prepare cake roll: Use the above ingredients and the directions for Chocolate Butter Sponge (Génoise) Cake Roll (p. 269) but roll cake up from a long side rather than a short one.
2. Combine 1 cup of the coffee buttercream with the melted chocolate. Beat until blended. Reserve.
3. Unroll cooled cake roll, spread with remaining coffee buttercream, and roll up.
4. Place cake on a long board or serving dish. A 16 x 4 1/2-inch strip of cardboard covered with green foil may be placed under the cake. Put a strip of wax paper under each of the sides and ends of the cake to protect the foil-covered cardboard and serving dish from frosting spills.
5. Cut a diagonal piece of cake off of each end. The cuts should be parallel to each other. Place one of these pieces on top of the cake near one end. Place the other on a side of the cake near the other end. These represent the stubs of cut-off branches.

6. Frost the cake with the chocolate buttercream. Use a table knife with a blunt tip to create a rough bark-like appearance. On the ends of the cake and stubs leave the coffee buttercream uncovered to resemble tree rings.

7. Remove paper strips by slowly pulling each of them away while holding the side of a knife at the bottom of the cake to prevent frosting from pulling away from the cake.

8. The yule log may be further decorated with meringue mushrooms and marzipan holly leaves, berries, and snowmen. A light sprinkling of confectioners' sugar will simulate snow.

9. Refrigerate until served.

Yield: One cake roll, 8 to 10 servings.

Lemon Chiffon Cake

A very light cake that reminds me of cotton candy.

6 large eggs, separated
1 1/8 cups granulated sugar
3 tablespoons lemon juice
1 tablespoon water
1 tablespoon finely grated
  lemon rind

1/2 teaspoon vanilla extract
1/2 teaspoon cream of tartar
3/4 cup all-purpose flour

1. In an electric mixer, with a wire whisk attachment, if available, beat egg yolks and sugar together until thick and light yellow.

2. Add lemon juice, water, rind, and vanilla. Stir until blended. Reserve.

3. Use an electric mixer to beat egg whites until foamy. Add cream of tartar and continue to beat until whites are stiff but not dry. Reserve.

4. Use a strainer to sift flour. Return flour to strainer and sift a third of the flour over the egg yolk mixture. Fold in flour until partially blended. Repeat with each remaining third of flour. Continue to fold until mixture is thoroughly blended but no more than necessary. A large rubber spatula, about 13 1/2-inches long, from a restaurant supply store, is quite helpful for folding in the large volume of ingredients in this recipe.

5. Fold about one-third of the egg whites into the batter. Gently but thoroughly fold in remaining whites.

6. Turn batter into a 10-inch unbuttered tube pan. Remove any air pockets by pressing the surface of the batter with a rubber spatula.

7. Bake in a preheated 325° F oven until a cake tester comes out clean, about 55 minutes.

8. Invert pan onto a wire rack. Be sure at least 6-inches of air can circulate under cake. This will prevent the cake from becoming wet as it cools. Cool cake completely. Use a metal spatula to loosen the cake from the sides of the pan and a narrow knife to loosen it from the inner cone.

Yield: One 10-inch tube cake, 10 to 12 servings.

Note: This cake may be frosted with Lemon Frosting (p. 294) or Lemon Buttercream (p. 291) and covered with 3/4 cup of toasted sliced almonds.

Orange Chiffon Cake

Prepare Lemon Chiffon Cake (p. 272) but instead of the lemon juice, water, and lemon rind, use 1 tablespoon of lemon juice, 3 tablespoons of orange juice, and 1 tablespoon of finely grated orange rind.

Note: This cake may be frosted with Orange Frosting (p. 294) or Orange Buttercream (p. 291).

Sour Cream Pound Cake

1 cup (2 sticks) butter
(no substitute), at room
temperature
3 cups granulated sugar
6 large egg yolks, at room
temperature
1 1/2 teaspoons vanilla
extract

3 cups sifted cake flour
1/4 teaspoon salt
1/4 teaspoon baking soda
1 cup sour cream, at room
temperature
6 large egg whites, at room
temperature

1. In an electric mixer, cream the butter. Add sugar and beat until fluffy, about 5 minutes. Add egg yolks and vanilla. Beat until smooth.

2. Sift flour, salt, and baking soda together. Add one-quarter of the flour mixture to the mixer alternately with one-third of the sour cream. Start and end with the flour mixture. Be sure ingredients are mixed thoroughly after each addition but no more than necessary. Use a rubber spatula to scrape sides of bowl as needed.

3. Beat egg whites until stiff but not dry. Use a large whisk to fold egg whites into batter. Turn batter into a buttered and floured 10-inch tube pan. Smooth the surface of the batter.

4. Bake in a preheated 300° F oven until golden brown and a cake tester comes out clean, about 1 1/2 hours.

5. Cool cake in pan for 10 minutes and then turn out onto a wire rack.

6. Store cooled cake in an airtight container. This cake freezes well.

Yield: One 10-inch tube cake, 12 to 16 servings.

Notes:

1. This cake may be served plain, dusted with confectioners' sugar, or frosted with Vanilla (p. 293), Lemon (p. 294), or Orange Frosting (p. 294).

2. The frosted cake may be covered with 3/4 cup of toasted sliced almonds, chopped pecans, or walnuts.

Marble Pound Cake

1/2 cup (1 stick) butter (no substitute), at room temperature
1 cup granulated sugar
1 teaspoon vanilla extract
2 large eggs, at room temperature

2 cups sifted cake flour
1 teaspoon baking powder
1/2 cup milk, at room temperature
2 ounces (2 squares) semisweet chocolate, melted

1. In an electric mixer, cream the butter. Add sugar and beat until fluffy.

2. Beat in vanilla and eggs, one at a time, until smooth and light in color.

3. Sift flour and baking powder together. Add one-quarter of the flour mixture to the mixer alternately with one-third of the milk. Start and end with the flour mixture. Be sure ingredients are mixed thoroughly after each addition but no more than necessary. Use a rubber spatula to scrape sides of bowl as needed.

4. Pour about one-third of the batter into a small bowl. Add chocolate and stir until blended.

5. Butter and flour an 8 1/2 x 4 1/2 x 2 1/2-inch loaf pan. Add alternate spoonfuls of the two batters to the pan in an overlapping pattern to create a marbled effect. A table knife drawn through the batter in a zigzag fashion will produce a more intricately marbled effect.

6. Bake in a preheated 350° F oven until a cake tester comes out clean, about 1 hour. Cool cake in pan for 5 minutes before turning out onto a wire rack.

7. Store cooled cake in an airtight container. This cake freezes well.

Yield: One 8-inch loaf cake, 8 servings.

Lemon Bundt Cake

3/4 cup (1 1/2 sticks) butter or margarine, at room temperature
1 1/2 cups granulated sugar
3 large eggs, separated, at room temperature
2 1/2 cups sifted all-purpose flour

1 tablespoon baking powder
1 cup milk, at room temperature
1/2 teaspoon vanilla extract
1 tablespoon lemon juice
1 1/2 teaspoons finely grated lemon rind

1. In an electric mixer, cream the butter. Add sugar and beat until fluffy. Add yolks and beat until smooth and light in color.

2. Sift flour and baking powder together. Add one-quarter of the flour mixture to mixer alternately with one-third of the milk. Start and end with the flour mixture. Then add vanilla, lemon juice, and rind. Be sure ingredients are mixed thoroughly after each addition but no more than necessary. Use a rubber spatula to scrape sides of bowl as needed.

3. Beat egg whites until they form soft peaks. Fold into batter.

4. Turn batter into a buttered and floured 10-inch bundt or tube pan.

5. Bake in a preheated 325° F oven until golden brown and a cake tester comes out clean, about 50 minutes.

6. Cool cake in pan for 5 minutes and then turn out onto a wire rack.

Yield: One 10-inch tube cake, 12 to 16 servings.

Note: This cake may be served plain, dusted with confectioners' sugar, or frosted with Lemon Frosting (p. 294) and covered with 3/4 cup of toasted sliced almonds.

Orange Bundt Cake

Follow the recipe for Lemon Bundt Cake (see above) with the following changes:

1. Use 1 tablespoon of finely grated orange rind instead of the lemon rind.

2. Substitute 1/2 cup of orange juice for 1/2 cup of the milk.

Yield: One 10-inch tube cake, 12 to 16 servings.

Note: This cake may be served plain, dusted with confectioners' sugar, spread with Coconut, Pecan, and Orange Topping (p. 297), or frosted with Orange Frosting (p. 294).

Pecan Bundt Cake

3/4 cup (1 1/2 sticks) butter or margarine, at room temperature
1 1/2 cups light brown sugar, firmly packed
1 teaspoon vanilla extract
3 large eggs, separated, at room temperature

2 1/2 cups sifted all-purpose flour
1 tablespoon baking powder
1 cup milk, at room temperature
1 cup finely chopped pecans

1. In an electric mixer, cream the butter. Add brown sugar and beat until fluffy. Add vanilla and egg yolks. Beat until smooth and light in color.

2. Sift flour and baking powder together. Add one-quarter of the flour mixture to the mixer alternately with one-third of the milk. Start and end with the flour mixture. Be sure ingredients are mixed thoroughly after each addition but no more than necessary. Use a rubber spatula to scrape sides of bowl as needed.

3. Stir in pecans.

4. Beat egg whites until they form soft peaks. Fold into batter.

5. Turn batter into a buttered and floured 10-inch bundt or tube pan.

6. Bake in a preheated 325° F oven until golden brown and a cake tester comes out clean, about 1 hour.

7. Cool cake in pan for 5 minutes and then turn out onto a wire rack.

Yield: One 10-inch tube cake, 12 to 16 servings.

Note: This cake may be served plain, dusted with confectioners' sugar, or frosted with Caramel Icing (p. 296) and covered with 1 1/4 cups of chopped pecans.

Applesauce Cake

1/2 cup (1 stick) butter or margarine, at room temperature
2 cups granulated sugar
2 large eggs, at room temperature
1 teaspoon vanilla extract
1 can (16 ounces) applesauce
3 cups sifted all-purpose flour, divided
2 teaspoons ground cinnamon
1/2 teaspoon grated nutmeg
1/4 teaspoon ground cloves
1/4 teaspoon ground allspice
2 teaspoons baking soda
2 cups raisins
3/4 cup chopped walnuts or pecans
Cream Cheese Frosting (p. 288) (optional)
Walnut or pecan halves for decoration (optional)
Raisins for decoration (optional)

1. In an electric mixer, cream the butter. Add sugar and beat until fluffy.

2. Add eggs and vanilla. Beat until smooth and light yellow. Stir in applesauce. Reserve.

3. In a bowl, combine 2 1/2 cups of the flour, spices, and baking soda. Mix thoroughly and then sift. Add to mixer bowl. Mix only until blended.

4. Toss raisins and nuts with 1/2 cup of flour. Add to batter and stir until evenly distributed.

5. Turn batter into a buttered 9-inch tube pan.

6. Bake in a preheated 350° F oven until a cake tester comes out clean, about 1 1/4 hours. Cool cake in pan for 5 minutes before turning out onto a wire rack.

7. Frost cake after it has cooled. A table knife is useful for frosting the center of the cake. Decorate cake with walnuts and raisins.

Yield: One 9-inch tube cake, 12 to 16 servings.

Note: The cake may be served with Vanilla Ice Cream (p. 368) or Whipped Cream for Desserts (p. 371).

Pineapple Upside-Down Cake

3 tablespoons butter or
  margarine
1/3 cup dark brown sugar,
  firmly packed
3 tablespoons dark corn
  syrup
1 can (20 ounces) pineapple
  slices (9 slices), drained

9 maraschino cherries
3 large eggs
1/2 teaspoon vanilla extract
1/2 cup granulated sugar
1 cup sifted cake flour

1. Melt butter in a 9-inch square baking pan. Add brown sugar and corn syrup. Stir until smooth. Arrange 9 pineapple slices in one layer on top of the syrupy mixture. Press a cherry into the center of each slice. Reserve.

2. Break eggs into an electric mixer bowl. Place bowl over hot water. Stir occasionally until eggs are warm. Add vanilla.

3. Use a wire whisk attachment, if available, to beat eggs at high speed for 1 minute. Gradually beat in granulated sugar and continue to beat until light yellow and thick, about 5 to 7 minutes.

4. After eggs are beaten, use a strainer to sift a third of the flour over the egg mixture. Fold in with a large rubber spatula until partially blended. Repeat with each remaining third of flour. Continue to fold until mixture is thoroughly blended but no more than necessary.

5. Pour batter into prepared pan and spread evenly.

6. Bake in a preheated 350° F oven until a cake tester comes out clean, about 30 minutes. Immediately turn cake out onto a serving plate.

7. Serve immediately or within several hours.

Yield: One 9-inch square cake, 6 to 9 servings.

Note: This cake may be served with Whipped Cream for Desserts (p. 371).

Dutch Apple Cake

A superb coffee cake.

CRUMBS

2 tablespoons all-purpose
  flour
2/3 cup granulated sugar
1/2 teaspoon ground
  cinnamon

1/4 teaspoon grated nutmeg
2 tablespoons (1/4 stick)
  butter or margarine, chilled

APPLES

3 or 4 baking apples such
  as Cortland, McIntosh, or
  Rome Beauty

1 tablespoon lemon juice

CAKE

1/2 cup (1 stick) butter or
  margarine, at room
  temperature
1/2 cup granulated sugar
2 large eggs, at room
  temperature
1 teaspoon vanilla extract

2 tablespoons milk, at
  room temperature
1 1/3 cups sifted all-purpose
  flour
1 1/2 teaspoons baking
  powder

TOPPING
Whipped Cream for Desserts (p. 371) (optional)

1. Prepare crumbs: In a food processor bowl with a steel blade, combine flour, sugar, cinnamon, and nutmeg. Process for a few seconds until mixed. Add butter, cut into 1/2-inch cubes, and process until crumbs form. If a food processor is not available, combine dry ingredients in a bowl and use a pastry blender to cut in butter. Reserve.

2. Peel, quarter, and core apples. Slice apples, keeping slices of each quarter together. Brush lemon juice on apples. Reserve.

3. Prepare cake batter: Cream the butter in an electric mixer. Add sugar and beat until fluffy. Add eggs, one at a time, and beat until smooth. Add vanilla and milk. Beat until blended.

4. Sift flour and baking powder together. Add to mixer bowl. Mix only until blended.

5. Spread batter in a buttered 9-inch square cake pan.

6. On top of batter, arrange sliced apples in 3 rows. Sprinkle crumbs over apples.

7. Bake in a preheated 350° F oven until apples are tender and a cake tester comes out clean, about 45 minutes.

8. Cool cake in pan for 5 minutes before turning out onto a wire rack or serving plate.

9. This cake is best served warm while the topping is still crisp but it may be served at room temperature.

10. Serve with whipped cream.

Yield: One 9-inch square cake, 6 to 8 servings.

Blueberry Crumb Cake

CRUMBS
1 1/4 cups all-purpose flour
1/3 cup granulated sugar
1/2 teaspoon baking powder
1/2 teaspoon ground
  cinnamon

1/8 teaspoon grated nutmeg
1/4 cup (1/2 stick) butter or
  margarine, chilled
Finely grated rind of a lemon
1 large egg white

FILLING
1/4 cup granulated sugar
1/4 teaspoon ground
  cinnamon

Pinch grated nutmeg
1 pint fresh blueberries
2 teaspoons lemon juice

CAKE
1/2 cup (1 stick) butter or
  margarine, at room
  temperature
1/2 cup granulated sugar
1 large egg, at room
  temperature
1 large egg yolk, at room
  temperature

1 teaspoon vanilla extract
2 tablespoons milk, at
  room temperature
1 1/4 cups sifted all-purpose
  flour
1 1/2 teaspoons baking
  powder

TOPPING
2 tablespoons confectioners' sugar

1. Prepare crumbs: In a food processor bowl with a steel blade, combine flour, sugar, baking powder, cinnamon, and nutmeg. Process for a few seconds until mixed. Add butter, cut into 1/2-inch cubes, and lemon rind. Process until mixture resembles cornmeal. Add egg white and process until crumbs form. If a food processor is not available, combine dry ingredients in a bowl and use a pastry blender to cut in butter. Add lemon rind and egg white. Stir until crumbs form. Reserve.

2. Prepare filling: In a bowl, mix sugar, cinnamon, and nutmeg together. Add blueberries and lemon juice. Use a rubber spatula to gently toss the ingredients. Reserve.

3. Prepare cake batter: Cream the butter in an electric mixer. Add sugar and beat until fluffy. Add egg, egg yolk, vanilla, and milk. Beat until smooth.

4. Sift flour and baking powder together. Add to mixer bowl. Mix only until blended.

5. Spread batter in a buttered 9-inch square cake pan. Pour blueberry mixture over batter. Sprinkle crumbs over blueberries.

6. Bake in a preheated 350° F oven until a cake tester comes out clean, about 45 minutes. Cool cake in pan for 5 minutes before turning out onto a wire rack.

7. Use a small strainer to sift confectioners' sugar over cake.

8. Serve cake warm or at room temperature.

Yield: One 9-inch square cake, 6 to 8 servings.

Note: This cake may be served with Whipped Cream for Desserts (p. 371).

Cheesecake

Prepare this creamy treat at least a day before serving.

CRUST (OPTIONAL) (SEE NOTE 1, NEXT PAGE)

1 cup vanilla wafer or graham cracker crumbs OR 1/2 cup vanilla wafer or graham cracker crumbs and 1/2 cup finely ground pecans or toasted almonds

1/3 cup confectioners' sugar
1/2 teaspoon ground cinnamon (optional)
1/4 cup (1/2 stick) butter or margarine, melted

FILLING

3 packages (8 ounces each) cream cheese
1 cup granulated sugar
1 tablespoon lemon juice

1 teaspoon vanilla extract
1 1/2 cups sour cream
1/2 cup whipping cream
4 large eggs

1. Prepare crust: In a food processor or small bowl, mix all crust ingredients together to form crumbs. Press crumbs evenly on the bottom of a buttered 9-inch springform pan. Reserve.

2. Prepare filling: In an electric mixer, beat cream cheese until soft. Add granulated sugar and beat until fluffy. Beat in each of the remaining ingredients, in order listed, until smooth. Pour batter into prepared pan.

3. Bake in a preheated 250° F oven for 1 1/2 hours. Turn off heat and leave cheesecake in oven for 2 hours. Do not open oven door during this time. Remove cheesecake from oven and cool at room temperature for 3 hours. If cheesecake is refrigerated before it reaches room temperature, it will become watery.

4. Cover pan with plastic wrap. Refrigerate for at least 12 hours before serving.

5. Remove sides of springform pan. Invert cake onto a plate. Use a sharp knife to loosen and remove bottom of pan. Invert cake onto a serving dish.

6. Cover with plastic wrap. Refrigerate until served. The cake may be cut cleanly and easily with a piece of dental floss stretched between your hands.

Yield: One 9-inch cheesecake, 10 to 12 servings.

Notes:

1. If the crust is omitted, place 1/4 cup of vanilla wafer or graham cracker crumbs in the buttered pan. Rotate pan until bottom and sides are evenly coated.

2. This cheesecake may be served plain or with fresh fruit such as strawberries, raspberries, peaches, and blueberries, and/or Whipped Cream for Desserts (p. 371).

Strawberry Cheesecake

**1/2 recipe Whipped Cream for
   Desserts (p. 371)
Cheesecake (p. 283)**

**1 pint fresh strawberries,
   washed and stemmed**

1. Use a pastry bag with a 1/2-inch star tube (#5) to pipe 16 rosettes of whipped cream around the top edge of the cheesecake. Pipe a larger rosette in center of cake.

2. Place largest strawberry on rosette in center of cake. Arrange strawberries of equal size on the other rosettes.

3. Cut 7 or 8 strawberries lengthwise into halves. Equally space the halves on the sides of the cake with their cut surfaces against the cake and stem ends next to the plate.

4. Pipe small rosettes of whipped cream between the strawberry halves.

5. Refrigerate until served. Serve within several hours.

Yield: One 9-inch cheesecake, 10 to 12 servings.

Grand Marnier or (Amaretto) Orange Cheesecake

Prepare Cheesecake (p. 283) with the following changes:

1. Prepare crust with vanilla wafer crumbs and almonds. Mix 1 teaspoon of finely grated orange rind into crust ingredients.

2. Reduce vanilla extract to 1/2 teaspoon.

3. Add the following ingredients before adding sour cream in Step 2:

**4 teaspoons finely
  grated orange rind**

**2 tablespoons Grand Marnier
  or Amaretto liqueur**

Yield: One 9-inch cheesecake, 10 to 12 servings.

Note: This cheesecake may be garnished with Chocolate Sauce (p. 373). Warm the sauce so it will flow easily and pour it into a plastic squeeze bottle or a plastic sandwich bag with a tiny hole cut in one corner. On each serving plate, squeeze out continuous back and forth rows of sauce or make an irregular design. Stand a slice of cheesecake in the middle of the plate. Squeeze a wavy line of sauce on top of the cake. A rosette of whipped cream (Whipped Cream for Desserts, p. 371) may be piped on the top of the cake at the outer edge. Sprinkle finely grated orange rind on the center of the rosette.

Pecan Orange Chiffon Cheesecake

In this recipe, only the crust is baked.

CRUST
**1/2 cup graham cracker
  crumbs**
**1/2 cup finely chopped
  pecans**
1/3 cup confectioners' sugar
**1/2 teaspoon ground
  cinnamon**

1/4 teaspoon grated nutmeg
**1/8 teaspoon ground dried
  ginger**
**1/4 cup (1/2 stick) butter
  (no substitute), melted**

FILLING
**1 envelope (1 tablespoon)
  unflavored gelatin**
1/4 cup cold water
**2 packages (8 ounces each)
  cream cheese**
**4 teaspoons finely grated
  orange rind**
2 tablespoons lemon juice
1/4 teaspoon grated nutmeg

3 large eggs, separated
**2/3 cup light brown sugar,
  firmly packed**
1/2 cup milk
1/4 cup granulated sugar
1 cup finely chopped pecans
**1 cup (1/2 pint) whipping
  cream**

Cakes 285

TOPPING
Whipped Cream for Desserts   **Pecan halves for garnish**
  (p. 371) (optional)   **(optional)**

1. Prepare crust: In a small bowl, mix all crust ingredients together to form crumbs. Press crumbs on the bottom of a buttered 9-inch springform cake pan. Bake crust in a preheated 350° F oven until light brown, about 10 minutes. Cool to room temperature before adding filling.

2. Prepare filling: In a cup, soften gelatin in water. Reserve.

3. In an electric mixer, beat cream cheese until soft. Beat in orange rind, lemon juice, and nutmeg. Reserve.

4. In a heavy 1 1/2-quart saucepan, whisk egg yolks and brown sugar together until smooth and light yellow. Add milk and stir until smooth. Stir over low heat until mixture is hot and slightly thickened. Do not boil or the yolks will curdle. Add gelatin and stir until melted. Remove from heat. Cool until warm or room temperature.

5. Gradually beat gelatin mixture into cream cheese mixture and continue to beat until smooth.

6. Beat egg whites until foamy. Gradually beat in granulated sugar and continue to beat until whites form soft peaks. Add egg whites and pecans to cream cheese mixture. Fold in ingredients.

7. Whip cream. Fold into filling.

8. Pour filling into cooled crust. Refrigerate until filling is firm, at least 1 1/2 hours.

9. The cake may be decorated with rosettes of whipped cream and each rosette topped with a pecan half.

Yield: One 9-inch cheesecake, 12 servings.

Rum or Liqueur Syrup

This syrup moistens cakes and gives them extra flavor.

1/4 cup granulated sugar
2 tablespoons water

2 tablespoons rum, Kahlúa,
Grand Marnier, or other
liqueur

1. In a 1/2-quart saucepan, combine sugar and water. Heat and stir until sugar is dissolved.
2. Cool to room temperature. Stir in rum.
3. Brush cake layers with syrup before frosting.

Yield: Syrup to brush three 9 or 10-inch cake layers.

Lemon Cake Filling

3/4 cup + 2 tablespoons
  granulated sugar
1/4 cup cornstarch
3/4 cup water
2 large egg yolks

1 teaspoon finely grated
  lemon rind
1/4 cup lemon juice
3 tablespoons butter or
  margarine

1. In a heavy 1 1/2-quart saucepan, whisk sugar and cornstarch together. Gradually stir in water. Cook over moderate heat, whisking almost constantly, until smooth and very thick.
2. In a small bowl, combine yolks, lemon rind, and juice. Beat until smooth. Add about one-third of the hot filling to the bowl. Mix together and return to saucepan.
3. Cook over moderate heat, stirring constantly, until very thick. Do not boil.
4. Remove from heat. Add butter and stir until melted. Transfer to a stainless steel bowl. Cool over cold water and ice cubes. Stir occasionally to prevent a film from forming.

Yield: 1 1/2 cups.

Pineapple Cake Filling

1 cup granulated sugar
3 tablespoons cornstarch
2 large eggs
2 tablespoons lemon juice
1 can (8 ounces) crushed
  pineapple, undrained

2 tablespoons (1/4 stick)
  butter or margarine
1 teaspoon vanilla extract

1. In a heavy 1 1/2-quart saucepan, whisk sugar and cornstarch together. Add eggs and beat until smooth. Stir in lemon juice and pineapple.

2. Stir over moderate heat until thick. Be careful mixture does not scorch.

3. Add butter and vanilla. Cook, stirring constantly, until very thick. Do not boil.

4. Transfer to a stainless steel bowl. Cool over cold water and ice cubes. Stir occasionally to prevent a film from forming.

Yield: 2 cups.

Cream Cheese Frosting

3 ounces cream cheese
2 tablespoons (1/4 stick)
  butter or margarine

2 cups confectioners' sugar
1/2 teaspoon finely grated
  lemon rind

1. In an electric mixer, beat cream cheese and butter together until fluffy.

2. Add remaining ingredients. Beat until smooth.

Yield: 1 cup.

Note: This frosting is perfect for Applesauce Cake (p. 278).

Buttercream

This buttercream should be made on a cool, dry day.

3/4 cup granulated sugar
1/3 cup water
4 large egg yolks
1 cup (2 sticks) butter
(no substitute), preferably
unsalted

Flavoring (see following
recipes, pp. 290 - 291)

1. In a heavy 1/2-quart saucepan, combine sugar and water. Bring to a boil while stirring occasionally until sugar is dissolved. If sugar crystals start to form on the sides of the saucepan, cover the pan for a few minutes until the crystals are dissolved by steam.

2. Boil syrup, uncovered, until a candy thermometer registers 240° to 245° F (soft ball stage).

3. Meanwhile, in an electric mixer with a wire whisk attachment, if available, beat egg yolks until light yellow and the consistency of mayonnaise.

4. While beating yolks, gradually add hot syrup and continue to beat until the mixture is smooth and very thick. Use a rubber spatula to scrape sides of bowl as needed. Cool to room temperature. Stir in flavoring. Reserve.

5. In another mixer bowl, using a paddle attachment, if available, whip butter. Reserve.

6. While beating egg yolk mixture with a wire whisk attachment, add butter, about 2 tablespoons at a time, beating until smooth and light after each addition.

7. Use immediately or refrigerate until needed. If refrigerated, let reach room temperature. Then, with a wire whisk attachment, beat for a few minutes before using.

8. Refrigerate frosted cake. Serve at room temperature.

Yield: About 2 1/4 cups, to fill and frost one 9-inch (2 or 3-layer) cake.

Note: You may prefer to make 1 1/2 times this recipe, especially if you plan to pipe rosettes or other decorations or like thicker layers of frosting.

Vanilla Buttercream

Add the following flavoring to Buttercream (p. 289):

2 teaspoons vanilla extract

Chocolate Buttercream

Add the folllowing flavoring to Buttercream (p. 289):

4 to 6 ounces (4 to 6 squares) semisweet chocolate, melted and cooled to room temperature

1 teaspoon vanilla extract (optional)

Chocolate Mocha Buttercream

Add the following flavoring and those for the above Chocolate Buttercream to Buttercream (p. 289):

2 teaspoons instant coffee granules dissolved in 1/2 teaspoon hot water

Coffee Buttercream

Add the following flavoring to Buttercream (p. 289):

1 tablespoon instant coffee granules dissolved in 1 teaspoon hot water

1 teaspoon vanilla extract (optional)

Lemon Buttercream

Add the following flavoring to Buttercream (p. 289):

1 tablespoon lemon juice
1 tablespoon finely grated
  lemon rind

1/4 teaspoon vanilla extract
  (optional)

Orange Buttercream

Add the following flavoring to Buttercream (p. 289):

1 tablespoon lemon juice
1 tablespoon finely grated
  orange rind

1/4 teaspoon vanilla extract
  (optional)

Quick Chocolate Buttercream

1 cup (2 sticks) butter
  (no substitute)
12 ounces semisweet or
  milk chocolate chips,
  melted and cooled to
  room temperature

2 large eggs
1 teaspoon vanilla extract
1 teaspoon instant coffee
  granules dissolved in 1
  teaspoon hot water
  (optional)

1. Use an electric mixer with a paddle attachment, if available, to cream the butter. Add remaining ingredients. Beat with a wire whisk attachment, if available, until light and fluffy.

2. If frosting is too thin, refrigerate until thick and then beat again.

Yield: 3 cups, to fill and frost one 9-inch (3-layer) cake.

Marshmallow Frosting

This frosting will hold its shape for 2 or 3 days although it is best served the day it is made.

FOR 7 CUPS, TO FILL AND FROST A 9-INCH (3-LAYER) CAKE

4 large egg whites
1/4 cup light corn syrup
1 1/3 cups granulated sugar
2 tablespoons water

1 1/2 teaspoons vanilla,
almond, or lemon extract
(optional)

FOR 3 CUPS, TO FROST A 9-INCH (3-LAYER) CAKE OR A CAKE ROLL

2 large egg whites
2 tablespoons light corn syrup
1/2 cup + 2 tablespoons granulated sugar

1 tablespoon water
3/4 teaspoon vanilla, almond, or lemon extract (optional)

1. In a deep 2-quart saucepan or double boiler, combine all ingredients except flavoring extract.

2. Place the pan in a larger saucepan of barely simmering water. Beat at high speed with a portable electric mixer for 7 minutes.

3. Transfer frosting to a stationary electric mixer. Add flavoring. Beat with a wire whisk attachment, if available, until very thick, about 2 to 3 minutes. Use immediately.

Brown Sugar Marshmallow Frosting

Follow the above recipe for Marshmallow Frosting (7 cups) with the following changes:

1. Use 1 1/2 cups of light brown sugar, firmly packed, instead of the granulated sugar.

2. Use 1 teaspoon of vanilla extract for flavoring (optional).

Yield: Frosting to fill and frost one 9-inch (3-layer) cake.

Note: This frosting is delicious on Spice Layer Cake (p. 254).

Vanilla Frosting

1/2 cup (1 stick) butter
(no substitute), preferably
unsalted
2 cups sifted confectioners'
sugar

1 large egg yolk
1/4 teaspoon vanilla
extract
1/2 teaspoon lemon juice

1. In an electric mixer, cream the butter.
2. Add remaining ingredients. Beat until light and fluffy.
3. This frosting is best if used immediately.

Yield: 1 3/4 cups, to frost one 10-inch tube cake.

Chocolate Frosting

FOR 1 1/3 CUPS, TO FROST ONE 10-INCH TUBE CAKE

1/2 cup (1 stick) butter or
margarine, at room
temperature
2 cups sifted confectioners'
sugar

2 ounces (2 squares)
unsweetened chocolate,
melted
1 large egg yolk
1/2 teaspoon vanilla extract

FOR 2 CUPS, TO FILL AND FROST ONE 9-INCH (2-LAYER) CAKE

10 tablespoons (1 1/4 sticks)
butter or margarine, at room
temperature
2 1/2 cups sifted
confectioners' sugar

3 ounces (3 squares)
unsweetened chocolate,
melted
2 large egg yolks
1 teaspoon vanilla extract

1. In an electric mixer, cream the butter.
2. Add remaining ingredients and beat until light and fluffy.
3. This frosting is best if used immediately.

Lemon Frosting

1/2 cup (1 stick) butter
(no substitute), preferably
unsalted
2 1/2 cups sifted
confectioners' sugar

1 1/2 teaspoons finely
grated lemon rind
1/4 teaspoon vanilla extract
3 to 5 teaspoons lemon juice

1. In an electric mixer, cream the butter.

2. Add remaining ingredients using 3 teaspoons of lemon juice. Beat until light and fluffy. If needed, add additional juice and beat until the desired consistency is reached.

3. This frosting is best if used immediately.

Yield: 1 1/2 cups, to frost one 10-inch tube cake.

Orange Frosting

1/2 cup (1 stick) butter
(no substitute), preferably
unsalted
2 1/2 cups sifted
confectioners' sugar
2 teaspoons finely grated
orange rind

1/4 teaspoon vanilla extract
1 teaspoon lemon juice
3 to 4 teaspoons orange juice

1. In an electric mixer, cream the butter.

2. Add remaining ingredients using 3 teaspoons of orange juice. Beat until light and fluffy. If needed, add additional juice and beat until the desired consistency is reached.

3. This frosting is best if used immediately.

Yield: 1 1/2 cups, to frost one 10-inch tube cake.

Frosting for Cake Decorating

This frosting has the proper consistency for forcing through a pastry bag and also has excellent flavor. For making roses, use as mixed. For rosettes, borders, and leaves, thin with a little milk.

1/4 cup (1/2 stick) butter
 (no substitute),
 preferably unsalted
2 cups sifted confectioners'
 sugar

1/4 teaspoon vanilla extract
1 teaspoon lemon juice
1 1/2 teaspoons milk
Food coloring (optional)

1. In an electric mixer, beat butter until light and fluffy.
2. Beat in remaining ingredients.
3. Cover with plastic wrap until used.

Yield: 1 cup.

Caramel Icing

1 1/2 cups light brown sugar,
 firmly packed
1/2 cup half-and-half

3 tablespoons butter or
 margarine
1/4 teaspoon vanilla extract

1. In a heavy 1 1/2-quart saucepan, combine sugar and half-and-half. Bring to a boil, stirring constantly, until sugar is dissolved. Then boil without stirring until a candy thermometer registers 235° to 240° F.
2. Remove from heat. Stir in butter and vanilla.
3. Place saucepan over cold water and ice cubes. Beat with a wooden spoon until icing is thick as molasses.
4. Immediately pour icing over cake until it reaches the edges and starts to drip down the sides. Use a metal spatula to spread the remaining frosting on the sides. Work fast as the icing hardens quickly. The spatula may be dipped in hot water and used to smooth any rough areas.

Yield: Icing to frost one 10-inch tube cake.

Penuche Frosting

1/2 cup (1 stick) butter or
  margarine
1 cup dark brown sugar
2 tablespoons light corn
  syrup

1/8 teaspoon salt
1/4 cup milk
2 teaspoons vanilla extract
2 1/2 cups sifted
  confectioners' sugar

1. In a heavy 1 1/2-quart saucepan, combine butter, brown sugar, corn syrup, salt, and milk.

2. Bring to a full boil, stirring constantly, until sugar is dissolved. Let boil, without stirring, for exactly 2 minutes.

3. Remove from heat. Place saucepan over cold water and ice cubes. Beat with a wooden spoon until mixture is thick and cool. Stir in vanilla.

4. Place confectioners' sugar in an electric mixer bowl. Add cooled mixture and beat until light and fluffy, about 3 minutes.

5. This frosting is best if used immediately.

Yield: Frosting to fill and frost one 9-inch (2-layer) cake.

Notes:

1. Chopped walnuts or pecans (1/2 cup) may be pressed on the sides of the frosted cake (p. 251).

2. This frosting is delectable on Chocolate Layer Cake (p. 256).

Chocolate Glaze

This glaze will remain soft and shiny even when refrigerated.

2 ounces (2 squares)
  unsweetened chocolate
3 tablespoons butter or
  margarine

1/2 cup confectioners' sugar
1 large egg
1/4 teaspoon vanilla extract
  (optional)

1. In a heavy 1 1/2-quart saucepan, melt chocolate and butter over low heat. Remove from heat.

2. Add remaining ingredients. Whisk until smooth. Place saucepan over cold water and beat until thick.

3. Spread warm glaze on cake or pastry.

Yield: 3/4 cup, to frost one 9-inch (1-layer) cake or one recipe of Eclairs (p. 348).

Coconut, Pecan, and Orange Topping

3/4 cup orange marmalade
1 tablespoon butter or
  margarine
1 cup grated fresh, frozen, or
  packaged coconut (p. 16)

3/4 cup chopped pecans
1 tablespoon Grand Marnier
  or other orange liqueur
  (optional)

1. In a 1 1/2-quart saucepan, combine marmalade and butter. Heat and stir until butter is melted.

2. Stir in remaining ingredients.

Yield: 1 3/4 cups, to cover a 10-inch tube cake.

Note: After the cake has been spread with this topping, 8 pecan halves may be placed in a circle on top of the cake.

Meringue Mushrooms

These are lots of fun and easy to make. You will be surprised at how much they look like real mushrooms. The mushrooms may be served alone or with ice cream. They are also used to decorate cakes such as Bûche de Noël (Yule Log Cake) (p. 271).

3 large egg whites　　　　　**Unsweetened cocoa**
1/4 teaspoon cream of tartar　　**(optional)**
3/4 cup granulated sugar

1. In an electric mixer, beat egg whites and cream of tartar until foamy. Gradually beat in sugar until thick glossy peaks are formed.

2. Use a pastry bag with a 3/8-inch plain, round tip (#4), to pipe small rounds resembling mushroom caps on a lightly oiled and floured baking sheet. Use a finger dipped in cold water to flatten any peaks. Make the stems by piping a little meringue on the baking sheet and pulling the tip straight up to make a pointed cone. The size of the caps and stems should be in balance. The mushrooms may all be the same size or a variety of sizes may be made. The meringues may be placed close together on the baking sheet since they do not spread. Save a tablespoon of meringue for attaching the stems to the caps after baking.

3. Bake in a warm oven (about 200° F) until meringues are completely dry, about 2 to 3 hours. Do not be tempted to use a higher temperature or the meringues will color and this will affect their taste and appearance. As soon as the meringues are cool, place in airtight containers since they readily absorb moisture.

4. Use the point of a sharp-tipped knife to drill a small hole in the center of the flat surface of each cap. Dip the top of each stem in the reserved meringue or use frosting as glue. Insert the stem into the hole in the cap.

5. The mushrooms may be lightly sprinkled with cocoa to simulate soil.

6. Keep in an airtight container until served. The mushrooms may be frozen.

Marzipan

With this confection you can make an endless variety of decorations for cakes.

1 can (8 ounces) almond paste
1 large egg white

About 3 cups confectioners' sugar

1. In a large bowl, use a wooden spoon to break almond paste into pieces. Blend in egg white and 1 cup of confectioners' sugar.
2. Add 1 1/2 cups of confectioners' sugar and knead until blended. Knead in additional confectioners' sugar until the consistency of modeling clay.
3. Store in a plastic bag. The marzipan may be frozen.
4. In order to prevent marzipan from sticking to your hands, rub them with a drop or two of vegetable oil. Also, very lightly oil any equipment used to shape marzipan. Use oil very sparingly. A medicine dropper is useful since it will dispense only one drop of oil at a time.

See the recipe for Bûche de Noël (Yule Log Cake) (p. 271) for an illustration of the following decorations:

HOLLY LEAVES
Color marzipan by kneading in green and yellow food coloring. Use a very lightly oiled rolling pin and work surface to roll the marzipan about 1/8-inch thick. The pattern below may be used to cut out the leaves. Use the dull side of a knife tip to mark veins on the leaves.

HOLLY BERRIES

Color marzipan by kneading in red food coloring. Roll into balls about 1/4-inch in diameter. On the cake, place two holly leaves with their stem ends near each other. Arrange 3 berries between the stem ends.

SNOWMAN

Use uncolored marzipan to make a small ball placed on top of a larger ball. Shape arms from additional marzipan and press them on the larger ball. Make a hat from pink marzipan or use another color. Mark eyes and buttons with a toothpick dipped in Chocolate Buttercream (p. 290) or melted chocolate.

Cookies

Toasted Almond Wafers

Paper-thin cookies that are wonderful with ice cream or sherbet (pp. 368 - 370), Bavarian cream (pp. 356 - 358), or fresh fruit.

1/4 cup (1/2 stick) butter (no substitute), at room temperature
1/3 cup granulated sugar
1 large egg, at room temperature
1/2 teaspoon almond extract

1 tablespoon milk, at room temperature
1/4 cup finely chopped almonds
1/2 cup all-purpose flour
3/4 cup sliced almonds, divided

1. In an electric mixer, beat butter and sugar together until fluffy. Add egg, almond extract, and milk. Beat until smooth and light.

2. Stir in chopped almonds. Add flour. Mix until blended. Do not overmix.

3. Use a teaspoon to place teaspoon amounts of batter on baking sheets lined with buttered aluminum foil. Use the back of a teaspoon or a spatula to spread batter into very thin circles about 2 1/2-inches in diameter. Twelve cookies, equally spaced, will fit on a 17 x 12-inch baking sheet. Sprinkle each set of 12 cookies with 1/4 cup of sliced almonds.

4. Bake cookies in a preheated 325° F oven until the edges are brown and the centers barely begin to brown, about 12 to 14 minutes. Be sure the cookies bake long enough so they will become crisp when cool.

5. Slide sheet of foil with cookies off baking sheet and onto a wire rack. After the cookies have cooled slightly, their edges will begin to loosen from the foil. Peel cookies from foil. Cool on wire racks. As soon as cookies are crisp, store them in an airtight container.

Yield: 3 dozen cookies.

Chocolate Leaves

1. Prepare batter for Toasted Almond Wafers (p. 302) through Step 2. The sliced almonds listed in the recipe are not used for these cookies.

2. Shape the cookies with a metal leaf-shaped stencil from a restaurant supply store (A) or a stencil from cardboard using the illustration below (B). Lay stencil on a baking sheet lined with buttered aluminum foil. Use a spatula to spread the batter as thinly as possible in the stencil and then carefully lift the stencil.

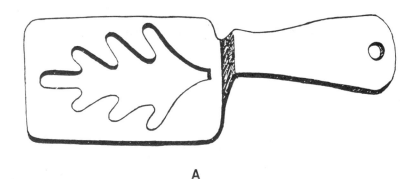

A

B

3. Bake and cool cookies following Steps 4 and 5 of the recipe for Toasted Almond Wafers (p. 302).

4. Melt 4 ounces (4 squares) of semisweet chocolate. Spread a thin layer of chocolate on the bottom surface (side that touched foil during baking) of each cookie. The chocolate may be marked with the tip of a knife to resemble veins of a leaf.

5. Refrigerate cookies for a few minutes until chocolate is firm.

6. Store in an airtight container.

Yield: 25 cookies using a leaf stencil measuring 4 x 2 1/2 -inches.

Viennese Butter Cookies

These crisp and delicious cookies are elegant yet quick to make.

COOKIES
1/2 cup (1 stick) butter
  (no substitute), at room
  temperature
1/4 cup granulated sugar
1 large egg yolk

BUTTERCREAM (OPTIONAL)
2 tablespoons (1/4 stick)
  butter (no substitute)
1/4 cup confectioners' sugar

1 teaspoon vanilla extract
3/4 cup sifted all-purpose
  flour
2 ounces (2 squares)
  semisweet chocolate,
  melted

1/8 teaspoon vanilla extract

Seedless raspberry jam (optional)

1. In an electric mixer, cream the butter. Add sugar and beat until fluffy. Add yolk and vanilla. Beat until smooth and light. Add flour and mix until blended. Do not overmix.

2. Place dough in a pastry bag with a fine tooth 1/2-inch star tip (#5B). Hold the tip 1/4-inch above a lightly buttered baking sheet and pipe out 3-inch lengths. When the end of each length is reached, release pressure on pastry bag. Then, in one quick motion, push the tip upward and backward over the length to separate the dough from the pastry bag. See illustration, p. 349. Space cookies about 1 1/2-inches apart since they spread during baking.

3. Bake cookies in a preheated 350° F oven until light golden brown, about 10 to 15 minutes. Let cookies cool on baking sheet for a minute or two before transferring them to wire racks.

4. If desired, the cookies may be sandwiched with buttercream and/or raspberry jam.

5. Prepare buttercream: In a small bowl, beat butter, confectioners' sugar, and vanilla until smooth. Spread this buttercream on the flat surface of half of the cookies.

6. On the unfrosted cookies, place a thin band of raspberry jam lengthwise down the center. Use a small spoon or a pastry bag with a narrow plain tip. Sandwich these cookies with those spread with buttercream.

7. Dip both ends of each cookie in the chocolate. Place cookies on a wire rack. Try not to let the chocolate ends touch the wires of the rack or the cookies may stick to the rack and be difficult to remove. Refrigerate for a few minutes until chocolate is firm.

8. Store cookies in an airtight container.

Yield: About 2 dozen cookies; 1 dozen if sandwiched.

Notes:
1. These cookies are great with ice cream or fresh fruit.
2. This recipe is easily doubled.

Cookie Press Cookies

1. Prepare Viennese Butter Cookies (p. 304) through Step 1 but use 1 1/4 cups of sifted flour.

2. Use a cookie press to form dough into cookies on a lightly buttered baking sheet. Space cookies about 1-inch apart.

3. A candied cherry half or a piece of candied pineapple may be pressed in the center of each cookie. Alternatively, a depression may be made in the center of each cookie with your thumb and the cookies filled with melted chocolate after baking.

4. Bake cookies in a preheated 350° F oven until the edges are light brown, about 14 minutes.

5. Remove cookies from baking sheets and cool on wire racks. Store in an airtight container.

Yield: About 3 dozen cookies.

Candied Fruit and Nut Wafers

These cookies are best made on a dry day.

2 large egg whites
1 large egg
1/2 cup + 2 tablespoons
  granulated sugar
1/4 teaspoon vanilla extract
1/2 cup sifted all-purpose
  flour
1/8 teaspoon ground
  cinnamon
1/8 teaspoon ground cloves
1/8 teaspoon ground nutmeg

1/8 teaspoon baking powder
1/4 cup finely chopped
  candied fruit (any individual
  fruit or a mixture)
3/4 cup coarsely chopped
  pecans or toasted almonds
4 ounces (4 squares)
  semisweet chocolate
  (optional)
18 candied cherries (optional)

1. In a small bowl, beat egg whites, egg, sugar, and vanilla together until smooth. Reserve.

2. Mix flour, cinnamon, cloves, nutmeg, and baking powder together. Add to egg mixture. Stir until blended. Add candied fruit and pecans. Mix thoroughly.

3. Cover baking sheets with aluminum foil. Lightly butter the foil. Use a teaspoon to drop teaspoon amounts on the foil. Use the back of the teaspoon or a spatula to spread batter into circles about 2 1/2-inches in diameter. Twelve cookies, equally spaced, will fit on a 17 x 12-inch baking sheet.

4. Bake in a preheated 300° F oven until cookies are almost completely golden brown, about 16 to 18 minutes. Slide sheet of foil with cookies off baking sheet and onto a wire rack. Cool to room temperature.

5. Peel cookies off foil. If they stick to the foil, they need to cool more or to bake for a longer time.

6. Use a plastic sandwich bag with a tiny hole cut in one corner or a small spoon to drizzle chocolate over cookies. Place half a candied cherry in the center of each cookie. Refrigerate for a few minutes until chocolate is firm.

7. Store in an airtight container.

Yield: About 3 dozen cookies.

Lemon Pecan Squares

CRUST
1 2/3 cups all-purpose flour
1/4 cup granulated sugar
1/8 teaspoon salt

3/4 cup (1 1/2 sticks) butter
(no substitute), melted
2/3 cup finely chopped
pecans

FILLING
1 1/2 cups granulated sugar
3 tablespoons all-purpose
flour
1/8 teaspoon salt
4 large eggs
6 tablespoons lemon juice

1 tablespoon finely grated
lemon rind
1/2 teaspoon vanilla extract
3 tablespoons all-purpose
flour

TOPPING
6 tablespoons confectioners' sugar

1. Prepare crust: In an electric mixer bowl, combine the flour, sugar, and salt. Add butter and mix until blended. Stir in pecans. Press the mixture evenly into a 15 x 11-inch jelly roll pan. Bake in a preheated 350° F oven until light brown, about 20 minutes.

2. Meanwhile, prepare filling: In an electric mixer, mix the sugar, flour, and salt together. Add the eggs, lemon juice, lemon rind, and vanilla. Beat until blended.

3. Pour filling into baked crust. Bake until filling is golden brown, about 25 minutes.

4. Cool in pan. Cut into 6 lengthwise and 8 crosswise rows to make 48 squares. Sift confectioners' sugar over the squares.

5. Store in an airtight container.

Yield: 48 cookies.

Toffee Squares

1 cup finely chopped pecans
1 cup (2 sticks) butter or
  margarine, at room
  temperature
1 cup light brown sugar,
  firmly packed
1 1/2 teaspoons vanilla
  extract
2 cups sifted all-purpose
  flour
1/4 teaspoon salt
12 ounces chocolate chips

1. Heat the pecans on a baking sheet in a preheated 350° F. oven until they give off a nutty aroma, about 5 to 7 minutes. Do not let the nuts brown or they will taste burned. Reserve.

2. In an electric mixer, cream the butter. Add brown sugar and beat until fluffy. Stir in vanilla.

3. Add flour and salt and mix only until blended.

4. Spread the mixture in an unbuttered 15 x 11-inch jelly roll pan. Bake in a preheated 350° F oven until dark golden brown, about 20 minutes.

5. Sprinkle chocolate chips on top and return to oven until chips have softened, about 1 minute (no longer or chocolate may become grainy). Spread the melted chocolate evenly over the surface.

6. Sprinkle the nuts evenly on top and press them into the chocolate.

7. While still warm, cut into 6 lengthwise and 8 crosswise rows to make 48 squares. Cool on wire racks.

8. Refrigerate cookies until chocolate is firm, about 30 minutes.

9. Store in an airtight container.

Yield: 48 cookies.

Chocolate Chip Cookies

1 cup (2 sticks) butter or
  margarine
1/2 cup granulated sugar
1 cup light brown sugar
2 large eggs
1 teaspoon vanilla extract
2 1/4 cups all-purpose flour
1 teaspoon baking soda
1/8 teaspoon salt
12 ounces chocolate chips
1 cup chopped pecans
  (optional)

1. In an electric mixer, cream the butter. Add granulated sugar and brown sugar. Beat until fluffy. Add eggs and vanilla. Beat until smooth and light.

2. Sift flour, baking soda, and salt together. Add to mixer. Mix until blended.

3. Stir in chocolate chips and pecans.

4. Use a teaspoon to place tablespoon amounts of batter on lightly buttered baking sheets. Twelve cookies, equally spaced, will fit on a 17 x 12-inch baking sheet.

5. Bake in a preheated 375° F oven until cookies are light brown, about 12 to 14 minutes. Remove cookies from baking sheets and cool on wire racks.

6. Store in an airtight container.

Yield: 5 dozen cookies.

Gingerbread Men

Let your children decorate these cookies. They will have a great time and their ideas will provide creative alternatives to the method described here. Also, use this dough to make spice cookies of any size and shape.

1/2 cup (1 stick) butter or
  margarine
1 cup dark brown sugar,
  firmly packed
1/2 cup molasses
1 large egg
1/2 teaspoon finely grated
  lemon rind
1 teaspoon finely grated
  orange rind
2 1/2 cups all-purpose flour
1/2 teaspoon baking soda
1/2 teaspoon salt

1 teaspoon ground dried
  ginger
2 1/2 teaspoons ground
  cinnamon
1/2 teaspoon grated nutmeg
1 teaspoon ground cloves
1/4 teaspoon ground allspice
1/2 to 1 recipe Frosting for
  Cake Decorating (p. 295)
Raisins for decoration
Cinnamon candies for
  decoration

1. In an electric mixer, cream the butter. Add brown sugar and molasses. Beat until fluffy. Add egg, lemon rind, and orange rind. Beat until smooth.

2. Mix flour, baking soda, salt, ginger, cinnamon, nutmeg, cloves, and allspice together. Sift and add to mixer. Mix until blended.

3. Place dough on a piece of plastic wrap. Flatten into a disc about 1-inch thick. Wrap in plastic wrap. Chill for 6 hours or longer.

4. Use a lightly floured pastry cloth and rolling pin cover to roll dough 3/8-inch thick. Roll one-quarter of the dough at a time, keeping the remainder refrigerated.

5. Use a 5-inch gingerbread man cutter or a cardboard pattern to cut out the gingerbread men. Form scraps into a ball, chill, and reroll.

6. Bake cookies on buttered baking sheets in a preheated 350° F oven until they barely begin to brown around the edges, about 10 to 12 minutes. Remove cookies from baking sheets and cool on wire racks.

7. Decorate the gingerbread men by piping frosting through a pastry bag. Use a 1/8-inch plain tube to pipe two dots for the eyes, another for the nose, and a semicircle for the mouth. Use a 1/4-inch star tube to pipe 3 dots for buttons. Place a piece of raisin on top of each of the eye dots and a cinnamon candy on top of each button dot.

8. Store cookies in an airtight container or wrap each one separately in plastic wrap. Gingerbread men freeze well.

Yield: About 3 dozen 5-inch gingerbread men.

Fudge Brownies

10 tablespoons (1 1/4 sticks)
  butter or margarine
3 ounces (3 squares)
  semisweet chocolate
1 ounce (1 square)
  unsweetened chocolate
1 pound (2 cups, firmly
  packed) light brown sugar

1 1/2 teaspoons vanilla
  extract
4 large eggs
1 1/4 cups all-purpose flour
2 teaspoons baking powder
1/4 teaspoon salt
1 1/2 cups chopped pecans
  or walnuts

1. In a 2-quart saucepan, melt butter, semisweet, and unsweetened chocolate over low heat. Stir until smooth. Remove from heat. Stir in brown sugar and vanilla. Whisk in eggs, one at a time, until smooth.

2. Sift flour, baking powder, and salt together. Add to saucepan. Stir until blended. Mix in nuts. Turn batter into a buttered 13 x 9 x 2-inch pan.

3. Bake in a preheated 350° F oven until a cake tester comes out clean, about 35 to 40 minutes. Cool brownies in pan.

4. Cut into 3 lengthwise and 8 crosswise rows to make 18 squares.

Yield: 18 brownies.

Note: For a delicious treat, serve these brownies with a scoop of Vanilla Ice Cream (p. 368) or other ice cream and Chocolate Fudge Sauce (p. 373) or Chocolate Sauce (p. 373).

Peanut Spice Cookies

1/2 cup (1 stick) butter or
  margarine, at room
  temperature
3/4 cup crunchy peanut
  butter
1/2 cup granulated sugar
1/2 cup light brown sugar,
  firmly packed
1 large egg, at room
  temperature

1 teaspoon vanilla extract
1 1/2 cups all-purpose flour
1 teaspoon baking soda
3/4 teaspoon ground
  cinnamon
1/2 teaspoon grated nutmeg
1/4 teaspoon ground cloves
3/4 cup unsalted chopped
  peanuts

1. In an electric mixer, cream the butter and peanut butter together. Add granulated sugar and brown sugar. Beat until fluffy. Add egg and vanilla. Beat until smooth and light.

2. Sift flour, baking soda, cinnamon, nutmeg, and cloves together. Add to mixer. Mix until blended. Stir in peanuts.

3. Cover bowl with plastic wrap and chill until dough is firm. If the dough is not sticky and you work quickly, this step may be omitted.

4. Form dough into balls about 1 1/2-inches in diameter and equally space them on unbuttered baking sheets. Twelve cookies will fit on a 17 x 12-inch baking sheet.

5. Use a table fork dipped in flour to flatten each cookie into a 2 1/2-inch circle. The fork will leave an attractive grooved design on the surface.

6. Bake cookies in a preheated 350° F oven until golden brown, about 12 minutes. Remove cookies from baking sheets and cool on wire racks.

Yield: 3 dozen cookies.

Pfeffernüsse Cookies

German Christmas cookies that look like little snowballs.

1/2 cup (1/2 stick) butter or margarine, at room temperature
1 cup dark brown sugar, firmly packed
1/3 cup honey
1 teaspoon finely grated lemon rind
2 large eggs, at room temperature
3 1/4 cups all-purpose flour
1/2 teaspoon salt
1 teaspoon ground cinnamon
1/2 teaspoon grated nutmeg

1/2 teaspoon ground allspice
1/2 teaspoon ground ginger
1/2 teaspoon ground cloves
1/4 teaspoon ground black pepper
1/2 teaspoon ground cardamom (optional)
1/4 teaspoon baking soda
1/2 cup finely chopped pecans or walnuts
1 cup granulated sugar
1/2 cup water
About 3 cups confectioners' sugar

1. In an electric mixer, cream the butter. Add brown sugar, honey, and lemon rind. Beat until smooth. Add eggs and beat until blended.

2. Stir flour, salt, spices, and baking soda together. Sift and add to mixer. Mix until blended. Add nuts and mix until evenly distributed.

3. Shape dough into 1-inch balls. Arrange cookies 1 1/2-inches apart on lightly buttered baking sheets.

4. Bake cookies in a preheated 350° F oven until bottom surfaces are light brown, about 12 to 15 minutes. Remove cookies from baking sheets and cool on wire racks.

5. Prepare glaze: In a heavy 1 1/2-quart saucepan, combine granulated sugar and water. Stir over high heat until sugar is dissolved. Boil without stirring until a light syrup is formed, about 2 minutes. Cool until warm or room temperature.

6. Sift confectioners' sugar into a pie pan.

7. Dip cookies in glaze and place on a wire rack. Roll each cookie in the confectioners' sugar while pressing on the sugar. Resift confectioners' sugar if it becomes lumpy.

8. Dry cookies on wire racks for at least 15 minutes. Roll again in confectioners' sugar.

9. The cookies may be served immediately but their flavor is greatly improved by freezing them in an airtight container for at least a week. If cookies have been frozen, roll them in more confectioners' sugar before serving.

Yield: 4 dozen cookies.

Linzer Cookies

These sandwiched cookies with raspbery jam showing through the center of the top cookie are elegant as well as delectable.

1/2 cup sliced almonds, toasted
1 1/2 cups all-purpose flour
1/2 cup dark brown sugar, firmly packed
1/4 cup granulated sugar
1/2 teaspoon baking powder
1 teaspoon ground cinnamon
1/4 teaspoon grated nutmeg
1/4 teaspoon ground cloves
1/2 cup (1 stick) butter (no substitute), chilled
1 large egg, slightly beaten
Confectioners' sugar for dusting
1 cup raspberry jam

1. Grind almonds in a food processor or finely chop them with a knife. Reserve.

2. In a food processor with a steel blade, combine flour, brown sugar, granulated sugar, baking powder, cinnamon, nutmeg, and cloves. Process until thoroughly mixed.

3. Cut butter into 1/2-inch cubes. Add to processor. Process until mixture resembles cornmeal. Transfer to a large bowl. If a processor is not available, combine dry ingredients in a bowl and use a pastry blender to cut in butter.

4. Use a wooden spoon to stir in almonds and then the egg. Stir until a smooth dough is formed. Do not overwork the dough. Form into a ball and then flatten into a disc about 1-inch thick. Wrap in plastic wrap. Refrigerate until chilled, about 30 minutes.

5. Roll dough 1/8 to 1/4-inch thick using a lightly floured pastry cloth and rolling pin cover. Roll one-third of the dough at a time, keeping the remainder refrigerated. Cut into rounds with a 2 1/2-inch cutter, preferably scalloped. Use a 1-inch cutter to remove the centers from half the cookies. Space cookies about 1 1/2-inches apart on lightly buttered baking sheets. Form scraps into a ball, chill, and reroll.

6. Bake in a preheated 350° F oven until cookies begin to brown at the edges, about 8 minutes. Remove cookies from baking sheets and cool on wire racks.

7. Store in an airtight container. The cookies may be frozen until ready to assemble and serve.

8. Use a tea strainer to sprinkle confectioners' sugar on top of the ring-shaped cookies. Spread the bottom surface of the other cookies with raspberry jam. Sandwich the ring-shaped cookies on top of those spread with jam.

9. Serve cookies within several hours since they are best when crisp.

Yield: About 2 dozen cookies.

Pastries

Pie Pastry

Lard, vegetable shortening, butter, and margarine are the shortenings commonly used for making pie pastry. The type of shortening affects the flakiness, tenderness, and flavor of the crust.

A crust made with lard will be the most flaky and tender, followed by one made with vegetable shortening, then margarine, and lastly butter. I prefer to use lard for double crust fruit pies and savory pies such as Chicken Pot Pie (p. 121) because of its flakiness, tenderness, and flavor.

Many cooks use vegetable shortening because of its flaky and tender qualities. I prefer not to use all vegetable shortening because it lacks flavor.

For pies other than fruit and savory ones, I prefer the taste of butter. However, a crust made with all butter tends to be the least flaky and tender. In order to have a buttery tasting crust that is also flaky and tender, use 3 parts butter and 1 part vegetable shortening.

A crust made with margarine is also quite tasty, flaky, and tender.

LARD OR VEGETABLE SHORTENING PIE PASTRY FOR A SINGLE CRUST 9, OR 10-INCH PIE, TART, OR FLAN

1/2 cup lard or vegetable
  shortening
1 1/2 cups all-purpose flour
1/4 to 1/2 teaspoon salt

About 2 to 4 tablespoons
ice water

LARD OR VEGETABLE SHORTENING PIE PASTRY FOR A DOUBLE CRUST 9, OR 10-INCH PIE, TART, OR FLAN

3/4 cup lard or vegetable
  shortening
2 1/2 cups all-purpose flour
1/2 to 1 teaspoon salt

About 4 to 6 tablespoons
ice water

BUTTER OR MARGARINE PIE PASTRY FOR A SINGLE CRUST
9-INCH PIE, TART, OR FLAN

6 tablespoons (3/4 stick)
  butter, preferably unsalted,
  and 2 tablespoons vegetable
  shortening OR 1/2 cup
  (1 stick) margarine

1 1/4 cups all-purpose flour
1/8 to 1/4 teaspoon salt
About 2 to 4 tablespoons
  ice water

BUTTER OR MARGARINE PIE PASTRY FOR A DOUBLE CRUST
9-INCH PIE, TART, OR FLAN

12 tablespoons (1 1/2 sticks)
  butter, preferably unsalted,
  and 1/4 cup vegetable
  shortening OR 1 cup
  (2 sticks) margarine

2 1/2 cups all-purpose flour
1/4 to 1/2 teaspoon salt
About 4 to 6 tablespoons
  ice water

DOUGH

1. Be sure all equipment is close at hand, including plastic wrap, wax paper, rolling pin, and pie plate or pan.

2. If a combination of shortenings is used, blend them together in an electric mixer. Spread the measured amount of lard, vegetable shortening, or shortening blend on a plate. Place in the freezer until very cold or frozen. When needed, use a knife to cut the chilled shortening into small pieces and to scrape it from the plate.

3. If only margarine is used, divide the stick(s) lengthwise into quarters. Cut the quarters crosswise into 1/2-inch cubes. Place in the freezer for a few minutes until very cold or frozen.

4. Use either the hand method or food processor method:

Hand Method

1. Place the flour in a large bowl. Use a pastry blender to cut in the shortening until the mixture resembles cornmeal. If overblended, the pastry will be tough and greasy. The blending must be done quickly to prevent the fat from melting.

2. If making a single crust, combine the salt and 1 tablespoon of the ice water. For a double crust, combine the salt with 2 tablespoons of the ice water. Stir until all or most of the salt is dissolved.

3. Sprinkle the salted ice water over the flour mixture and mix lightly with a fork. Continue to add water, 1 tablespoon at a time, while mixing lightly with a fork until the flour is evenly moistened and is just able to be pressed into a ball of dough that will not crumble. First, use a rubber

spatula to press the dough together. The spatula makes the process easier and reduces the time that your hands are in contact with the dough which can cause the shortening to melt. Then, use floured hands to press the dough into a ball. Enough water must be added to prevent the dough from cracking and falling apart when it is rolled. If too much water is added, the dough will be sticky and difficult to roll out, and the crust will shrink and become tough when baked.

4. Flatten dough into a disc about 1-inch thick. Wrap in plastic wrap and refrigerate for at least 1 hour and preferably 2 to 4 hours, or up to 24 hours.

Food Processor Method

1. Place the flour in a food processor with a steel blade.

2. Add shortening. Process with 15 to 30 rapid on and off pulses until mixture resembles cornmeal. Do not overprocess.

3. Transfer to a large bowl and follow Steps 2 to 4 of the Hand Method (p. 317).

ROLLING OUT THE PASTRY

1. Soften the refrigerated dough at room temperature until it can be rolled but is still cold, about 2 to 10 minutes. Lightly dust the dough with flour.

2. Marble, granite, and the new solid surface products for counters are ideal surfaces for rolling pastry since they absorb heat from the dough and keep it cold. However, any counter surface can be used.

3. Although dough can be rolled on a lightly floured surface or with a lightly floured pastry cloth and rolling pin cover, I prefer to roll it between two pieces of wax paper. The dough is less likely to tear, is more easily turned, and is less likely to be touched and warmed by the hands. Sheets of wax paper should measure about 16 x 12-inches.

4. Roll the dough using strokes of even pressure that always start from the center. I prefer to use a French spindle-shaped rolling pin which causes more pressure to be placed on the center of the dough than at the edges. The thickness of the pastry in the center becomes equal to that of the edges faster than if a rolling pin of uniform diameter is used. A marble rolling pin also works well since its weight helps to flatten the dough and the marble keeps the dough cool.

5. While rolling, occasionally peel off one of the sheets of wax paper to be sure the dough is not sticking to the paper. If so, sprinkle the dough lightly with flour.

6. Roll dough until it is about 1/8-inch thick and 12 to 13-inches in diameter. If dough is not rolled thin enough, the crust may not be tender.

LINING A PIE PAN OR PLATE

1. Peel off top layer of wax paper. Lightly flour the rolling pin and place it on the edge of the dough nearest to you. Roll dough up on the rolling pin, gradually peeling off the wax paper and dusting lightly with flour as needed to prevent the dough from sticking to itself. Unroll the dough over the pie plate or pan.

2. Ease dough into pan using floured fingers. Do not stretch the dough. Repairs can be made by cutting off pieces at the edge and pressing them in place.

3. For a single crust pie, use scissors to cut the pastry so 3/4-inch of dough hangs evenly over the rim. Fold the overhanging dough under the dough covering the rim to make the rim twice as thick as the rest of the crust. Lightly roll a rolling pin over the rim of the pan to make the rim evenly thick.

4. A decorative edge can be made by one of the following methods:

   A. Fork-Pressed Edge: Dip tines of a fork into flour and press into pastry around the rim.

   B. Fluted Edge: Press pastry between the thumb and index finger of one hand held on the inner edge of the rim and the index finger of the other hand on the outside of the rim. Repeat around the rim.

   C. Rope Edge: Press the side of a thumb, held at an angle to the rim, into the pastry. Then pinch pastry between the thumb and index finger so it forms a ridge. Repeat around the rim.

5. Cover the crust with wax paper and refrigerate for at least 30 minutes before baking.

LINING A TART PAN OR FLAN

1. Place flan or tart pan on a baking sheet.

2. Follow Steps 1 & 2 above for lining a pie pan.

3. Push dough down the sides to make them a little thicker than the bottom.

4. Pass a rolling pin over the top edge of the tart pan or flan to cut off the excess crust.

5. If using a flan ring, press sides upward about 3/8-inch above the rim. A decorative edge can be made by pressing the tines of a fork at an angle on top of the pastry rim.

6. Cover crust with wax paper and refrigerate for at least 30 minutes before baking.

Note: For lining tart pans smaller than 4-inches, rolled dough is much easier to handle if it is chilled before using. Keep refrigerated rolled dough between sheets of wax paper on a baking sheet. Cut chilled dough into rounds or squares that are slightly larger than the pans being lined.

PREPARING A COMPLETELY BAKED PIE, TART, OR FLAN SHELL

1. Prick crust all over with the tines of a fork to prevent it from rising unevenly.

2. Most cookbooks recommend lining the pastry shell with foil and filling the foil with dried beans or rice. The crust is baked for a time, the foil and beans removed, and then the crust is baked until brown. This method is supposed to prevent the sides of the pastry from collapsing and to keep the bottom from rising above the bottom of the pan. My experience has shown no benefits from this procedure. Some shrinkage of the crust will occur with or without the use of foil and beans. If the sides of the crust are properly made, as described above, they should not collapse. The crust will brown faster and more evenly if foil and beans are not used.

2. Bake pastry in a preheated 400° F oven when using a metal pan or flan, or in a 375° F oven when using a glass or ceramic plate. Even though the crust has been pricked before baking, part of the bottom crust will probably rise and form one or more bubbles during the first 8 minutes of baking. Watch pastry carefully during this time and be prepared to prick the bubble with the tip of a sharp knife. Prick the bubble in only one place. If multiple holes are made, cracks may form in the crust.

3. Bake crust until the bottom and sides are golden brown, about 20 to 25 minutes. Cool crust in the pan or plate.

Tart Pastry

This delicious buttery crust tastes like a cookie, cuts without shattering, and resists moisture. The dough tolerates handling without the crust becoming tough.

PASTRY FOR A SINGLE CRUST 9 OR 10-INCH TART PAN OR FLAN

1/2 cup (1 stick) butter (no substitute), preferably unsalted, chilled
2 large egg yolks
1/2 teaspoon vanilla extract
1 1/3 cups all-purpose flour

1/4 teaspoon salt (if using unsalted butter) or 1/8 teaspoon salt (if using salted butter)
1/2 cup confectioners' sugar

1. Be sure all equipment is close at hand including plastic wrap, wax paper, rolling pin, and tart pan or flan ring.

2. Divide butter lengthwise into 4 quarters. Cut crosswise into 1/2-inch cubes. Place in freezer for a few minutes until very cold but not frozen.

3. In a cup, beat egg yolks and vanilla together until blended. Refrigerate until needed.

4. Use either hand method or food processor method:

Hand Method

1. In a large bowl, mix the flour, salt, and confectioners' sugar together. Use a pastry blender to cut in butter until mixture resembles cornmeal.

2. Pour egg yolks and vanilla over flour mixture. Stir with a fork until flour is evenly moistened and dough starts to come together. Using lightly floured hands, press mixture into a ball of dough.

3. Flatten dough into a disc about 1-inch thick. Wrap in plastic wrap. Refrigerate for at least 2 hours or up to 24 hours.

4. Roll dough, line tart pan or flan, and bake as described in the recipe for Pie Pastry (pp. 318 - 320). Use an oven temperature of 375° F.

Food Processor Method

1. In a food processor with a steel blade, place the flour, salt, and sugar. Process a few seconds to mix ingredients.

2. Add butter and process with a pulsing action until mixture resembles cornmeal, about 20 seconds.

3. Remove processor lid and pour egg yolks and vanilla over flour mixture. Pulse until mixture barely begins to come together. Transfer to a large bowl. With lightly floured hands, form dough into a ball.

4. Continue with Step 3 of the Hand Method (p. 321).

Graham Cracker or Cookie Crumb Pie Crust

1 1/3 cups graham cracker, vanilla wafer, or chocolate wafer crumbs
2 tablespoons granulated sugar

6 tablespoons (3/4 stick) butter or margarine, melted
1/8 teaspoon ground cinnamon (optional)

1. In a 9-inch pie pan or plate, stir all ingredients together until thoroughly mixed. A food processor with a steel blade can be used to make the crumbs and mix in the remaining ingredients.

2. Press crumbs evenly on sides and bottom of pan. Do not cover the rim.

3. Bake in a preheated 375° F oven until crust begins to brown, about 8 minutes. Cool before using.

Yield: One 9-inch pie crust.

Apple Cheese Pie

PIE PASTRY
1 unbaked 9-inch pie shell (Pie Pastry, p. 316)

APPLE FILLING
2 tablespoons (1/4 stick)
  butter or margarine, at
  room temperature
6 cups peeled, cored, and
  sliced, 1/2-inch thick, baking
  apples such as Cortland,
  McIntosh, or Rome Beauty
1/3 cup raisins or currants
2 tablespoons lemon juice
Finely grated rind of a lemon

1/2 cup granulated sugar
1 tablespoon cornstarch
1 teaspoon ground
  cinnamon
1/4 teaspoon grated nutmeg
Pinch ground cloves
  (optional)
3 tablespoons dark rum
  (optional)

CHEESE TOPPING
1 cup creamy cottage cheese
1/3 cup granulated sugar
1/3 cup sour cream
1 tablespoon lemon juice

2 large eggs
1 teaspoon vanilla extract
Grated nutmeg for garnish

1. Refrigerate pie shell until needed.

2. Prepare apple filling: Spread the butter over the bottom of a 13 1/2 x 8 1/2-inch glass baking dish. Add apples, raisins, lemon juice, and lemon rind. Toss until mixed. Stir sugar, cornstarch, cinnamon, nutmeg, and cloves together. Sprinkle over apples. Toss until mixed.

3. Bake in a 400° F oven until apples are barely tender, about 15 to 20 minutes. Use a large spoon to stir mixture several times while baking. Cool for several minutes. Stir in rum.

4. Prepare cheese topping: In a food processor with a steel blade, process cottage cheese until very smooth. Add all remaining ingredients except nutmeg. Process until blended.

5. Turn apple filling into pie shell. Cover with cheese topping.

6. Bake pie on a rack in the lower third of a preheated 400° F oven for 10 minutes. Reduce oven temperature to 350° F and bake until the cheese topping is firm, about 20 to 25 minutes.

7. Sprinkle with nutmeg. Serve warm or at room temperature.

Yield: One 9-inch pie, 8 servings.

Apple Crumb Tart

The crumb crust in this tart is quickly and easily prepared.

CRUST
1 1/4 cups all-purpose flour
1/4 cup granulated sugar
1/4 teaspoon salt
1/2 cup (1 stick) butter or
  margarine, chilled

Finely grated rind of a lemon
  (optional)
1/3 cup finely chopped
  almonds (optional)

FILLING
1/2 cup granulated sugar
1 tablespoon cornstarch
1/3 cup dry white wine
2 tablespoons (1/4 stick)
  butter or margarine
1 teaspoon vanilla extract

6 cups peeled, cored, and
  sliced, 1/2-inch thick,
  baking apples such as
  Cortland, McIntosh, or
  Rome Beauty

TOPPING
Whipped Cream for Desserts (p. 371) (optional)

1. Prepare crust: In a food processor with a steel blade, combine flour, sugar, and salt. Process for a few seconds until mixed. Add butter, cut into 1/2-inch cubes, and lemon rind. Process until mixture resembles cornmeal.

2. If a food processor is not available, mix flour, sugar, and salt together and use a pastry blender to cut in butter. Stir in lemon rind.

3. Mix 1/2 cup of the crumbs and almonds together. Reserve. Press remaining crumbs on the bottom and up an inch on the sides of a buttered 9-inch springform pan. Refrigerate.

4. Prepare filling: In a heavy, nonreactive 1 1/2-quart saucepan, mix sugar and cornstarch together. Stir in wine. Stir over moderate heat until smooth and boiling. Remove from heat. Add butter and vanilla. Stir until butter is melted.

5. Pour mixture over apple slices. Toss until apple slices are evenly coated.

6. Turn filling into crust. Bake in a preheated 425° F oven for 20 minutes.

7. Sprinkle the crumb mixture on top. Continue to bake tart until apples are tender and crumbs are brown, about 35 minutes.

8. Serve warm or chilled with whipped cream.

Yield: One 9-inch tart, 8 servings.

French Apple Tart

PASTRY
1 unbaked 9-inch tart or flan shell (Tart Pastry, p. 321)

FILLING
5 medium baking apples
such as Cortland,
McIntosh, or Rome
Beauty
1 tablespoon lemon juice

1/4 cup granulated sugar
1 teaspoon cornstarch
1 tablespoon butter or
margarine

TOPPING
1/2 cup apricot jam or
apple jelly (optional)

Whipped Cream for
Desserts (p. 371) (optional)

1. Prepare filling: Peel, core, and slice apples. Coarsely chop the small and broken slices. Sprinkle the chopped apples over the bottom of the pastry shell.
2. Starting at the edge of the shell, arrange the apple slices in overlapping circles working toward the center of the shell. The completed arrangement should resemble a large open rose. Brush lemon juice over apples.
3. In a small bowl, mix sugar and cornstarch together. Sprinkle over apples. Dot surface with butter.
4. Bake in a preheated 375° F oven until apples are tender and crust is golden brown, about 1 hour.
5. In a heavy 1/2-quart saucepan, melt jam over low heat while stirring constantly. Force through a tea strainer. Brush the warm tart with the glaze.
6. Serve warm or chilled with whipped cream.

Yield: One 9-inch tart, 6 to 8 servings.

Blueberry Pie

Pie Pastry for a Double Crust
  9-inch Pie (p. 316)
1 quart blueberries
1 tablespoon lemon juice
1/2 teaspoon finely grated
  orange rind
3/4 cup granulated sugar
1/4 cup cornstarch
1/8 teaspoon ground
  cinnamon

2 tablespoons (1/4 stick)
  butter or margarine
Milk to brush top crust
  (optional)
1 tablespoon granulated
  sugar for top crust
  (optional)

1. Line a 9-inch pie plate using a little more than half the pastry. Refrigerate pie shell and remaining pastry while filling is prepared.

2. In a large bowl, toss blueberries with lemon juice and orange rind.

3. In a small bowl, mix sugar, cornstarch, and cinnamon together. Sprinkle over blueberries. Toss gently but thoroughly. Turn filling into pie shell. Dot with butter.

4. Roll remaining pastry and make a lattice or plain top crust. Brush crust with milk. Sprinkle top of pie with sugar.

5. Bake pie on a rack in the lower third of a preheated 400° F oven for 20 minutes. Reduce temperature to 350° F and bake until crust is golden brown and filling is bubbling, about 40 minutes. Place an aluminum foil covered baking sheet on the rack below the pie to catch any drips.

6. Serve warm or chilled.

Yield: One 9-inch pie, 8 servings.

Blueberry Sour Cream Pie

This pie can be prepared quickly since the crust is made with crumbs.

CRUMBS
1 1/4 cups all-purpose flour
1/2 cup granulated sugar
1/2 teaspoon baking powder
1 teaspoon ground cinnamon

1/4 teaspoon grated nutmeg
10 tablespoons (1 1/4 sticks)
  butter or margarine, chilled
Finely grated rind of a lemon

FILLING
1/2 cup granulated sugar
2 tablespoons all-purpose
  flour
2 large eggs

1 cup sour cream
2 teaspoons lemon juice
1 pint blueberries

TOPPING
2 tablespoons confectioners' sugar

1. Prepare crumbs: In a food processor with a steel blade, combine flour, sugar, baking powder, cinnamon, and nutmeg. Process for a few seconds until mixed. Add butter, cut into 1/2-inch cubes, and lemon rind. Process until crumbs form.

2. If a food processor is not available, combine dry ingredients in a bowl and use a pastry blender to cut in butter. Stir in lemon rind.

3. Reserve 3/4 cup of crumbs. Press remaining crumbs on bottom and sides of a buttered 9-inch pie pan to form a crust.

4. Prepare filling: In a large bowl, stir sugar and flour together. Add eggs and whisk until smooth and light yellow. Stir in sour cream and lemon juice. Add blueberries. Mix gently.

5. Pour filling into crust. Cover with remaining crumbs.

6. Bake in a preheated 375° F oven until crumbs are brown and a knife inserted about 1 1/2-inches from the center comes out clean, about 30 minutes. Cool.

7. Sift confectioners' sugar over pie. Serve warm or chilled.

Yield: One 9-inch pie, 8 servings.

Poached Pear or Apple Tart

This delicious tart should be assembled immediately before serving or the moisture from the fruit will cause the glaze to become watery.

2 cups water
1/3 cup dry white wine
2/3 cup granulated sugar
1 teaspoon vanilla extract
3 ripe pears or 3 1/2 apples, peeled, halved, and cored
1/4 cup guava or apple jelly
1 teaspoon pear or apple liqueur (optional)

1 completely baked 9-inch tart or flan shell (Tart Pastry, p. 321)
1 1/4 cups Cream Filling for Pastries (Crème Pâtissière) (p. 350) flavored with pear or apple liqueur, kirsch, or vanilla extract
1/4 cup sliced or slivered almonds, toasted

1. In a nonreactive 4 1/2-quart pot, combine water, wine, sugar, and vanilla. Bring to a boil, stirring until sugar is dissolved.

2. Add pear or apple halves and simmer until just tender when pierced with a knife, about 10 to 15 minutes. Turn halves once halfway through this time. Use a slotted spoon to transfer the halves to a plate. When cool, cut the halves crosswise into 1/4-inch slices keeping the slices of each half together. Reserve.

3. Boil the cooking liquid until reduced to 1/2 cup. Add jelly and liqueur and stir until smooth. Transfer this glaze to a heavy 1/2-quart saucepan and reserve.

— This recipe may be prepared ahead to this point. —

4. At serving time, brush a little of the glaze on the bottom of the pastry shell. Fill shell with cream filling.

5. Arrange pear or apple halves on top of filling. Place one half in the center and the others around it. Coat fruit with glaze.

6. Sprinkle almonds around edge of tart. Serve immediately.

Yield: One 9-inch tart, 8 servings.

Peach Crumb Pie

PASTRY
1 unbaked 9-inch pie shell (Pie Pastry, p. 316)

FILLING
2 tablespoons (1/4 stick)
butter or margarine, at
room temperature
4 cups peeled and sliced
peaches
1 teaspoon lemon juice

6 tablespoons light brown
sugar, firmly packed
3/4 teaspoon ground
cinnamon
1/4 teaspoon grated nutmeg
1 tablespoon cornstarch

CRUMBS
1/2 cup all-purpose flour
1/2 cup light brown sugar,
firmly packed
1 teaspoon ground cinnamon

1/4 teaspoon grated nutmeg
1/4 cup (1/2 stick) butter or
margarine, chilled
3/4 cup chopped pecans

TOPPING
Whipped Cream for Desserts (p. 371) (optional)

1. Refrigerate pie shell while filling is prepared.
2. Spread the butter on the bottom of an 11 x 7-inch (2-quart) baking dish. Add peaches, sprinkle with lemon juice, and toss.
3. In a small bowl, mix brown sugar, cinnamon, nutmeg, and cornstarch together. Sprinkle over peaches.
4. Bake in a 400° F oven until peaches are just tender, about 20 minutes. Use a large spoon to stir mixture every 5 minutes while baking. Cool to room temperature.
5. Prepare crumbs: In a food processor with a steel blade, combine flour, sugar, cinnamon, and nutmeg. Process for a few seconds until mixed.
6. Add butter, cut into 1/2-inch cubes. Process until crumbs form. If a food processor is not available, combine dry ingredients in a bowl and use a pastry blender to cut in butter.
7. Spread 1/2 cup of the crumb mixture over the bottom of the pie shell. Fill shell with peaches.
8. Stir pecans into remaining crumbs. Spread over peaches.
9. Bake pie on a rack in the lower third of a preheated 400° F oven until crumbs are golden brown, about 20 minutes.

10. Serve warm or chilled with whipped cream.

Yield: One 9-inch pie, 8 servings.

Peach Tart

5 or 6 peaches, preferably
  freestone
2 teaspoons lemon juice
2 teaspoons water
1/2 cup apricot jam
2 tablespoons peach liqueur,
  Grand Marnier, or water
Whipped Cream for Desserts
  (p. 371) or 1 2/3 cups Cream
  Filling for Pastries (Crème
  Pâtissière) (p. 350)

1 completely baked 10-inch
  tart or flan shell (Tart Pastry,
  p. 321)
1/2 cup slivered almonds,
  toasted
Mint leaves for garnish
  (optional)

1. Drop peaches into boiling water for 30 seconds. Transfer to cold water. Peel and quarter peaches. Cut each quarter in half crosswise to form triangular pieces. Combine lemon juice and water. Sprinkle over peaches and toss gently. Refrigerate until needed.

— This recipe may be prepared ahead to this point. —

2. Assemble tart as close to serving time as possible, no longer than 3 hours ahead. In a heavy 1/2-quart saucepan, combine apricot jam and peach liqueur. Stir over low heat until jam is melted. Strain through a tea strainer. Brush pastry shell with half of this glaze.
3. Spread whipped cream or cream filling in pastry shell.
4. Arrange peaches, peeled side down, on top of filling. The peaches should be in one layer and close to each other. Brush peaches with remaining glaze.
5. Sprinkle almonds on outer edge of tart. Garnish with mint leaves.
6. Refrigerate until served.

Yield: One 10-inch tart, 8 servings.

Strawberry Tart or Pie

FOR A 10-INCH TART OR 9-INCH PIE

1 1/4 cups Cream Filling for Pastries (Crème Pâtissière) (p. 350) or Pastry Cream (p. 351), flavored with 2 tablespoons framboise (raspberry liqueur) or Grand Marnier or 1 teaspoon vanilla extract

1 completely baked 10-inch tart or flan shell (Tart Pastry, p. 321) or 9-inch pie shell (Pie Pastry, p. 316)

3 pints fresh ripe strawberries, washed and stemmed

2/3 cup currant jelly

2 tablespoons framboise (raspberry liqueur) (optional)

1/3 cup sliced almonds, toasted (optional)

Confectioners' sugar for dusting (optional)

FOR A 9-INCH TART

1 1/4 cups Cream Filling for Pastries (Crème Pâtissière) (p. 350)

1 completely baked 9-inch tart or flan shell (Tart Pastry, p. 321)

2 pints fresh ripe strawberries, washed and stemmed

1/3 cup currant jelly

1 tablespoon framboise (raspberry liqueur) (optional)

1/4 cup sliced almonds, toasted

Confectioners' sugar for dusting (optional)

1. Assemble tart as close to serving time as possible, no longer than 3 hours ahead.

2. Spread cream filling or pastry cream in pastry shell.

3. Arrange strawberries, stem sides down, on top of filling. Place the largest berries in the center.

4. In a heavy 1/2-quart saucepan, stir currant jelly and framboise over low heat until melted. Brush strawberries with this glaze.

5. Sprinkle almonds or confectioners' sugar on strawberries at edge of tart.

6. Refrigerate until served.

Yield: One 9 or 10-inch tart or 9-inch pie, 8 to 10 servings.

Coconut Ambrosia Pie or Tart

3/4 cup grated fresh, frozen,
or packaged coconut (p. 16),
divided
Pastry Cream (p. 351),
flavored with 2 tablespoons
Grand Marnier or other
orange liqueur
1 completely baked 9-inch pie
shell (Pie Pastry, p. 316) or
10-inch flan or tart shell
(Tart Pastry, p. 321)

2 bananas, peeled and sliced
1/4-inch thick
2 oranges, peeled and cut
into sections
1/2 cup apricot jam
2 tablespoons Grand Marnier
or water
6 to 8 maraschino cherries,
halved (optional)

1. Assemble pie as close to serving time as possible, no longer than 3 hours ahead.

2. Stir 1/2 cup of the coconut into the pastry cream. Fill pastry shell with pastry cream.

3. Place a ring of banana slices on the outer edge of the pastry cream.

4. Arrange a ring of orange sections inside the banana slices with one narrow end of each section touching the bananas and the other pointing inward.

5. Starting at the inner edge of the orange sections, cover the center of the pastry with the remaining banana slices in an overlapping rose petal pattern.

6. In a heavy 1/2-quart saucepan, stir apricot jam and Grand Marnier over low heat until jam is melted. Strain through a tea strainer. Brush glaze over bananas and oranges.

7. Sprinkle remaining coconut on top of the orange sections.

8. Place a cherry half in the center of the pastry and on every other banana slice around the edge of the pie.

9. Refrigerate until served.

Yield: One 9-inch pie or 10-inch tart, 8 servings.

Pineapple Rum Tart or Pie

1 fresh pineapple
1 completely baked 10-inch
  tart or flan shell (Tart Pastry,
  p. 321) or 9-inch pie shell
  (Pie Pastry, p. 316)
Pastry Cream (p. 351),
  flavored with 2 tablespoons
  dark rum

2/3 cup pineapple jam
1 tablespoon dark rum
1/2 cup whipping cream
2 tablespoons confectioners'
  sugar
9 maraschino cherries

1. Cut the crown of leaves off the pineapple. Cut a thin slice off the stem end so the pineapple will stand upright. Use a large serrated knife to remove the peel in lengthwise strips. Split the pineapple lengthwise. Cut out the core in each half. Cut each pineapple half crosswise into 1/4-inch slices. Reserve.

— This recipe may be prepared ahead to this point. —

2. Assemble this pie as close to serving time as possible, no longer than 3 hours ahead.

3. Fill shell with pastry cream. Starting at the edge of the shell, arrange the pineapple slices in overlapping circles working toward the center of the shell. The completed arrangement should resemble a large open rose.

4. In a heavy 1/2-quart saucepan, combine jam and rum. Stir over low heat until melted. Spread this glaze on the pineapple slices.

5. Whip cream with confectioners' sugar. Use a pastry bag with a 1/2-inch star tip (#5) to pipe 16 rosettes of cream around the edge and a larger rosette in the center of the pastry.

6. Dry cherries on paper towels. Place a whole cherry on top of the center rosette and half a cherry on each of the rosettes at the edge.

7. Refrigerate until served.

Yield: One 10-inch tart or 9-inch pie, 8 servings.

Banana Cream Pie or Tart

1 completely baked 9-inch pie
  shell (Pie Pastry, p. 316) or
  10-inch flan or tart shell
  (Tart Pastry, p. 321)
Pastry Cream (p. 351),
  flavored with 2 tablespoons
  dark rum
3 bananas, peeled and sliced
  1/4-inch thick

1/2 cup apricot jam
1 tablespoon dark rum
1/2 cup whipping cream
  (optional)
2 tablespoons confectioners'
  sugar (optional)

1. Assemble this pie as close to serving time as possible, no longer than 3 hours ahead.

2. Fill shell with pastry cream.

3. Cover pastry cream with banana slices. The slices should be in one layer and close to each other.

4. In a heavy 1/2-quart saucepan, combine apricot jam and rum. Stir over low heat until jam is melted. Strain through a tea strainer. Brush banana slices with this glaze.

5. Whip cream with confectioners' sugar. Use a pastry bag with a 1/2-inch star tip (#5) to pipe 16 rosettes of cream around the edge of the pastry.

6. Refrigerate until served.

Yield: One 9-inch pie or 10-inch tart, 8 servings.

Coconut Cream Pie or Tart

1 1/4 cups grated fresh, frozen, or packaged coconut (p. 16), divided
1 completely baked 9-inch pie shell (Pie Pastry, p. 316) or 10-inch flan or tart shell (Tart Pastry, p. 321)

2 1/2 cups Cream Filling for Pastries (Crème Pâtissière) (p. 350)
1 cup (1/2 pint) whipping cream
1/4 cup confectioners' sugar
1/4 teaspoon vanilla extract

1. Toast 1/4 cup of the coconut by stirring it frequently on a baking sheet in a 350° F oven. A toaster oven is useful for this. Reserve.

2. Stir remaining 1 cup of coconut into cream filling. Refrigerate until needed.

— This recipe may be prepared ahead to this point. —

3. Assemble this pie as close to serving time as possible, no longer than 3 hours ahead. Fill pastry shell with cream filling. Reserve.

4. In an electric mixer bowl, combine whipping cream, confectioners' sugar, and vanilla. Use a wire whisk attachment, if available, and beat at moderate speed until the cream holds the impressions made by the beater and is thick enough to retain its shape. Do not overbeat or the cream will become grainy and separate.

5. If desired, reserve about 1/2 cup of the whipped cream to make rosettes. Spread remaining whipped cream evenly over cream filling. Use a pastry bag and a 1/2-inch star tip (#5) to pipe 12 rosettes around the edge of the pastry. A large rosette may be piped in the center. Also, six rosettes may be piped in a circle midway between the center and outer circle of rosettes.

6. Sprinkle the toasted coconut between the rosettes.

7. Refrigerate until served.

Yield: One 9-inch pie or 10-inch tart, 8 servings.

Nesselrode Pie or Tart

8 ounces chopped mixed
  candied fruit
1/4 cup dark rum
Pastry Cream (p. 351),
  flavored with 2 tablespoons
  dark rum
1 completely baked 9-inch pie
  shell (Pie Pastry, p. 316) or
  10-inch flan or tart shell
  (Tart Pastry, p. 321)

Whipped Cream for Desserts
  (p. 371)
3 ounces (3 squares) coarsely
  shaved semisweet chocolate
16 candied or maraschino
  cherries

1. Soak candied fruit in rum for 12 hours or longer.

2. Assemble this pie as close to serving time as possible, no longer than 3 hours ahead.

3. Fold candied fruit into pastry cream. Spread pastry cream in shell.

4. Reserve one-quarter of the whipped cream to make rosettes. Spread remaining cream evenly on top of filling. Use a pastry bag with a 1/2-inch star tip (#5) to pipe 16 rosettes around the edge of the pastry. Top each rosette with a cherry.

5. Sprinkle shaved chocolate on pie.

6. Refrigerate until served.

Yield: One 9-inch pie or 10-inch tart, 8 to 12 servings.

Pumpkin Pie

1 unbaked 9-inch pie shell
  (Pie Pastry, p. 316)
1 can (16 ounces) pumpkin
1 cup light brown sugar,
  firmly packed
3 large eggs
1 1/2 teaspoons ground
  cinnamon
1/4 teaspoon grated nutmeg

1/4 teaspoon ground dried
  ginger
1/8 teaspoon ground cloves
1 cup half-and-half
2 tablespoons (1/4 stick)
  butter or margarine,
  melted (optional)

1. Refrigerate pie shell while preparing filling.

2. Use an electric mixer or whisk to blend remaining ingredients in order listed. Pour into pie shell

3. Bake pie on a rack in the lower third of a preheated 400° F oven for 10 minutes. Reduce oven temperature to 350° F and bake until a knife inserted in the center comes out clean, about 45 to 50 minutes.

4. Serve warm or chilled.

Yield: One 9-inch pie, 8 servings.

Note: The pie may be garnished with Whipped Cream for Desserts (p. 371) and pecan halves.

Pecan Pie

1 unbaked 9-inch pie shell
 (Pie Pastry, p. 316)
4 large eggs
1 cup granulated or light
 brown sugar
1 cup dark corn syrup
1/4 teaspoon salt

3 tablespoons butter or
 margarine, melted
1 1/2 teaspoons vanilla
 extract
1 1/4 cups pecan halves or
 broken pieces

1. Refrigerate pie shell while preparing filling.

2. In a large bowl, combine eggs and sugar. Beat with a whisk until smooth. Stir in remaining ingredients. Pour into shell.

3. Bake pie on a rack in the lower third of a preheated 400° F oven for 10 minutes. Reduce oven temperature to 350° F and bake until a knife inserted halfway between the center and edge of the pie comes out clean, about 40 to 45 minutes.

4. Serve at room temperature.

Yield: One 9-inch pie, 8 servings.

Note: This pie may be served with Whipped Cream for Desserts (p. 371).

Miniature Pecan Tarts

PASTRY
1 large egg yolk
1/2 teaspoon vanilla extract
1 cup all-purpose flour
2 tablespoons granulated
  sugar

1/2 cup (1 stick) butter or
  margarine, divided
  lengthwise into quarters and
  cut crosswise into 1/2-inch
  cubes, chilled

FILLING
1 large egg
1/4 cup granulated sugar
1 teaspoon all-purpose flour
1/2 teaspoon vanilla extract
1/2 cup dark corn syrup

2 tablespoons (1/4 stick)
  melted butter or margarine
3/4 cup coarsely chopped
  pecans
24 pecan halves

1. Prepare pastry: In a cup, stir egg yolk and vanilla together. Refrigerate until needed. Combine flour and sugar in a food processor with a steel blade. Add butter. Process with a pulsing action until mixture resembles cornmeal.

2. Pour egg yolk and vanilla over flour mixture. Process until ingredients are just blended, about 5 seconds.

3. If a food processor is not available, use a pastry blender to cut butter into flour and sugar. Then stir in egg yolk and vanilla mixture.

4. Form dough into a ball and flatten into a disc about 1-inch thick. Wrap in plastic wrap and chill for at least 1 hour.

5. Roll dough 1/8-inch thick between two pieces of wax paper. Chill rolled dough between the sheets of wax paper. This will make the dough easier to handle. Divide dough into 24 squares or circles. Use the pastry pieces to line two buttered miniature muffin pans each having twelve 1 3/4-inch cups. Refrigerate the lined pans.

6. Prepare filling: In a small bowl, whisk egg and sugar together until smooth. Stir in flour, vanilla, corn syrup, butter, and chopped pecans.

7. Fill cups no higher than 1/8-inch below the top edge of the crust. Be sure the pecans are evenly distributed among the tarts. Top each tart with a pecan half.

8. Bake tarts in a preheated 350° F oven until golden brown, about 30 minutes. Immediately loosen tarts from pans using a knife with a sharp tip. Transfer tarts to a wire rack to cool.

Yield: 24 tarts.

Mincemeat Pie

MINCEMEAT
1/2 pound beef suet
5 cups peeled, cored, and
   coarsely chopped apples
15 ounces (3 cups) seedless
   black raisins
10 ounces (2 cups) dried
   currants
1 cup seedless white raisins
12 ounces (1 1/2 cups)
   chopped mixed candied fruit
1 1/2 cups light brown sugar,
   firmly packed

1 teaspoon ground cinnamon
1/2 teaspoon grated nutmeg
1/2 teaspoon ground allspice
1/4 teaspoon ground cloves
Finely grated rind and juice
   of 2 lemons
Finely grated rind and juice
   of 1 orange
1 cup brandy

MINCEMEAT PIE
Pie Pastry for a Double Crust
   9-inch Pie (p. 316)

1/3 recipe (2 3/4 cups) of
   the above Mincemeat

MINCEMEAT

1. Cut suet into 1-inch cubes. Grind in a food processor with a steel blade or use a meat grinder. In a heavy 4 1/2-quart pot, stir suet over moderate heat until fat melts and suet becomes golden brown.

2. Add apples. Stir over moderate heat until apples are barely tender.

3. Add all remaining ingredients except brandy. Heat and stir until ingredients are mixed and hot. Remove from heat and stir in brandy.

4. Although the mincemeat may be used immediately, it will develop more flavor if refrigerated for at least 4 weeks before using. Store in a covered glass, plastic, or earthenware container. Stir the mincemeat once a week.

Yield: 8 1/2 cups, enough for three 9-inch pies.

Notes:

1. I like to double or triple this recipe and give the mincemeat as presents a week or so before Christmas. The mincemeat may be packed in decorative or plain 1 1/2 pint jars. One recipe will fill three jars and each jar will contain enough mincemeat for one 9-inch pie. The jars may be decorated with red and green ribbon.

2. Instead of making pies, the mincemeat may be heated and served over Vanilla Ice Cream (p. 368).

MINCEMEAT PIE
1. Line a 9-inch pie plate using a little more than half the pastry. Fill pie shell with mincemeat. Use remaining pastry to form a top crust (lattice or plain).

2. Bake pie in a preheated 375° F oven until crust is golden brown, about 45 minutes.

3. Serve pie warm or at room temperature.

Yield: One 9-inch pie, 6 to 8 servings.

Note: The pie may be dusted with confectioners' sugar and served with Whipped Cream for Desserts (p. 371) or Vanilla Ice Cream (p. 368).

Lemon Meringue Pie or Tart

PASTRY SHELL
1 completely baked 9-inch pie shell (Pie Pastry, p. 316) or 10-inch tart or flan shell (Tart Pastry, p. 321)

2 tablespoons dry bread crumbs
2 tablespoons granulated sugar

LEMON FILLING
1/2 cup cornstarch
1 1/2 cups granulated sugar
1 2/3 cups cold water
4 large egg yolks

2 teaspoons finely grated lemon rind
1/2 cup lemon juice
3 tablespoons butter or margarine

MERINGUE
4 large egg whites
1/4 teaspoon cream of tartar

1/2 cup granulated sugar

1. Prepare pastry shell: Mix bread crumbs and granulated sugar together. Spread this mixture over the bottom of the crust to help prevent it from becoming soggy.

2. Prepare filling: In a heavy 2 1/2-quart saucepan, mix cornstarch and sugar together. Gradually stir in water until smooth. Stir over

moderate heat until very thick and clear. Reduce heat. Simmer and stir for 3 minutes.

3. In a small bowl, beat egg yolks, lemon rind, and juice together until blended. Add one-third of the hot filling to the bowl. Mix thoroughly and return to saucepan. Stir over moderate heat until very thick, about 7 minutes. Do not let boil. Remove from heat. Stir in butter.

4. Transfer filling to a stainless steel bowl. Place over cold water and ice cubes. Stir occasionally until cold. Spread filling in crust.

5. Prepare meringue: Beat egg whites and cream of tartar until foamy. Gradually beat in granulated sugar and continue to beat until thick glossy peaks are formed. Use a rubber spatula to cover the pie with meringue. The meringue should be higher in the middle than at the edges.

6. Starting at the center of the pie, press the flat side of the rubber spatula into the meringue and raise it quickly to form tall peaks all over the surface of the pie.

7. Bake pie in a preheated 350° F oven until the meringue has browned, about 10 minutes.

8. Serve chilled or at room temperature.

Yield: One 9-inch pie or 10-inch flan, 8 servings.

Lemon or Lime Chiffon Pie

This pie may be decorated with flair or served plain.

1 envelope (1 tablespoon)
unflavored gelatin
1/3 cup cold water
4 large eggs, separated
1 cup granulated sugar,
divided
6 tablespoons lemon or lime
juice
1/2 teaspoon finely grated
lemon or lime rind (avoid
the bitter white part)

1 completely baked 9-inch pie
shell (Pie Pastry, p. 316) or
Graham Cracker or Cookie
Crumb Pie Crust (p. 322)
Whipped Cream for Desserts
(p. 371) (optional)
1 lemon slice cut into 8
wedges, each about 1/4-inch
wide (optional)
8 mint leaves (optional)
1/3 cup sliced almonds,
toasted (optional)

1. In a cup, soften gelatin in water. Reserve.

2. In a heavy, nonreactive 1 1/2-quart saucepan, combine egg yolks and 1/2 cup of sugar. Whisk until light yellow. Stir in lemon or lime juice and rind.

3. Using a wooden spatula or spoon, stir mixture over low heat until thick. The mixture is done when a mark made with a finger on the spatula holds its shape. Do not overcook. Remove from heat and add gelatin. Stir until dissolved.

4. Immediately transfer mixture to a stainless steel bowl placed over cold water and ice cubes. Stir occasionally until mixture begins to gel around edges. Do not let mixture gel anymore or it will be difficult to fold in the egg whites in the next step. If mixture becomes too thick, remove bowl from ice water and whisk until soft.

5. Meanwhile, in an electric mixer, beat egg whites until foamy. Gradually beat in 1/2 cup of sugar and continue to beat until whites are stiff but not dry. Fold whites, one-third at a time, into lemon mixture.

6. Pour filling into pie shell. Refrigerate until filling is set, at least 1 hour.

7. If desired, reserve one-fifth of the whipped cream to make rosettes. Spread remaining cream evenly over filling. For easier serving, the pie may be cut into 8 pieces at this time.

8. Use a pastry bag and a 1/2-inch star tip (#5) to pipe 8 rosettes around the edge of the pastry. Top each rosette with a tiny lemon wedge.

9. Place mint leaves so the base of each leaf touches a rosette and the tip points upward and toward the center of the pie.

10. Sprinkle pie with toasted almonds.

11. Chill until served.

Yield: One 9-inch pie, 8 servings.

Lemon Coconut Chess Pie

1 unbaked 9-inch pie shell
   (Pie Pastry, p. 316)
1 1/2 cups granulated sugar
2 tablespoons all-purpose
   flour
4 large eggs
1 1/2 teaspoons finely grated
   lemon rind

1/3 cup lemon juice
1/2 cup (1 stick) butter or
   margarine, melted
3/4 cup grated fresh, frozen,
   or packaged coconut,
   firmly packed (p. 16)

1. Refrigerate pie shell while filling is prepared.

2. In an electric mixer, mix sugar and flour together. Add eggs. Beat until smooth and light yellow.

3. Mix in remaining ingredients. Pour into pie shell.

4. Bake pie on a rack in the lower third of a preheated 400° F oven for 10 minutes. Reduce oven temperature to 350° F. Bake until filling is golden brown and a cake tester placed in the center comes out clean, about 20 minutes.

5. Serve at room temperature or chilled.

Yield: One 9-inch pie, 8 to 10 servings.

Note: This pie may be served with Whipped Cream for Desserts (p. 371).

Bakewell Tarts

A British specialty for tea time or anytime.

Pie Pastry for a Single Crust
8 or 9-inch Pie (p. 316)
1/4 cup (1/2 stick) butter
(no substitute), at room
temperature
1/4 cup granulated sugar
1 large egg, at room
temperature
1/4 + 1/8 teaspoon almond
extract, divided
2 tablespoons all-purpose
flour
1/4 cup finely ground
almonds, toasted
About 2 tablespoons
raspberry jam
1/2 cup confectioners' sugar
1 1/2 teaspoons milk
1 teaspoon lemon juice
Sliced almonds, toasted,
for garnish (optional)
Raspberry jam for garnish
(optional)

1. Prepare pastry: Roll dough 1/8-inch thick between two pieces of wax paper. Chill dough between the sheets of wax paper. Cut dough into 24 squares or circles. Use the pastry pieces to line two buttered miniature muffin pans each having twelve 1 3/4-inch cups. Refrigerate the lined pans.

2. Prepare filling: Beat butter until smooth. Add sugar and beat until fluffy. Add egg and 1/4 teaspoon of almond extract. Beat until smooth and light. Stir in flour until blended. Stir in almonds.

3. Place about 1/4 teaspoon of raspberry jam in the center of each tart shell. Fill shells with filling.

4. Bake tarts in a preheated 375° F oven until golden brown, about 20 minutes. Cool in pans for 5 minutes before turning out onto wire racks.

5. Prepare frosting: In a small bowl, combine confectioners' sugar, milk, lemon juice, and 1/8 teaspoon of almond extract. Beat until smooth. Spread on the cooled tarts.

6. Decorate each tart with an almond slice placed in the center. Apply almond slices while frosting is still moist so they will adhere. Use a toothpick to place a drop of raspberry jam in the center of each almond slice.

7. Serve tarts warm or at room temperature. These tarts are elegant when served in fluted paper cups.

Yield: 24 tarts.

Apple Strudel

A lot of trouble but great fun and my favorite dessert. This strudel is always the star of my Christmas dinner parties. Give it a try. You can do it!

1 1/3 cups warm water
(105° - 115° F)
1 large egg
2 tablespoons vegetable oil
About 4 to 4 1/2 cups all-
purpose flour
Apple Filling for Strudel
(p. 347)
1 cup fine dry bread crumbs

1 cup granulated sugar
1/2 teaspoon grated nutmeg
1 1/4 cups (2 1/2 sticks) butter
(no substitute), melted,
divided
1/2 cup raisins
1 1/4 cups chopped pecans
Confectioners' sugar for
dusting

1. In an electric mixer bowl, combine water, egg, and vegetable oil. Add 2 1/2 cups of flour. Use a paddle attachment, if available, and beat at medium speed until blended, about 2 minutes.

2. Stop mixer and add 1 1/2 cups of flour. Using a dough hook at low speed, begin to knead the dough. Gradually add additional flour by tablespoon amounts until the dough gathers on the dough hook and completely cleans the bottom and sides of the bowl, about 3 to 4 minutes. About 4 to 8 tablespoons of flour will be needed. Then knead the dough for an additional 5 minutes. If an electric mixer is not available, the dough can be kneaded by hand.

3. Turn dough onto a lightly floured work surface. Knead by hand until it becomes elastic and forms a smooth ball, about 1 minute. Place in an oiled bowl, turning to coat the top with oil. Cover bowl with plastic wrap and let rest at room temperature for 45 minutes.

4. The apple filling may be prepared while the dough is resting. Reserve.

5. Combine bread crumbs, sugar, nutmeg, and 1/2 cup of melted butter. Reserve.

6. Cover a rectangular table, about 48 to 56 x 30 to 42-inches, with a clean bed sheet. Dust the sheet with flour and rub it in. Place the dough in the center of the table. Stretch or roll it into a circle about 16-inches in diameter. Brush dough with vegetable oil.

7. Stretch the dough to the edges of the table or to an area of at least 48 x 30-inches. The thinner the dough is stretched, the flakier the strudel will become. Place your hands under the dough and use the back of your

hands to gently stretch the dough. First stretch the center of the dough until it is thin. Then work outward, stretching the surrounding dough. At times, use the tips of your fingers to gently pull the edges of the dough outward. Work toward getting the edges to hang over the table. This will anchor the dough and keep it stretched. Immediately repair any tears by overlapping the torn edges and pressing them together.

8. After the dough is completely stretched, cut off the thick edges with a scissors or sharp knife. Let dough dry until it starts to wrinkle, about 15 minutes.

9. Place the apple filling along the edge of one of the short sides of the dough (see Note 2).

10. Sprinkle bread crumb mixture evenly over the entire half of dough that has the apple filling at its edge. Sprinkle raisins and then pecans over bread crumb mixture.

11. Use 1/2 cup of the melted butter to brush the half of dough not covered with bread crumbs.

12. Fold the edge of each long side inward a few inches by lifting up the edge of the sheet. Starting at the side with the apple filling, roll up the strudel like a jelly roll by lifting and pulling the sheet.

13. Use part of the remaining butter to brush a 17 x 12-inch rimmed baking sheet. Transfer strudel to baking sheet bending it into a horseshoe shape. Brush strudel with butter.

14. Bake in a preheated 375° F oven until the surface is golden brown, about 40 minutes. Brush strudel with melted butter 20 and 30 minutes after the start of baking.

15. Use large spatulas to remove the strudel from the pan as soon as it is baked. Cool on a wire rack. Cut into serving pieces.

16. The strudel may be served immediately, refrigerated, or frozen. Reheat, uncovered, in a 325° F oven. If the strudel has been frozen, let it reach room temperature before reheating.

17. Sift confectioners' sugar over the strudel just before serving.

Yield: About 15 to 20 servings.

Notes:

1. Whipped Cream for Desserts (p. 371) makes a delicious topping. The whipped cream may be garnished with a light sprinkling of grated nutmeg.

2. Strudel may be made in small pieces to serve at parties. Place the apple filling along the edge of a long side rather than a short one (see Step 9). Cut the rolled strudel into strips that will fit on the baking sheet. The baking time will be about 30 minutes.

Apple Filling for Strudel

1/4 cup (1/2 stick) butter
(no substitute)
12 cups peeled, cored, and
sliced, 1/2-inch thick, baking
apples such as Cortland,
McIntosh, or Rome Beauty
2/3 cup raisins
1/4 cup lemon juice

Finely grated rind of 2 lemons
1 cup granulated sugar
2 tablespoons cornstarch
2 teaspoons ground
cinnamon
1/2 teaspoon grated nutmeg
Pinch ground cloves
(optional)

1. Spread the butter on the bottom of a 15 x 10-inch (4-quart) baking dish or pan. Add apples, raisins, lemon juice, and lemon rind. Toss gently.

2. In a small bowl, combine remaining ingredients. Mix thoroughly. Sprinkle over apples. Toss gently.

3. Bake in a 400° F oven until apples are barely tender, about 25 minutes. Use a large spoon to stir mixture several times while baking.

4. Cool to room temperature.

Yield: 6 cups.

Cream Puffs and Eclairs

CREAM PUFF PASTRY
(PÂTE À CHOUX)

6 tablespoons (3/4 stick)
  butter or margarine
1 cup water
1/16 teaspoon grated nutmeg
  (optional)

1 teaspoon granulated sugar
  (only for dessert cream
  puffs and eclairs) (optional)
1 1/3 cups sifted all-purpose
  flour
4 large eggs

1. In a heavy 2-quart saucepan, bring butter, water, nutmeg, and sugar to a boil. Remove from heat. Immediately add flour all at once. Use a wooden spoon or spatula to beat ingredients into a smooth thick paste. Cool until warm or room temperature.

2. Transfer mixture to a food processor with a steel blade. Add eggs, one at a time, processing after each egg is added until mixture is blended. If a food processor is not available, use a wooden spoon to beat in eggs one at a time.

3. Line a large baking sheet with aluminum foil. Do not butter the foil or the cream puffs or eclairs will spread and not rise properly while baking. Shape the paste into cream puffs or eclairs according to the following directions:

CREAM PUFFS

Divide the paste into 8 to 12 spoonfuls evenly spaced on the baking sheet. Use a spatula to shape each spoonful into a smooth circular mound. Alternatively, a pastry bag with a 3/4-inch plain round tip (#9) may be used to shape the puffs.

ECLAIRS

Use a pastry bag with a 3/4-inch plain round tip (#9) to pipe the paste onto the baking sheet. See illustration, next page. Each shape should be about 5-inches long and 1 1/2-inches wide. When the end of each length is reached (A), release pressure on the pastry bag. Then, in one quick motion, push the tip upward and backward over the length to separate the paste from the pastry bag (B). The tip of a table knife may be used to smooth any irregular areas. There will be enough paste to make 8 to 10 eclairs.

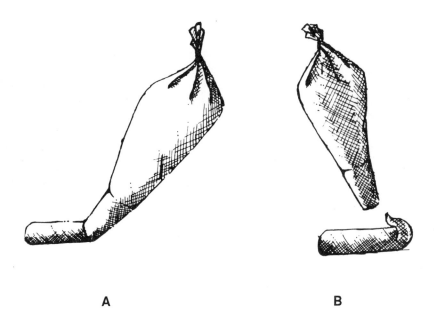

A   **B**

4. Bake cream puffs or eclairs in a preheated 425° F oven for 20 minutes. Reduce temperature to 375° F and continue to bake until golden brown, about 10 to 15 minutes.

5. Immediately remove pastries from foil. Split pastries in half horizontally. Eclairs may be split leaving one long side uncut. Use a spoon to scrape out the moist centers. Return pastries to baking sheet with inside surfaces upward.

6. Turn off oven. Place pastries in oven, with door partially open, until centers are dry, about 15 minutes.

7. Store pastries in a plastic bag until needed. They may be frozen. If pastries become soft, they can be crisped by placing them in a 400° F oven for a few minutes.

8. Assemble pastries just before serving. Fill the cream puffs or eclairs with ice cream, Whipped Cream for Desserts (p. 371), Pastry Cream (p. 351), Coffee Pastry Cream (p. 352), Cream Filling for Pastries (Crème Pâtissière) (p. 350), or Chocolate Cream Filling for Pastries (Crème Pâtissière) (p. 351). The pastries may be dusted with confectioners' sugar or topped with Chocolate Fudge Sauce (p. 373), Chocolate Sauce (p. 373), or Butterscotch Sauce (p. 374). Eclairs may be frosted with Chocolate Glaze (p. 297).

Yield: 10 to 12 cream puffs or 8 to 10 eclairs, 8 to 12 servings.

Miniature Cream Puffs and Eclairs

1. Follow the recipe for Cream Puffs and Eclairs (p. 348) but use a 1/2-inch plain round tip (#7) to pipe the dough into 24 shapes. After baking, use a sharp knife to cut a slit in the bottom of each cream puff or in the end of each eclair to let steam escape. It is not necessary to split these small pastries and remove their centers.

2. For dessert cream puffs or eclairs, see Step 8 (p. 349) for filling and topping suggestions. A pastry bag with a 3/8-inch plain round tip (#4) may be used to pipe filling through the slit of each pastry.

3. For cream puffs for appetizers see Miniature Cream Puffs with Assorted Fillings (p. 31).

Yield: 24 cream puffs or eclairs.

Cream Filling for Pastries (Crème Pâtissière)

FOR 1 1/4 CUPS FILLING (1 2/3 CUPS WITH THE OPTIONAL WHIPPED CREAM), FOR BOSTON CREAM PIE OR A 9 OR 10-INCH TART OR FLAN SHELL

1/4 cup granulated sugar
2 large egg yolks
2 tablespoons cornstarch
1 cup half-and-half or milk
1 tablespoon butter
  (no substitute)

1 teaspoon vanilla extract
  OR 1 1/2 teaspoons dark
  rum, Grand Marnier, or
  other liqueur (optional)
1/4 cup whipping cream
  (optional)

FOR 2 1/2 CUPS FILLING (3 1/4 CUPS WITH THE OPTIONAL WHIPPED CREAM), FOR CREAM PUFFS OR ECLAIRS

1/2 cup granulated sugar
4 large egg yolks
5 tablespoons cornstarch
2 cups half-and-half or milk
2 tablespoons (1/4 stick)
  butter (no substitute)

2 teaspoons vanilla extract
  OR 1 tablespoon dark
  rum, Grand Marnier, or
  other liqueur (optional)
1/2 cup whipping cream
  (optional)

1. In a heavy, nonreactive 1 1/2 or 2-quart saucepan, whisk sugar and egg yolks together until thick and light yellow. Stir in cornstarch until smooth.

2. Scald the half-and-half or milk and gradually stir it into the egg yolk mixture. Stir constantly over moderate heat until smooth and thick. Reduce heat to low. Cook for a few minutes, stirring constantly, to prevent scorching. Add butter and stir until melted.

3. Transfer to a stainless steel bowl placed over cold water and ice cubes. Add flavoring. Stir occasionally until cold.

4. Whip cream until soft peaks form. Fold into filling.

5. Refrigerate until needed.

Chocolate Cream Filling for Pastries (Crème Pâtissière)

Prepare Cream Filling for Pastries (Crème Pâtissière) (p. 350) with the following changes:

1. Use half the amount of vanilla.

2. After Step 2, stir 3 ounces (3 squares or 1/2 cup chips) of melted semisweet chocolate into 1 1/4 cups of Cream Filling for Pastries (Crème Pâtissière) (Yield: 1 1/2 cups) or 6 ounces (6 squares or 1 cup chips) of melted semisweet chocolate into 2 1/2 cups of Cream Filling for Pastries (Crème Pâtissière) (Yield: 3 cups).

Pastry Cream

1 envelope (1 tablespoon)
  unflavored gelatin
1/4 cup cold water
1/2 cup granulated sugar
2 large eggs, separated
3 tablespoons all-purpose
  flour

1 cup milk
1 cup (1/2 pint) whipping
  cream
2 teaspoons vanilla extract
  OR 2 tablespoons dark
  rum, Grand Marnier, or
  other liqueur

1. Soften gelatin in water. Reserve.

2. In a heavy, nonreactive 2-quart saucepan, whisk sugar and egg yolks together until smooth and light yellow. Stir in flour until smooth.

3. Scald milk and gradually stir it into egg yolk mixture. Stir constantly over moderate heat until smooth and thick. Reduce heat to low. Cook for a few minutes, stirring constantly, to prevent scorching. Remove from heat. Add gelatin and stir until dissolved.

4. Transfer to a stainless steel bowl placed over cold water and ice cubes. Stir occasionally until mixture begins to gel around edges. Do not let mixture gel anymore or it will be difficult to fold in the egg whites in the next step. If mixture becomes too thick, remove bowl from ice water and whisk until soft.

5. Meanwhile, beat egg whites until stiff but not dry. Gently fold egg whites into mixture.

6. Whip cream until soft peaks form. Fold into pastry cream. Stir in vanilla or other flavoring.

7. Cover with plastic wrap. Refrigerate until firm.

Yield: 4 1/2 cups, for one 9-inch pie shell or one 10-inch tart or flan. This pastry cream may also be used to fill Cream Puffs and Eclairs (p. 348).

Coffee Pastry Cream

Prepare Pastry Cream (p. 351) flavoring it with 1 teaspoon of instant coffee granules dissolved in 1 teaspoon of cold water. One tablespoon of Kahlúa (coffee liqueur) may also be added.

Yield: 4 1/2 cups, for one 9-inch pie shell or one 10-inch tart or flan. This pastry cream may also be used to fill Cream Puffs and Eclairs (p. 348).

Desserts

and

Dessert

Sauces

Grand Marnier Soufflé

I prefer to bake soufflés in individual soufflé dishes rather than in one large dish. When served, an individual soufflé is far more attractive than a spoonful of soufflé scooped from one large dish. Also, individual soufflés bake faster and stay puffed longer than one large soufflé. Individual soufflés may be prepared for baking up to an hour before serving. While you and your guests are finishing the main course, simply place the soufflés in the oven and in about 20 minutes, they will be ready to serve. I like to use ten 6-ounce (3/4-cup) soufflé dishes. This size is ample for most guests. For those with larger appetites, serve additional soufflés that have been kept warm in the oven.

3 tablespoons butter
  (no substitute)
1/4 cup all-purpose flour
1 cup milk
1 tablespoon finely grated
  orange rind
1/2 cup granulated sugar,
  divided, and additional to
  coat soufflé dishes

4 large egg yolks
1/4 cup Grand Marnier
1 teaspoon vanilla extract
5 large egg whites
1/4 teaspoon cream of tartar
Confectioners' sugar for
  dusting

1. Butter ten 6-ounce (3/4-cup) soufflé dishes. Roll 1/2 teaspoon of granulated sugar around the inside of each dish to coat sides and bottom. Place dishes on a rimmed baking sheet. Reserve.

2. In a heavy 2-quart saucepan, melt the butter. Whisk in flour until smooth. Stir over low heat for 2 minutes without browning. Add milk, orange rind, and 1/4 cup of granulated sugar. Stir over moderate heat until smooth and very thick.

3. Remove from heat and let cool for a minute. Add egg yolks and beat until smooth. Stir in Grand Marnier and vanilla. Reserve.

4. Beat egg whites with cream of tartar until foamy. Gradually beat in 1/4 cup of granulated sugar and continue to beat until whites are stiff but not dry.

5. Fold about one-quarter of the egg whites into the egg yolk mixture. Transfer this mixture to the bowl with the remaining egg whites. Fold together gently but thoroughly.

6. Pour mixture into prepared dishes. Each dish should be filled no higher than 1/4-inch below the rim. The dishes may be covered and set aside for up to an hour before baking.

— This recipe may be prepared ahead to this point. —

7. Place the baking sheet on the middle rack of a preheated 375° F oven. Bake, uncovered, until soufflés rise and are golden brown, about 15 to 20 minutes.

8. Sprinkle each soufflé with confectioners' sugar and serve immediately. If the soufflés must wait a few minutes, keep them in the oven with the heat turned off. This will help prevent them from collapsing.

Yield: 10 individual soufflés, 10 servings.

Chocolate Soufflé

1/3 cup + 1/4 cup granulated
  sugar, divided, and
  additional to coat soufflé
  dishes
1/3 cup unsweetened cocoa
2 tablespoons all-purpose
  flour
1/2 cup milk
2 tablespoons (1/4 stick)
  butter (no substitute)

4 large eggs, separated
1/4 teaspoon cream of tartar
Confectioners' sugar for
  dusting
Whipped Cream for Desserts
  (p. 371) (optional)
Chocolate Sauce (p. 373)
  (optional)

1. Butter six 6-ounce (3/4-cup) soufflé dishes. Roll 1/2 teaspoon of granulated sugar around the inside of each dish to coat sides and bottom. Place dishes on a rimmed baking sheet. Reserve.

2. In a heavy 2-quart saucepan, combine 1/3 cup of granulated sugar, cocoa, and flour. Mix thoroughly. Gradually add milk while stirring until smooth.

3. Stir over moderate heat until very thick and smooth.

4. Remove from heat. Add butter and stir until melted. Beat in egg yolks until smooth. Reserve.

5. Beat egg whites with cream of tartar until foamy. Gradually beat in 1/4 cup of granulated sugar and continue to beat until whites are stiff but not dry.

6. Fold about one-quarter of the egg whites into the egg yolk mixture. Transfer this mixture to the bowl with the remaining egg whites. Fold together gently but thoroughly.

7. Pour mixture into prepared dishes. Each dish should be filled no higher than 1/4-inch below the rim. The dishes may be covered and set aside for up to an hour before baking.

— This recipe may be prepared ahead to this point. —

8. Place the baking sheet on the middle rack of a preheated 375° F oven. Bake until soufflés rise and barely begin to brown around the edges, about 22 minutes.

9. Sprinkle each soufflé with confectioners' sugar and serve immediately. If the soufflés must wait a few minutes, keep them in the oven with the heat turned off. This will help prevent them from collapsing.

10. Each soufflé may be served with whipped cream and Chocolate Sauce (p. 373).

Yield: 6 individual soufflés, 6 servings.

Vanilla Bavarian Cream

This Bavarian cream is a spectacular dessert when surrounded with raspberry or strawberry sauce and garnished with rosettes of whipped cream and fresh berries.

1 envelope (1 tablespoon)
  unflavored gelatin
1/4 cup cold water
6 large egg yolks
2/3 cup granulated sugar
1 1/2 cups half-and-half
  OR 1 cup milk and 1/2 cup
  whipping cream
1 1/2 teaspoons vanilla
  extract
4 large egg whites

1 cup whipping cream
Raspberry Sauce (p. 371) or
  Strawberry Sauce (p. 372)
  (optional)
1/2 recipe Whipped Cream
  for Desserts (p. 371)
  (optional)
Raspberries, strawberries,
  or other fruit for garnish
  (optional)

1. Soften gelatin in water. Reserve.

2. In a heavy, nonreactive 2-quart saucepan, whisk egg yolks and sugar together until smooth and light yellow. Stir in half-and-half.

3. Using a wooden spatula or spoon, stir mixture over low heat until thick. The mixture is done when a mark made with a finger on the back

of the spatula holds its shape. Do not overcook or let boil or mixture will curdle. Remove from heat. Add gelatin and stir until dissolved.

4. Immediately transfer mixture to a stainless steel bowl placed over cold water and ice cubes. Stir occasionally until mixture begins to gel around edges. Do not let mixture gel anymore or it will be difficult to fold in the egg whites in the next step. If mixture becomes too thick, remove bowl from ice water and whisk until soft. Stir in vanilla.

5. Meanwhile, beat egg whites until stiff but not dry. Use a whisk to gently fold egg whites into mixture.

6. Whip cream until soft peaks form. Fold into mixture.

7. Turn mixture into twelve 4-ounce (1/2-cup) molds or one 1 1/2-quart mold sprayed with nonstick cooking spray or lightly oiled. The mixture may also be placed in nine 7-ounce wine glasses. Cover with plastic wrap. Refrigerate until firm, at least 2 hours.

8. If a mold was used, dip it in hot water for a few seconds to loosen the edges. Do not immerse too long or the cream will melt. Invert onto a serving plate and shake the mold to release the cream. If necessary, use your fingers or a knife to help loosen the cream from the mold. Molded creams are more easily unmolded the day after they are made.

9. Unmolded Bavarian creams may be surrounded with raspberry or strawberry sauce. Use about 2 tablespoons for each individual Bavarian cream and all the sauce for one 1 1/2-quart Bavarian cream. Garnish with rosettes of whipped cream and fruit.

10. Bavarian creams in wine glasses may also be garnished with rosettes of whipped cream, fruit, and raspberry or strawberry sauce.

Yield: 1 1/2-quarts, 8 to 12 servings.

Liqueur Bavarian Cream

Follow the recipe for Vanilla Bavarian Cream (p. 356) with the following changes:

1. Reduce vanilla extract to 1 teaspoon.

2. After vanilla is added, add 2 tablespoons of framboise (raspberry liqueur), Grand Marnier, rum, or other liqueur.

Yield: 1 1/2 quarts, 8 to 12 servings.

Chocolate Bavarian Cream

Follow the recipe for Vanilla Bavarian Cream (p. 356) with the following changes:

1. After completing Step 3, add 6 ounces (6 squares) of melted semisweet chocolate. Stir until blended.
2. Reduce vanilla extract to 1 teaspoon. Add 2 tablespoons of dark rum or Kahlúa (optional) with the vanilla.

Yield: 1 1/2 quarts, 8 to 12 servings.

Chocolate Mocha Bavarian Cream

Follow the recipe for Vanilla Bavarian Cream (p. 356) with the following changes:

1. After completing Step 3, add 2 teaspoons of instant coffee granules. Stir until dissolved. Then add 6 ounces (6 squares) of melted semisweet chocolate. Stir until blended.
2. Reduce vanilla extract to 1 teaspoon.

Yield: 1 1/2 quarts, 8 to 12 servings.

Coffee Bavarian Cream

Follow the recipe for Vanilla Bavarian Cream (p. 356) with the following changes:

1. After completing Step 3, add 4 teaspoons of instant coffee granules. Stir until coffee is dissolved.
2. Reduce vanilla extract to 1 teaspoon. Add 2 tablespoons of Kahlúa (optional) with the vanilla.

Yield: 1 1/2 quarts, 8 to 12 servings.

Lemon Mousse

1 envelope (1 tablespoon)
unflavored gelatin
1/4 cup cold water
4 large eggs, separated
1 1/4 cups granulated sugar,
divided
1/2 cup lemon juice
1 1/2 teaspoons finely grated
lemon rind
1/4 teaspoon vanilla extract

1 cup (1/2 pint) whipping
cream
1/4 cup chopped or sliced
almonds, toasted, for
garnish (optional)
1/2 recipe Whipped Cream for
Desserts (p. 371) (optional)
1 lemon slice cut into 6 to 8
wedges, each about 1/4-
inch wide (optional)

1. This mousse may be served in six 6-ounce (3/4-cup) individual soufflé dishes or in one 1-quart soufflé dish. For an impressive effect with the mousse extending above the rim of the soufflé dish (see illustration, next page), construct a collar of double thickness wax paper. For individual soufflés, fold a 15 x 12-inch piece of wax paper lengthwise into quarters. Unfold the paper and cut it along the middle fold. Fold each piece of paper along the fold to make a 15 x 3-inch strip. Repeat with 2 more pieces of wax paper to make a total of 6 strips. For the 1-quart dish, fold a 30 x 12-inch length of wax paper in half lengthwise. Place each collar around the dish with half of it extending above the rim. Hold collar in place with a rubber band.

2. Soften gelatin in water. Reserve.

3. In a heavy, nonreactive 1 1/2-quart saucepan, beat egg yolks and 3/4 cup of sugar until smooth and light in color. Stir in lemon juice and lemon rind. Using a wooden spatula or spoon, stir mixture over low heat until thick. The mixture is done when a mark made with a finger on the spatula holds its shape. Do not overcook or let boil or mixture will curdle. Remove from heat. Add gelatin and stir until dissolved.

4. Immediately transfer mixture to a stainless steel bowl placed over cold water and ice cubes. Stir occasionally until mixture begins to gel around edges. Do not let mixture gel anymore or it will be difficult to fold in the egg whites in the next step. If mixture becomes too thick, remove bowl from ice water and whisk until soft.

5. Meanwhile, beat egg whites and vanilla until foamy. Gradually beat in 1/2 cup of sugar and continue to beat until whites are stiff but not dry. Fold egg whites into lemon mixture.

6. Whip cream until soft peaks form. Fold into mixture.

7. Pour mixture into dish(es). Refrigerate until firm, about 2 hours.

8. Remove collar(s). Press almonds on the sides that extend above the dish(es).

9. Decorate each individual mousse with a rosette of whipped cream topped with a small section of lemon slice. If the mousse is made in a 1-quart dish, place 8 or more rosettes around the edge.

10. Refrigerate until served.

Yield: 7 cups, 6 to 8 servings.

Note: This mousse may be served with Toasted Almond Wafers (p. 302) or Viennese Butter Cookies (p. 304).

Maple Custard

4 large eggs
1 cup maple syrup
1 teaspoon vanilla extract
2 1/2 cups milk, scalded

8 teaspoons maple syrup
  (optional)
1/3 cup chopped walnuts
  or pecans (optional)

1. In a large bowl, lightly beat the eggs. Stir in maple syrup, vanilla, and milk. Try not to let the mixture foam since this will cause an irregular surface on the finished custard. Pour mixture through a tea strainer to remove any foam.

2. Pour into eight 6-ounce (3/4-cup) buttered custard cups or individual soufflé dishes.

3. Equally space the cups in a pan measuring about 15 x 11-inches. Place pan on a rack in the middle of a preheated 325° F oven. Pour hot water into pan until it covers half the depth of the cups. Bake the custards until a knife inserted midway between the center and rim comes out clean, about 45 minutes.

4. Remove cups from water bath and cool to room temperature. Chill.

5. Each custard may be topped with 1 teaspoon of maple syrup and nuts.

Yield: 8 servings.

Rice Pudding

By using flour in this unique recipe, a rich, creamy, and smooth custard base is created for the rice and raisins.

PUDDING

4 cups milk	**1 teaspoon vanilla extract**
1/2 cup long-grain rice	**1 tablespoon lemon juice**
4 large egg yolks	**1/2 teaspoon grated nutmeg**
1/2 cup granulated sugar	**1/2 cup raisins**
Finely grated rind of a lemon	
3 tablespoons all-purpose flour	

MERINGUE

4 large egg whites	**1/2 teaspoon vanilla extract**
1/4 teaspoon cream of tartar	**1/2 cup granulated sugar**

1. Prepare pudding: Scald milk and pour into a 2-quart casserole. Add rice and stir until the grains are separated. Cover, and bake in a 300° F oven until rice is tender, about 45 minutes. Remove from oven and stir to separate the grains of rice. Reserve.

2. In a heavy, nonreactive 2-quart saucepan, whisk egg yolks, sugar, and lemon rind until smooth and light yellow. Add flour and stir until blended. Strain the milk from the rice into the egg yolk mixture. Return rice to casserole.

3. Stir egg yolk mixture over moderate heat until smooth and thick. Stir in vanilla, lemon juice, and nutmeg. Add raisins. Pour this mixture over the rice. Mix gently until raisins are evenly distributed. Reserve.

4. Prepare meringue: Beat egg whites until foamy. Add cream of tartar and vanilla. Gradually beat in sugar and continue to beat until thick glossy peaks are formed.

5. Use a rubber spatula to cover the pudding with meringue. Press the flat side of the spatula into the meringue and raise it quickly to form peaks.

6. Bake pudding in a preheated 350° F oven until meringue has browned, about 12 to 15 minutes.

7. Serve warm or chilled.

Yield: 6 to 8 servings.

Pearl Tapioca Pudding

PUDDING

1/2 cup pearl tapioca
4 cups milk
4 large egg yolks
1/2 cup granulated sugar
Finely grated rind of a lemon

3 tablespoons all-purpose flour
1 teaspoon vanilla extract
1 tablespoon lemon juice

MERINGUE

4 large egg whites
1/4 teaspoon cream of tartar

1/2 teaspoon vanilla extract
1/2 cup granulated sugar

1. Prepare pudding: Combine tapioca and milk in a covered 2-quart casserole. Soak overnight in refrigerator.

2. Transfer to a heavy 2-quart saucepan. Heat mixture until it scalds. Stir occasionally to be sure milk does not scorch. Transfer to a covered 2-quart casserole.

3. Bake in a preheated 325° F oven until the tapioca pearls enlarge and become translucent, about 30 minutes. Stir occasionally.

4. In a heavy, nonreactive 2-quart saucepan, whisk egg yolks, sugar, and lemon rind until smooth and light yellow. Add flour and stir until blended. Strain the milk from the tapioca into the egg yolk mixture. Return tapioca to casserole.

5. Stir egg yolk mixture over moderate heat until smooth and thick. Stir in vanilla and lemon juice. Pour this mixture over the tapioca. Mix gently until tapioca pearls are evenly distributed. Reserve.

6. Prepare meringue: Beat egg whites until foamy. Add cream of tartar and vanilla. Gradually beat in sugar and continue to beat until thick glossy peaks are formed.

7. Use a rubber spatula to cover the pudding with meringue. Press the flat side of the spatula into the meringue and raise it quickly to form peaks.

8. Bake pudding in a preheated 350° F oven until meringue has browned, about 12 to 15 minutes.

9. Serve warm or chilled.

Yield: 6 to 8 servings.

Lemon Sponge Pudding

This pudding is easy to make and is especially attractive when served in individual soufflé dishes.

1 1/4 cups granulated sugar	1/3 cup lemon juice
1/4 cup (1/2 stick) butter or margarine, at room temperature	1/4 cup all-purpose flour
	1 1/2 cups milk, at room temperature
4 large eggs, separated	1/8 teaspoon cream of tartar
1 1/2 teaspoons finely grated lemon rind	

1. In an electric mixer with a paddle attachment, if available, beat sugar, butter, egg yolks, and lemon rind together until smooth and light yellow. Mix in lemon juice. Add flour and mix until smooth. Stir in milk. Reserve.

2. Beat egg whites and cream of tartar together until whites are stiff but not dry. Use a whisk to fold whites into lemon mixture.

3. Pour into nine 6-ounce (3/4-cup) buttered soufflé dishes or custard cups or one 2-quart baking dish. Place dish(es) in a pan measuring about 15 x 11-inches.

4. Place pan on a rack in the middle of a preheated 350° F oven. Pour hot water into pan until it covers half the depth of the cups. Bake until light brown and a cake tester placed in the center comes out clean, about 30 to 35 minutes.

5. Serve warm or chilled.

Yield: 4 cups, 6 to 9 servings.

Bread Pudding

This homey dessert is fit for a king when served as described in Step 7.

2/3 cup raisins (if desired, half the raisins may be golden)
1/3 cup dark rum or water
10 slices (3/8-inch thick) White Bread (p. 210) or firm commercial bread, toasted
4 large eggs
2/3 cup granulated sugar

1 cup half-and-half and 1 1/2 cups milk OR 2 1/2 cups milk
1 teaspoon vanilla extract
1/4 cup (1/2 stick) butter or margarine
Ground cinnamon (optional)
English Custard Sauce (Crème Anglaise) (p. 372) (optional)

1. Soak raisins in rum or water overnight or for at least 1/2 hour.

2. This pudding may be baked in a buttered 8-inch square baking dish or in nine 6-ounce (3/4-cup) soufflé dishes or custard cups. If using a baking dish, cut each bread slice into 4 triangles. If using soufflé dishes, cut each slice into 8 triangles. Arrange the bread in the dish(es). Sprinkle with raisins and rum. Reserve.

3. In a heavy 2-quart saucepan, combine eggs and sugar. Whisk until smooth. Stir in milk and vanilla. Add butter.

4. Heat, stirring with a wooden spatula, until butter melts and mixture is quite hot. Do not let boil. Pour over bread and raisins. Sprinkle with cinnamon.

5. Place baking dish(es) in a pan measuring about 15 x 11-inches. Place pan on a rack in the middle of a preheated 350° F oven. Pour hot water into pan until it covers half the depth of the dish(es). Bake until a knife inserted in the center of the pudding comes out clean, about 20 to 25 minutes.

6. Serve warm or chilled.

7. For an elegant presentation, bake the pudding in individual soufflé dishes. Unmold each pudding and place it with the browned top up on a dessert plate. I prefer to place the pudding off center on the plate. Surround each pudding with 3 tablespoons of English custard sauce.

Yield: 4 1/2 cups, 6 to 9 servings.

Crêpes Normandy

4 dessert crêpes (use
1/2 recipe Crêpes for
Desserts, p. 248)
8 tablespoons (1 stick) butter
(no substitute), preferably
unsalted, divided
2 apples, preferably
Golden Delicious, unpeeled,
cored, and each cut into 18
slices, about 3/8-inch thick

1/2 cup apple liqueur
2 teaspoons granulated sugar
4 small scoops Vanilla Ice
Cream (p. 368) or other ice
cream

1. Warm the crêpes and 4 dessert plates while preparing apples and sauce.

2. In a 10-inch skillet, preferably nonstick, melt 2 tablespoons of butter. Add half the apple slices and sauté over moderately high heat until light golden brown on both sides. Remove apple slices from skillet. Add another 1 to 2 tablespoons of butter to skillet and sauté remaining slices.

3. Meanwhile, place a crêpe on each dessert plate. Arrange 9 apple slices, wheel spoke fashion, on top of each crêpe.

4. Add liqueur and sugar to skillet. Bring to a boil while stirring to dissolve sugar. Add remaining butter and boil until a light syrup is formed. Immediately pour over apple slices.

5. Place a scoop of ice cream on the center of each crêpe. Serve immediately.

Yield: 4 servings.

Apple Crisp

5 medium cooking apples
such as Cortland, McIntosh,
or Rome Beauty, peeled,
cored, and sliced 1/4-inch
thick
1 tablespoon lemon juice
3/4 cup granulated sugar,
divided
1 1/2 teaspoons ground
cinnamon, divided
1/8 teaspoon ground allspice
1/2 cup all-purpose flour
1/4 cup dark brown sugar,
firmly packed
1/2 cup dry bread crumbs
6 tablespoons (3/4 stick)
butter or margarine, cut
into 1/2-inch cubes

1. Toss apples with lemon juice. Mix 1/4 cup of granulated sugar with 1/2 teaspoon cinnamon. Add to apples and toss gently. Place apple slices in a buttered 8-inch square or 11 x 7-inch baking dish. Reserve.

2. In a food processor with a steel blade, combine 1/2 cup granulated sugar, 1 teaspoon ground cinnamon, allspice, flour, brown sugar, and bread crumbs. Process until mixed. Add butter and process until crumbs form. If a food processor is not available, combine dry ingredients in a bowl and use a pastry blender to cut in butter.

3. Spread crumbs over apples.

4. Bake in a 350° F oven until crumbs are brown and apples are tender, about 1 hour.

5. Serve warm or at room temperature.

Yield: 8 servings.

Note: This crisp may be served with Vanilla Ice Cream (p. 368), Whipped Cream for Desserts (p. 371), or English Custard Sauce (Crème Anglaise) (p. 372).

Spiced Apple Slices

4 medium cooking apples
such as Cortland, McIntosh,
or Rome Beauty
2/3 cup water
1/2 cup granulated sugar
1/2 teaspoon ground
cinnamon
1/8 teaspoon grated nutmeg
1 tablespoon butter or
margarine

1. Peel, quarter, and core apples. Cut each quarter in half lengthwise. Reserve.

2. In a heavy 4 1/2-quart pot, combine remaining ingredients. Bring to a boil, stirring until sugar is dissolved and butter melted. Add apples, cover, and boil gently over moderate heat for 3 minutes.

3. Uncover and continue to cook apples, stirring occasionally, until they are barely tender and the liquid becomes syrupy, about 8 to 10 minutes. Immediately transfer apples to a serving dish or storage container.

4. Serve warm or at room temperature.

Yield: 2 1/4 cups, 4 to 8 servings.

Note: The apple slices may be served alone, with ice cream, or Whipped Cream for Desserts (p. 371). They may be used as a topping for waffles or pancakes. The apples also make a tasty accompaniment for pork or poultry.

Poached Pears in Red Wine

3/4 cup granulated sugar
1 1/2 cups dry red wine
1/2 cup water
3-inch cinnamon stick
5 whole cloves
Peel from half a lemon
  (use a vegetable peeler)

4 pears, peeled, halved, and cored (use a small knife, grapefruit knife, or melon baller; the stems may be left on the pear halves)

1. In a heavy, nonreactive 4 1/2-quart pot, combine sugar, wine, water, cinnamon, cloves, and lemon rind. Bring to a simmer, stirring until sugar dissolves.

2. Add pear halves, core sides up, and simmer until just tender when pierced with a knife, about 10 to 15 minutes. Turn the pears once halfway through cooking time. Use a slotted spoon to transfer pears to a serving dish.

3. Boil the liquid down, stirring occasionally, until there is about 1 cup of syrup. Strain syrup over pears.

4. Serve chilled.

Yield: 8 poached pear halves with syrup, 4 servings.

Notes:

    1. These pears look like gigantic rubies when served in crystal dishes.

    2. Vanilla Ice Cream (see below) is a delicious accompaniment.

Vanilla Ice Cream

2 large egg yolks
2 large eggs
1 cup granulated sugar
3 cups milk, divided

1 cup (1/2 pint) whipping
  cream
2 teaspoons vanilla extract

    1. In a heavy 2-quart saucepan, combine egg yolks, eggs, and sugar. Beat until smooth and light in color. Stir in 2 cups of milk.

    2. Using a wooden spatula or spoon, stir over low heat until mixture is thick. The mixture is done when a mark made with a finger on the spatula holds its shape. Do not overcook or let boil or mixture will curdle.

    3. Immediately transfer to a bowl. Stir in 1 cup of milk, cream, and vanilla. Refrigerate until chilled.

    4. Freeze in an ice cream maker according to the manufacturer's directions.

Yield: 1 quart.

Note: This recipe is easily halved or doubled.

Butter Pecan Ice Cream

1 cup coarsely chopped
  pecans
1 tablespoon butter
  (no substitute), melted

Vanilla Ice Cream (see
  above), prepared through
  Step 3

    1. Spread pecans in one layer on a rimmed baking sheet. Heat in a 350° F oven until pecans give off a nutty aroma. Do not brown pecans or they will have a bitter taste.

    2. Toss pecans with butter. Reserve.

3. Using manufacturer's directions for ice cream maker, begin to freeze ice cream. When ice cream is partially frozen, stir in pecans and finish freezing.

Yield: 1 quart.

Chocolate Ice Cream

Prepare Vanilla Ice Cream (p. 368) with the following changes:

1. After the mixture has been transferred to a bowl in Step 3, sift 6 tablespoons of unsweetened cocoa over the mixture. Whisk until smooth.
2. Reduce vanilla extract to 1 teaspoon.

Yield: 1 quart.

Note: Each serving may be topped with a spoonful of Kahlúa, Grand Marnier, or other liqueur and toasted almonds.

Orange Ice Cream

2 cups orange juice
2 tablespoons lemon juice
1 tablespoon finely grated
** orange rind**

2 cups (1 pint) whipping
** cream**
1 1/2 cups granulated sugar

1. Combine all ingredients. Stir until sugar is dissolved.
2. Refrigerate until chilled.
3. Freeze in an ice cream maker according to the manufacturer's directions.

Yield: 1 quart.

Notes:
1. This recipe is easily halved or doubled.
2. Each serving may be topped with a spoonful of Grand Marnier or other liqueur and toasted almonds.

Lemon or Lime Sherbet

1 1/3 cups water
1 1/3 cups granulated sugar
2/3 cup lemon or lime juice

1 teaspoon finely grated
  lemon or lime rind
2 large egg whites

1. Combine water and sugar in a 1 1/2-quart saucepan. Bring to a boil, stirring until sugar dissolves. Boil, without stirring, for 2 minutes. Cool syrup to room temperature.

2. Pour syrup into a 4-cup measuring cup. Stir in lemon or lime juice and rind. Add water to make 4 cups of liquid. Reserve.

3. In an electric mixer, beat egg whites until soft peaks form. Pour syrup into egg whites. The egg whites will be blended with the syrup when the mixture is frozen in Step 5.

4. Chill in refrigerator or freezer.

5. Freeze in an ice cream maker according to the manufacturer's directions. If an ice cream maker is not available, freeze in a refrigerator tray until almost frozen. Then blend in a food processor or electric mixer until smooth. Refreeze. For best results, repeat the blending and freezing process.

Yield: 1 quart.

Strawberry Sherbet

1 pint strawberries, washed
  and hulled
1 1/2 tablespoons lemon juice

6 tablespoons granulated
  sugar

1. Purée strawberries in a food processor with a steel blade or use a food mill. Add lemon juice and sugar. Stir until sugar dissolves.

2. Chill in refrigerator or freezer.

3. Freeze in an ice cream maker according to the manufacturer's directions. If an ice cream maker is not available, freeze in a refrigerator tray until almost frozen. Then blend in a food processor or electric mixer until smooth. Refreeze. For best results, repeat the blending and freezing process.

Yield: 1 pint.

370 Desserts and Dessert Sauces

Whipped Cream for Desserts

1 cup (1/2 pint) whipping
 cream
2 to 4 tablespoons
 confectioners' sugar

1/4 teaspoon vanilla extract

1. Combine all ingredients in an electric mixer bowl. Use a wire whisk attachment, if available, and beat at moderate speed until the cream holds the impressions made by the beater and is thick enough to retain its shape. Do not overbeat or the cream will become grainy and separate.

2. If an electric mixer is not available, use a large whisk and a stainless steel bowl placed over cold water and ice cubes.

3. Cover, refrigerate, and use as soon as possible.

4. If the whipped cream softens, beat for a minute or two until stiff.

Yield: About 2 1/2 cups.

Raspberry Sauce

12 ounces frozen raspberries,
 partially thawed
1/2 cup granulated sugar
1 teaspoon lemon juice

1 tablespoon framboise
 (raspberry liqueur)
 (optional)

1. Place all ingredients in a food processor. Process until raspberries are puréed.

2. The sauce may be strained through a tea strainer or other fine sieve to remove seeds.

3. Refrigerate until served.

Yield: 1 1/2 cups.

Note: Serve with Bavarian Creams (pp. 356 - 358), Cheesecake (p. 283), or ice cream.

Strawberry Sauce

Prepare Raspberry Sauce (p. 371) but substitute 1 pint of fresh strawberries for the raspberries.

Yield: 1 3/4 cups.

English Custard Sauce (Crème Anglaise)

1 1/2 cups milk
4 large egg yolks
1/2 cup granulated sugar

1/4 teaspoon vanilla extract,
1 tablespoon rum, or other
liqueur

1. Scald milk. Meanwhile, in a heavy, nonreactive 2-quart saucepan, beat yolks and sugar with a whisk until thick and light yellow. Gradually whisk milk into yolks and sugar.

2. Using a wooden spatula or spoon, stir mixture over low heat until thick. The sauce is done when a mark made with a finger on the spatula holds its shape. Do not overcook or let boil or mixture will curdle. If the sauce begins to curdle, immediately remove from heat and beat vigorously with a whisk until smooth.

3. Immediately transfer the sauce to a stainless steel bowl placed over cold water and ice cubes. Stir occasionally until cold. Stir in vanilla or liqueur.

4. Refrigerate until served. Serve at room temperature, chilled, or warm.

Yield: 1 3/4 cups.

Note: Serve this sauce with Bread Pudding (p. 364), fresh or poached fruit, cake, or pie.

Chocolate Fudge Sauce

This sauce becomes thick and gooey when poured over ice cream.

1/2 cup unsweetened cocoa
or 3 ounces (3 squares)
unsweetened chocolate
3/4 cup granulated sugar
1/2 cup light or dark corn
syrup

1/2 cup milk
1/4 cup (1/2 stick) butter or
margarine
1 teaspoon vanilla extract

1. If cocoa is used, mix the cocoa and sugar together in a heavy 2-quart saucepan. Stir in corn syrup and milk. If chocolate is used, combine sugar, corn syrup, and milk in the saucepan. Add chocolate squares, broken into halves.

2. Bring to a boil while stirring constantly. Boil gently over moderate heat for 5 minutes. Stir occasionally to prevent sauce from sticking to saucepan. Remove from heat.

3. Stir in butter and vanilla.

4. Serve hot or cold. The sauce will thicken when chilled. It may be thinned by stirring over low heat and adding a little water.

Yield: 1 3/4 cups.

Note: Serve this sauce with Cream Puffs or Eclairs (p. 348), ice cream, or cake.

Chocolate Sauce

This sauce is rich and creamy.

4 ounces (4 squares)
semisweet chocolate
1 tablespoon butter or
margarine
6 tablespoons whipping
cream or half-and-half

1 tablespoon dark rum,
Grand Marnier, or Kahlúa
(optional)

1. Combine chocolate, butter, and whipping cream in a heavy 1 1/2-quart saucepan.
2. Stir over low heat until chocolate melts and sauce is smooth.
3. Remove from heat and stir in rum.
4. Serve warm or chilled. The sauce will thicken when chilled.

Yield: 3/4 cup.

Note: Serve this sauce with Cream Puffs or Eclairs (p. 348), ice cream, or cake.

Butterscotch Sauce

Thick and gooey with a rich buttery flavor.

**1 cup light brown sugar,
  firmly packed**
1/2 cup light corn syrup
1/4 cup milk

**1/4 cup (1/2 stick) butter
  (no substitute)**
1 teaspoon vanilla extract

1. In a heavy 2-quart saucepan, combine sugar, corn syrup, and milk. Bring to a boil while stirring constantly. Boil gently over moderate heat for 5 minutes. Stir occasionally to prevent sauce from sticking to saucepan. Remove from heat.
2. Stir in butter and vanilla.
3. Serve hot or cold. The sauce will thicken when chilled. It may be thinned by stirring over low heat and adding a little water.

Yield: 1 1/3 cups.

Note: Serve this sauce with ice cream or cake.

Table for Changing the Yield of a Recipe

This table lists fraction amounts of common measurements. For example, if a recipe requires 1 tablespoon of an ingredient and you wish to prepare only one-third of the recipe, find the 1 tablespoon amount in the original quantity column and then look to the right until you find the 1/3 column. The table indicates that 1 teaspoon should be used since this amount is one-third of 1 tablespoon.

Fraction of Original Quantity

Original Quantity	1/4	1/3	1/2	2/3	3/4
1/4t	1/16t	1/16t	1/8t	1/8t	3/16t
1/2t	1/8t	1/8t	1/4t	1/3t	3/8t
3/4t	3/16t	1/4t	3/8t	1/2t	1/2t
1t	1/4t	1/3t	1/2t	2/3t	3/4t
1/2T (1 1/2t)	3/8t	1/2t	3/4t	1t	1 1/8t
1T	3/4t	1t	1 1/2t	2t	2 1/4t
1/8c (2T)	1 1/2t	2t	1T	4t	4 1/2t
1/4c (4T)	1T	4t	1/8c	2T&2t	3T
1/3c (5 1/3T)	4t	5 1/3t	2T&2t	3T&1 3/4t	1/4c
1/2c (8T)	1/8c	2T&2t	1/4c	5T&1t	6T
2/3c (10 2/3T)	2T&2t	3T&1 3/4t	5T&1t	7T&1/3T	1/2c
3/4c (12T)	3T	1/4c	6T	1/2c	9T
1c (16T)	1/4c	1/3c	1/2c	2/3c	3/4c

(t = teaspoon, T = tablespoon, c = cup)

Index

Index

A

Acorn Squash
  and Apple Soup, 52
  Baked, 148
Advice
  yeast baking, 202
  frosting cakes, 250
Almond(s)
  blanching, 15
  Cake, Lemon, 263
  toasting, 15
  Wafers, Toasted, 302
Amaretto Orange Cheesecake, 284
Ambrosia, 65
Appetizers
  Apples with Cheese Spread and
    Pecans, Sliced, 39
  Cheddar Cheese with Port Wine,
    38
  Cheese Spread, 40
  Cheese Wafers, 22
  Chicken or Turkey Breasts
    Marsala for Appetizers, 37
  Chicken Mushroom Meatballs in
    Velouté Sauce, 35
  Clams on the Half Shell, Broiled,
    33
  Crab Salad for Appetizers, 30
  Fruit, Fresh, with Honey Lemon
    Salad Dressing, 38
  Green Beans, Carrots, Broccoli,
    and/or Cauliflower with
    Vinaigrette and Mustard
    Mayonnaise, 23
  Grouper Salad for Appetizers, 30
  Ham and Egg Canapés, 34
  Meatballs for Appetizers, Swedish,
    36
  Mushrooms Stuffed with Ham, 26
  Miniature Cream Puffs with
    Assorted Fillings, 31
  Oysters with Mornay Sauce, 31

  Pineapple with Rum, 37
  Salmon Pâté, 27
  Shrimp, Lemon-Lime Marinated,
    29
  Vegetable Cheese Spread, 40
Apple(s)
  Cake, Dutch, 280
  coring and slicing, 15
  Crisp, 366
  Filling for Strudel, 347
  Pie, Cheese, 323
  Salad, and Cheese, 66
  Sliced, with Cheese Spread and
    Pecans, 39
  Slices, Spiced, 366
  Soup, Acorn Squash and, 52
  Strudel, 345
  Stuffing, and Prune, 128
  Tart, Crumb, 324
  Tart, French, 325
  Tart, Poached, 328
Applesauce Cake, 278
Apricot and Raisin Stuffing, 129
Asparagus Soup, Cream of, 48

B

Bakewell Tarts, 344
Banana
  Bread, Nut, 240
  Muffins, Pecan, 242
  Pie or Tart, Cream, 334
Barbecue(d)
  Beef Ribs, 138
  Chicken, 108
  Chicken, Lemon and Wine, 109
  Sauce, 196
  Spareribs, 142
Barley
  Pilaf, 171
  Soup, and Beef, 44

Bavarian Cream
  Chocolate, 358
  Chocolate Mocha, 358
  Coffee, 358
  Liqueur, 357
  Vanilla, 356
Bean(s)
  Soup, Kidney Bean and Tomato, 57
  Soup, Sausage and, 58
Beef
  Braised, in Red Wine, 135
  Broth, 43
  London Broil, Marinated, 134
  Meat Loaf, or Beef and Pork, 140
  Rib Roast, 132
  Ribs, Barbecued, 138
  Sauerbraten, 133
  Soup, and Barley, 44
  Stew, Old-Fashioned, 136
  Stir-Fry, and Broccoli, 139
Beet(s)
  Soup, Fresh, 55
  Blue Cheese Salad Dressing, 77
Blueberry
  Bread, Orange, 239
  Crumb Cake, 281
  Muffins, 242
  Pie, 326
  Pie, Sour Cream, 327
Boston Cream Pie, 258
Bread Pudding, 364
Bread(s), Quick
  Banana Nut, 240
  Blueberry Orange, 239
  Coffee Cake, Streusel Nut, 241
  Cornbread, Skillet, 238
  Muffins, Banana Pecan, 242
  Muffins, Blueberry, 242
  Muffins, Pumpkin Raisin, 243
  Pancakes, Whole Wheat, 245
  Popovers, 245
  Scones, 244
  Yorkshire Pudding, 246
Bread(s), Yeast. See also Buns;
  Rolls
  advice on yeast baking, 202
  Challah (Egg Bread), 219

Cinnamon Swirl Raisin, 214
Cornmeal and Honey, 218
Crumb Cake, 231
dough
  braiding, 205
  kneading, 203
  rising, 204
  shaping loaves, 206
  shaping rolls, 207
French, 222
Herb Toast, 213
Italian, 225
Kugelhopf (Austrian
  Sweet Bread), 230
Melba Toast, 213
Pain de Mie (Sandwich Bread), 213
Rye, 217
Stollen, (German Christmas
  Bread), 234
Sweet Dough, 226
White, 210
White – Sponge Method, 211
Whole Wheat, 215
Whole Wheat Braid, 217
Whole Wheat French, 225
Whole Wheat Raisin, 216
Broccoli
  and Beef Stir-Fry, 139
  and Cheese Rice Pilaf, 172
  and/or Green Beans, Carrots,
    Cauliflower with Vinaigrette and
    Mustard Mayonnaise, 23
  Bright Green, 149
  Soup, Cream of, 48
Broth
  Beef, 43
  Chicken, 42
Brownies, Fudge, 311
Browning Sauce, 15
Bûche de Noël (Yule Log Cake), 271
Buns
  Cinnamon Raisin, 228
  Hot Cross, 229
  Pecan Caramel, 227

Butter
   about, 16
   Honey, 236
   Maple, 236
Butternut Squash, Baked, 148
Butter Pecan Ice Cream, 368
Butter Sponge (Genoise) Cake, 260
Butter Sponge (Genoise) Cake Roll, 266
Buttercream, 289
   Chocolate, 290
   Chocolate Mocha, 290
   Chocolate, Quick, 291
   Coffee, 290
   Lemon, 291
   Orange, 291
   Vanilla, 290
Butterscotch Sauce, 374

C

Cabbage
   Spiced Red, 151
   Steamed, 150
   Steamed with Bacon, 151
   Steamed with Mirepoix, 150
Caesar Salad, 64
Cake Filling(s)
   Chocolate Cream, for Pastries (Crème Pâtissière), 351
   Cream, for Pastries (Crème Pâtissière), 350
   Lemon, 287
   Pineapple, 288
Cake(s)
   Applesauce, 278
   Blueberry Crumb, 281
   Boston Cream, 258
   Bûche de Noël (Yule Log Cake), 271
   Butter Sponge (Génoise), 260
   Butter Sponge (Génoise) Cake Roll, 266
   Chocolate Buttercream, 265
   Chocolate Butter Sponge (Génoise), 264
   Chocolate Butter Sponge (Génoise) Cake Roll, 269
   Chocolate Cake Roll, 270
   Chocolate Layer, 256
   Coconut Layer, 255
   Coconut Lemon Layer, 255
   Coconut Pineapple Layer, 255
   Crumb, 231
   Devil's Food, 257
   Dutch Apple, 280
   Easter Bunny, 258
   frosting, advice, 250
   Fruit Shortcake, 262
   Jelly Roll, 268
   Lemon Almond, 263
   Lemon Bundt, 276
   Lemon Cake Roll, 267
   Lemon Chiffon, 272
   Lemon Layer, 253
   Lemon Coconut Layer, 255
   Marble Pound, 275
   nuts for frosted cakes, 251
   Orange Bundt, 276
   Orange Chiffon, 273
   Orange Layer, 254
   Pecan Bundt, 277
   Pineapple Cake Roll, 267
   Pineapple Upside-Down, 279
   Sour Cream Pound, 274
   Spice Layer, 254
   Strawberry and Other Fruit Shortcakes, 262
   Strawberry Cake Roll, 268
   Streusel Nut Coffee, 241
   Yellow Layer, 252
Candied Fruit and Nut Wafers, 306
Cannelloni, Chicken, 183
Caramel Icing, 295
Carrot(s)
   and/or Green Beans, Broccoli, Cauliflower with Vinaigrette and Mustard Mayonnaise, 23
   and Rutabaga Timbales, 153
   Glazed, 152
   Maple Glazed, 152
   Soup, Cream of, 46
   Steamed Yellow Squash, Zucchini, and, with Butter and Wine Sauce, 160

Cauliflower
  and/or Green Beans, Carrots,
    Broccoli with Vinaigrette and
    Mustard Mayonnaise, 23
  with Mornay Sauce, 155
  with Tomatoes, 156
Challah (Egg Bread), 219
Cheddar Cheese
  Sauce, 198
  Soup, 54
  Spread, 40
  with Port Wine, 38
Cheese
  Cheddar with Port Wine, 38
  Macaroni and, 188
  Manicotti, 185
  Salad, Apple and, 66
  Salad Dressing, Blue, 77
  Sauce, Cheddar, 198
  Soup, Cheddar, 54
  Spread, Cheddar, 40
  Spread, Vegetable, 40
  Wafers, 22
Cheesecake, 283
  Amaretto Orange, 284
  Grand Marnier Orange, 284
  Pecan Orange Chiffon, 285
  Strawberry, 284
Chess Pie, Lemon Coconut, 343
Chicken
  Baked, Dijon, 105
  Baked with Wine, 106
  Barbecued, 108
  Barbecued, Lemon and Wine, 109
  Breasts Cordon Bleu, 113
  Breasts, Italian, 112
  Breasts, Marsala, 116
  Breasts Marsala for Appetizers, 37
  Breasts with Dijon Sauce,
    Sautéed, 111
  Breasts with Mushrooms and
    Cream, Sautéed, 110
  Broiled, with Wine, 104
  Broth, 42
  Cannelloni, 183
  Crêpes, and Mushroom, 122
  Cutlets Tarragon, 114
  Dijon, Baked, 105

Divan, 111
Fricassee, 119
Greek, 110
Ham and, with Cornbread and
  Cheddar Cheese Sauce, 146
Lasagna, and Vegetable, 179
Lemon and Wine Barbecued, 109
Loaf with Parsley Cream Sauce,
  123
Meat Balls in Sour Cream Sauce,
  118
Meat Balls in Velouté Sauce,
  Mushroom, 35
Pot Pie, 121
Roast, 98
Salad, Curried, 72
Sauce, Pasta, and Tomato, 192
Sauce, Allemande, 195
Sauteed, 107
Sautéed, with Sour Cream or
  Heavy Cream, 108
Sautéed with Vinegar, 108
Soup, and Bok Choy, 46
Soup, Cream of, 49
Stir-Fry, and Vegetable, 117
Tetrazzini, 187
Chinese
  Rice, 174
  Spareribs, 143
Chocolate
  Bavarian Cream, 358
  Bavarian Cream, Mocha, 358
  Buttercream, 290
  Buttercream, Mocha, 290
  Buttercream, Quick, 291
  Cake, Buttercream, 265
  Cake, Butter Sponge (Génoise),
    Layer, 264
  Cake, Layer, 256
  Cake Roll, 270
  Cake Roll, Butter Sponge
    (Génoise), 269
  Cookies, Chocolate Chip, 308
  Cream Filling for Pastries
    (Crème Pâtissière), 351
  Frosting, 293
  Glaze, 297
  Ice Cream, 369

382 Index

Leaves, 303
Sauce, 373
Sauce, Fudge, 373
Soufflé, 355
Chowder, Clam, 61
Cinnamon
  Bread, Swirl Raisin, 214
  Buns, Raisin, 228
Clam(s)
  Chowder, 61
  on the Half Shell, Broiled, 33
Coconut
  Cake, Layer, 255
  Cake, Lemon Layer, 255
  Cake, Pineapple Layer, 255
  grating, 16
  opening, 16
  Pie or Tart, Ambrosia, 332
  Pie or Tart, Cream, 335
  Pie, Lemon Chess, 343
  removing sweet packaged taste,
    16
Cod
  Baked in Onion Mustard Sauce, 83
  Fish Cakes, 88
Coffee
  Bavarian Cream, 358
  Buttercream, 290
  Pastry Cream, 352
Coffee Cake
  Blueberry Crumb, 281
  Crumb, 231
  Dutch Apple, 280
  Streusel Nut, 241
Cole Slaw, 68
Confetti Corn, 157
Containers, 9
Cookbook protection, 10
Cookie Press Cookies, 305
Cookies
  Brownies, Fudge, 311
  Chocolate Chip, 308
  Chocolate Leaves, 303
  Cookie Press, 305
  Gingerbread Men, 309
  Linzer, 313
  Peanut Spice, 311
  Pfeffernüsse, 312

Toffee Squares, 308
Wafers, Almond, Toasted, 302
Wafers, Candied Fruit and Nut,
  306
Viennese Butter, 304
Cookware, 9
Corn
  Confetti, 157
  Soup, Cream of, 47
Cornbread and Sausage Stuffing,
  127
Cornbread, Skillet, 238
Cornmeal Bread, and Honey, 218
Cornstarch, 16
Crab
  and Mushroom Crêpes, 95
  and Shrimp Hollandaise, 92
  Salad, and Grapefruit, 67
  Salad for Appetizers, 30
Cranberry
  Relish, 200
  Salad, Molded, 65
  Sauce, Orange, 199
Cream
  Coffee Pastry, 352
  Filling, for Pastries (Crème
    Pâtissière), 350
  Filling, Chocolate, for
    Pastries (Crème Pâtissière), 351
  Pastry, 351
  Puffs, 348
  Puffs, Miniature, 350
  Puffs, Miniature with Assorted
    Fillings, 31
  Whipped, for Desserts, 371
Cream Cheese
  Frosting, 288
  Whipped, with Maple Syrup, 236
Crème
  Anglaise (English Custard Sauce),
    372
  Pâtissière, Chocolate Cream
    Filling for Pastries, 351
  Pâtissière, Cream Filling for
    Pastries, 350
Crêpes
  Chicken and Mushroom, 122
  Crab and Mushroom, 95

for Desserts, 248
for Entrées, 247
Normandy, 365
Croutons, 64
Crumb
Cake, 231
Crust, Graham Cracker or Cookie, 322
Pie, Peach, 329
Tart, Apple, 324
Crust
Graham Cracker or Cookie Crumb Pie, 322
Pie Pastry, 316
Tart Pastry, 321
Crusty Rolls, 225
Curried Chicken Salad, 72
Custard
Maple, 360
Sauce, English (Crème Anglaise), 372

D

Dessert Sauces,
Butterscotch, 374
Chocolate, 373
Chocolate Fudge, 373
English custard (Crème Anglaise), 372
Raspberry, 371
Strawberry, 372
Devil's Food Cake, 257
Dinner Rolls, 221
Dough blade, scraper, or knife, 12
Dressing. See also Stuffing
Noodle and Mushroom, 130
Duchess Potatoes, 162
Duck a l'Orange, 125
Dutch Apple Cake, 280

E

Easter Bunny Cake, 258
Eclairs, 348
Egg(s)
Canapés, and Ham, 34
Hard-Cooked, 29

warming, 16
whites, beating, 17
English Custard Sauce (Crème Anglaise), 372
Equipment, Restaurant, 12

F

Fan-Tan Roasted Potatoes, 164
Fish
Baked, with Wine, 82
Broiled, with Wine, 80
Broiled, with Wine and Garlic Butter, 81
Broiled or Baked, with Orange Butter Sauce and Pecans, 85
Broiled or Baked, with Tomato and Green Pepper, 84
Cod, Baked, in Onion Mustard Sauce, 83
Codfish Cakes, 88
Flounder Amandine, 83
Flounder Dugléré, 85
Mackerel with Mustard Hollandaise, Broiled, 82
Mackerel with Mustard Sauce, Broiled, 81
Salmon with Tarragon, Broiled, 82
Sautéed, in Cracker Meal, 86
Shallow-Poached, in Wine, 87
Flour, 17
Fluted Mushroom Caps, 157
French
Apple Tart, 325
Bread, 222
Bread, Whole Wheat, 225
Onion Soup, 45
Frosting(s) and Icing(s)
advice, 250
Brown Sugar Marshmallow Frosting, 292
Buttercream. See Buttercream
Cake Decorating, Frosting for, 295
Caramel Icing, 295
Chocolate Frosting, 293
Chocolate Glaze, 297
Coconut, Pecan, and Orange Topping, 297

Cream Cheese Frosting, 288
Lemon Frosting, 294
Marshmallow Frosting, 292
Orange Frosting, 294
Penuche Frosting, 296
Rum or Liqueur Syrup, 287
Vanilla Frosting, 293
Fruit
Fresh, with Honey Lemon Salad
Dressing, 38
Shortcakes, Strawberry and Other,
262
Fudge
Brownies, 311
Sauce, Chocolate, 373

G

Garlic, 17
Garlic Lime Mayonnaise, 76
Gingerbread Men, 309
Graham Cracker or Cookie Crumb
Pie Crust, 322
Grand Marnier
Orange Cheesecake, 284
Soufflé, 354
Gravy
Cream, for Poultry, 101
for Poultry or Meat using
Cornstarch (Jus Lié), 99
Poultry or Meat, with Mushrooms,
100
Green Beans
Amandine, 148
and/or Carrots, Broccoli,
Cauliflower with Vinaigrette
and Mustard Mayonnaise, 23
Grouper Salad for Appetizers, 30

H

Ham
and Egg Canapés, 34
and Turkey or Chicken with
Cornbread and Cheddar Cheese
sauce, 146
Herb(s)
about, 17

Mayonnaise, 76
Toast, 213
Hollandaise Sauce, 193
Honey
Butter, 236
Salad Dressing, Lemon, 78
Horseradish Sauce, 198
Hot Cross Buns, 229

I

Ice cream
Butter Pecan, 368
Chocolate, 369
Orange, 369
Vanilla, 368
Icing. See Cake(s): Frosting(s) and
Icing(s)
Improvisational Stir-Fry, 93
Italian
Bread, 225
Chicken Breasts, 112
Salad Dressing, 74
Salad Dressing, Creamy, 77

J

Jelly Roll, 268

K

Kidney Bean and Tomato Soup, 57
Knives, 10
Kugelhopf (Austrian Sweet Bread),
230

L

Lamb Stew, 145
Lasagna, 178
Lasagna, Chicken and Vegetable,
179
Lemon
Buttercream, 291
Cake, Almond, 263
Cake, Bundt, 276
Cake, Chiffon, 272
Cake, Coconut Lemon, 255
Cake, Filling, 287

Cake, Layer, 253
Cake Roll, 267
Chicken, Barbecued, and Wine,
    109
Frosting, 294
Mousse, 359
Pie, Chiffon, 342
Pie, Coconut Chess, 343
Pie or Tart, Meringue, 340
Pudding, Sponge, 363
rind, grating, 17
Salad Dressing, Basil, 74
Salad Dressing, Honey, 78
Sauce (Beurre Blanc), Butter, 194
Sherbet, 370
Squares, Pecan, 307
Lemon-Lime Marinated Shrimp, 29
Lentil Pilaf, Brown Rice and, 171
Lime
    Pie, Chiffon, 342
    Sherbet, 370
    Shrimp, Lemon-Lime Marinated,
    29
Linzer Cookies, 313
Liqueur Bavarian Cream, 357
London Broil, Marinated, 134

M

Macaroni and Cheese, 188
Mackerel
    Broiled, with Mustard Hollandaise,
    82
    Broiled with Mustard Sauce, 81
Manicotti
    Cheese, 185
    Spinach, 185
Maple
    Butter, 236
    Custard, 360
Marble Pound Cake, 275
Marinated London Broil, 134
Marshmallow Frosting, 292
Marzipan, 299
Mayonnaise, 75
    Garlic Lime, 76
    Herb, 76
    Mustard, 76

Meat Loaf, Beef or Beef and Pork,
    140
Meatballs
    Chicken, in Sour Cream Sauce,
    118
    Chicken, in Velouté Sauce,
    Mushroom, 35
    Swedish, 141
    Swedish, for Appetizers, 36
Melba Toast, 213
Meringue
    Lemon, Pie, 340
    Mushrooms, 298
Mincemeat, 339
Mincemeat Pie, 339
Minestrone, 56
Miniature Cream Puffs and
    Eclairs, 350
Miniature Cream Puffs with
    Assorted Fillings, 31
Mousse, Lemon, 359
Muffins
    Banana Pecan, 242
    Blueberry, 242
    Pumpkin Raisin, 243
Mushroom(s)
    Caps, Fluted, 157
    Chicken Breasts, Sautéed, with,
    and Cream, 110
    Chicken, Meatballs in Velouté
    Sauce, 35
    Crêpes, and Chicken, 122
    Crêpes, and Crab, 95
    Dressing, Noodle and, 130
    Meringue, 298
    Soup, Cream of, 49
    Stuffed with Ham, 26
Mustard
    Hollandaise, 194
    Mayonnaise, 76
    Vinaigrette Salad Dressing, 73

N

Nesselrode Pie or Tart, 336
Noodle(s), 176
    Dressing, and Mushroom, 130
    Lasagna, 178

Nut(s)
  Bread, Banana, 240
  for cakes, 251
  Wafers, Candied Fruit and, 306

O

Onion(s)
  about, 18
  slicing, chopping, or mincing, 18
  Soup, French, 45
Orange
  Bread, Blueberry, 239
  Buttercream, 291
  Cake, Bundt, 276
  Cake, Chiffon, 273
  Cake, Layer, 254
  Cheesecake, Amaretto, 284
  Cheesecake, Grand Marnier, 284
  Cheesecake, Pecan Chiffon, 285
  Frosting, 294
  Ice Cream, 369
  Rice Pilaf, Pecan, 173
  Rice Pilaf with Parsley, 173
  Sauce (Beurre Blanc), Butter, 195
  Topping, Coconut, Pecan, and,
    297
Ovens, 11
Oysters with Mornay Sauce, 31

P

Pain de Mie, 213
Pancakes, Whole Wheat, 245
Parsnips
  Glazed, 152
  Maple Glazed, 152
Pasta,
  Chicken Cannelloni, 183
  Chicken Tetrazzini, 187
  cooking, 177
  Dough, 176
  Lasagna, 178
  Lasagna, Chicken and Vegetable,
    179
  Macaroni and Cheese, 188
  Manicotti, Cheese, 185
  Manicotti, Spinach, 185

Noodles, 176
Noodles, Lasagna, 177
Salad, Shrimp and, 70
Sauce, Chicken and Tomato, 192
Spinach, 178
Squares, 177
Ziti, Baked, 186
Pastry(-ies). *See also* Pie; Tart(s)
  Apple Strudel, 345
  bag and tips, 11
  Cream, 351
  Cream, Coffee, 352
  Cream Filling for Pastries (Crème
    Pâtissière), 350
  Cream Filling for Pastries (Crème
    Pâtissière), Chocolate, 351
  Cream Puffs, 348
  Cream Puffs, Miniature, 350
  Cream Puffs, Miniature with
    Assorted Fillings, 31
  Crust, Graham Cracker or Cookie
    Crumb Pie, 322
  Pie, 316
  Tart, 321
  Eclairs, 348
  scraper, 12
Peach
  Pie, Crumb, 329
  Tart, 330
Peanut
  Cookies, Spice, 311
  Soup, Pumpkin, 62
Pear(s)
  Poached in Red Wine, 367
  Tart, Poached, 328
Pearl Tapioca Pudding, 362
Pecan
  Bundt Cake, 277
  Buns, Caramel, 227
  Cheesecake, Orange Chiffon, 285
  Ice Cream, Butter, 368
  Muffins, Banana, 242
  Pie, 337
  Rice Pilaf, Orange, 173
  Squares, Lemon, 307
  Tarts, Miniature, 338
  Topping, Coconut, and Orange,
    297

Penuche Frosting, 296
Peppers, Bell, Slicing, 19
Pfeffernüsse Cookies, 312
Pie. *See also* Pastry(-ies); Tart(s)
  Apple Cheese, 323
  Banana Cream, 334
  Blueberry, 326
  Blueberry Sour Cream, 327
  Boston Cream, 258
  Chess, Lemon Coconut, 343
  Coconut Ambrosia, 332
  Coconut Cream, 335
  Crust, Graham Cracker or Cookie
    Crumb, 322
  Lemon Chiffon, 342
  Lemon Meringue, 340
  Lime Chiffon, 342
  Mincemeat, 339
  Nesselrode, 336
  Pastry, 316
  Peach Crumb, 329
  Pecan, 337
  Pineapple Rum, 333
  Pumpkin, 336
  Strawberry, 331
Pilaf
  Barley, 171
  Broccoli and Cheese Rice, 172
  Brown Rice, 170
  Brown Rice and Lentil, 171
  Orange Pecan Rice, 173
  Orange Rice, with Parsley, 173
  Quinoa, 171
  White Rice, 170
Pineapple
  Cake, Layer, Coconut, 255
  Cake Roll, 267
  Cake, Upside-Down, 279
  Filling, Cake, 288
  Rum Tart or Pie, 333
  with Rum, 37
Popovers, 245
Pork
  Barbecued Spareribs, 142
  Chinese Spareribs, 143
  Scrapple, 144
  Swedish Meatballs, 141

Potato(es)
  Boulangère, 165
  Duchess, 162
  Fingers, 162
  Mashed, 161
  Roasted, Fan-Tan, 164
  Roasted New, with Garlic and
    Rosemary, 165
  Salad, Cold German, 69
  Salad, Hot German, 68
  Scalloped, with Cheese, 166
  Stuffed Baked, with Cream
    Cheese and Bacon, 163
Poultry. *See* Chicken; Turkey; Duck
    Rock Cornish Hens
Pound Cake
  Marble, 275
  Sour Cream, 274
Pudding
  Bread, 364
  Lemon Sponge, 363
  Pearl Tapioca, 362
  Rice, 361
Pumpkin
  Muffins, Raisin, 243
  Pie, 336
  Soup, Peanut, 62

Q

Quinoa Pilaf, 171

R

Raisin
  Bread, Cinnamon Swirl, 214
  Bread, Whole Wheat, 216
  Buns, Cinnamon, 228
  Muffins, Pumpkin, 243
Raspberry Sauce, 371
Recipe Collections, 12
Restaurant Equipment, 12
Rib Roast of Beef, 132
Rice
  Brown, Steamed, 168
  Brown, with Mushrooms, 169
  Chinese, 174

Oven Method for White or Brown, 168
Pilaf, Broccoli and Cheese, 172
Pilaf, Brown, 170
Pilaf, with Lentils, 171
Pilaf, Orange Pecan, 173
Pilaf, Orange, with Parsley, 173
Pilaf, White, 170
Pudding, 361
Rock Cornish Hens, Broiled, 105
Rolls
  Challah, 219
  Crusty, 225
  Dinner, 221
  Rye, 217
  shaping, 207
  Whole Wheat, 217
Rosettes, Shaping, 251
Rum or Liqueur Syrup, 287
Rutabaga
  Mashed, with Pecans, 154
  Timbales, and Carrot, 153
Rye
  Bread, 217
  Rolls, 217

S

Salad
  Ambrosia, 65
  Apple and Cheese, 66
  Caesar, 64
  Curried Chicken, 72
  Cole Slaw, 68
  Crab and Grapefruit, 67
  Crab, for Appetizers, 30
  Cranberry, Molded, 65
  Grouper, for Appetizers, 30
  Potato, Cold German, 69
  Potato, Hot German, 68
  Shrimp and Pasta, 70
  Tuna, 71
Salad Dressings
  Blue Cheese, 77
  Honey Lemon, 78
  Italian, 74
  Italian, Creamy, 77
  Lemon Basil, 74

Mayonnaise, 75
Mayonnaise, Garlic Lime, 76
Mayonnaise, Herb, 76
Mayonnaise, Mustard, 76
Mustard Vinaigrette, 73
Salmon
  Broiled, with Tarragon, 82
  Pâté, 27
Salt, 19
Sauce. See also Gravy; Dessert
    Sauces
  Barbecue, 196
  browning, 15
  Cheese, Cheddar, 198
  Chicken and Tomato Pasta, 192
  Chicken Allemande, 195
  Cranberry Orange, 199
  Hollandaise, 193
  Hollandaise, Mustard, 194
  Horseradish, 198
  Lemon Butter (Beurre Blanc), 194
  Orange Butter (Beurre Blanc), 195
  Sour Cream and Mustard, 197
  Sour Cream and Shallot, 197
  Tomato, 190
  Tomato, Fresh, 190
  Tomato Meat, 191
Sauerbraten, 133
Sausage and Bean Soup, 58
Scalloped Potatoes with Cheese, 166
Scallops Mornay, 90
Scones, 244
Scrapple, 144
Sherbet
  Lemon, 370
  Lime, 370
  Strawberry, 370
Shrimp
  and Scallops Mornay, 91
  and Vegetable Stir-Fry, 94
  Bisque, 60
  Hollandaise, Crab and, 92
  Lemon-Lime Marinated, 29
  Salad, and Pasta, 70
  Scampi, 89
Skillet Cornbread, 238

Soufflé
  Chocolate, 355
  Grand Marnier, 354
Soup
  Acorn Squash and Apple, 52
  Asparagus, Cream of, 48
  Beef and Barley, 44
  Beef Broth, 43
  Beet, Fresh, 55
  Broccoli, Cream of, 48
  Carrot, Cream of, 46
  Cheddar Cheese, 54
  Chicken and Bok Choy, 46
  Chicken Broth, 42
  Chicken, Cream of, 49
  Clam Chowder, 61
  Corn, Cream of, 47
  Kidney Bean and Tomato, 57
  Minestrone, 56
  Mushroom, Cream of, 49
  Onion, French, 45
  Peanut Pumpkin, 62
  Sausage and Bean, 58
  Shrimp Bisque, 60
  Spinach, Cream of, 50
  Split Pea, 59
  Sweet Potato, 53
  Tomato, Cream of, 51
Sour Cream
  Cake, Pound, 274
  Pie, Blueberry, 326
  Sauce, and Mustard, 197
  Sauce, and Shallot, 197
Spareribs
  Barbecued, 142
  Beef, 138
  Chinese, 143
Spice(s)
  about, 17
  Layer Cake, 254
Spiced Apple Slices, 366
Spinach
  Manicotti, 185
  Pasta, 178
  Soup, Cream of, 50
Split Pea Soup, 59
Spread
  Cheese, Cheddar, 40

Vegetable Cheese, 40
Squash
  Acorn, Baked, 148
  Butternut, Baked, 148
  Soup, Acorn, and Apple, 52
  Yellow, Steamed, Zucchini, and
    Carrots with Butter Wine
    Sauce, 160
Stew
  Beef, Old-Fashioned, 136
  Lamb, 145
Stir-Fry
  Beef and Broccoli, 139
  Chicken and Vegetable, 117
  Improvisational, 93
  Shrimp and Vegetable, 94
Stollen (German Christmas Bread),
  234
Strawberry
  Cake Roll, 268
  Cheesecake, 284
  Sauce, 372
  Sherbet, 370
  Shortcake, 262
  Tart or Pie, 331
Streusel Nut Coffee Cake, 241
Strudel, Apple, 345
Stuffing
  Apple and Prune, 128
  Apricot and Raisin, 129
  Cornbread and Sausage, 127
  Poultry, Old-Fashioned, 126
Swedish Meatballs, 141
Swedish Meatballs for Appetizers,
  36
Sweet Dough, 226
Sweet Potato(es)
  Mashed, with Pineapple, 167
  Soup, 53

T

Table for Changing the Yield of
  a Recipe, 375
Tapioca, Pudding, Pearl, 362
Tart(s)
  Apple Crumb, 324
  Apple, Poached, 328

Bakewell, 344
French, 325
Pastry, 321
Peach, 330
Pear, Poached, 328
Pecan, Miniature, 338
Pineapple Rum, 333
Strawberry, 331
Toffee Squares, 308
Tomato(es)
  Baked Stuffed, 159
  peeling, 19
  Sauce, 190
  Sauce, Chicken and Pasta, 192
  Sauce, Fresh, 190
  Sauce, Meat, 191
  seeding, 19
  Soup, Cream of, 51
  Soup, Kidney Bean and, 57
Towels, 13
Tuna Salad, 71
Turkey
  Breast, Roast Boneless, with
    Stuffing, 102
  Breasts, Marsala, 116
  Breasts Marsala, for Appetizers,
    37
  Loaf with Parsley Cream Sauce,
    123
  with Cornbread and Cheddar
    Cheese Sauce, Ham and, 146

V

Vanilla
  Bavarian Cream, 356
  Frosting, 293
  Ice Cream, 368
Vegetable(s). See also individual
    vegetables
  Cheese Spread, 40
  Sandwich Spread, 72
Vinaigrette
  Green Beans, Carrots, Broccoli,
    and/or Cauliflower with, and
    Mustard Mayonnaise, 23
  Mustard, Salad Dressing, 73

W

Wafers
  Almond, Toasted, 302
  Cheese, 22
Whipped Cream for Desserts, 371
Whipped Cream Cheese with Maple
  Syrup, 236
Whisks, 13
White Bread, 210
White Bread – Sponge Method, 211
Whole Wheat
  Braid, 217
  Bread, 215
  Bread, Raisin, 216
  Pancakes, 245
  Rolls, 217

Y

Yeast. See also Bread(s)
  about, 202
Yellow Layer Cake, 252
Yellow Squash, Steamed, Zucchini,
  and Carrots with Butter Wine
  Sauce, 160
Yorkshire Pudding, 246

Z

Ziti, Baked, 186
Zucchini, Steamed Yellow Squash,
  and Carrots with Butter and
  Wine Sauce, 160

About the Author

John L. Leonard, D.V.M., has practiced small animal veterinary medicine in Wilmington, North Carolina for over 20 years. He holds veterinary degrees from Cornell University and Auburn University. He has taken culinary continuing education courses at Johnson and Wales University and the Culinary Institute of America. Dr. Leonard shares his hobbies of cooking and bonsai with his wife, Betsy; two sons, Christopher and Will; English setter, Maybelle; and Labrador retriever, Georgia.

ORDER BLANK

**Heron Hill Press
7915 Masonboro Sound Road
Wilmington, NC 28409-2674**

Please send _____ copies of **YUM!** @ $17.95 per book.   _____

Postage and handling @ $3.00 per book.   _____

North Carolina residents add 6% sales tax ($1.08) per book   _____

                                             TOTAL ENCLOSED   _____

Please make checks payable to Heron Hill Press.

NAME _____

ADDRESS _____

CITY_____STATE _____ ZIP _____

COOKBOOKS MAKE SUPER GIFTS!

ORDER BLANK

**Heron Hill Press
7915 Masonboro Sound Road
Wilmington, NC 28409-2674**

Please send _____ copies of **YUM!** @ $17.95 per book.   _____

Postage and handling @ $3.00 per book.   _____

North Carolina residents add 6% sales tax ($1.08) per book   _____

                                             TOTAL ENCLOSED   _____

Please make checks payable to Heron Hill Press.

NAME _____

ADDRESS _____

CITY_____STATE _____ ZIP _____

COOKBOOKS MAKE SUPER GIFTS!

Reorder Additional Copies